THE MARRYING KIND?

Lives of gay & bi men
who marry women

CHARLES NEAL

Dedication

I dedicate this book to my husband of thirty-two years, Jeremy Cole. We both turned out to be of 'the marrying kind' it seems – having 'married' one another twice so far – and we're looking forward to more occasions on which to express our deep and lifelong love and commitment. I could not do much of what I do without the stability and nurture that his love affords me.

Acknowledgements

Mostly I wish to acknowledge – and profoundly thank – the men who entrusted me with their life stories over the five and more years that this book has taken to gestate. Their patience, honesty, openness, commitment and integrity have been remarkable. Thanks also to all the other courageous gay and bi men with whom I've been privileged to share stories and journeys in individual and group therapy over all the years.

I'd like to thank my former wife, Sally for so many years of warmth and friendship while we were married and ever since and my magnificent sons, Sam and Jago for their always loving and vital part in my own life journey.

Finally I have been encouraged – and painstakingly checked and given valuable feedback – along the way with this book by Jan Dryden and Giles Collinge Genovese in particular as well as by Judy Davies, Cath Fletcher, Jax Freedman, Jill Gabriel, Rosemary Pitt and Debbi Burch. I had help with resources from Dominic Davies, sound publishing advice from Marion Eaton and transcription from Kate Lott as well as the expertise of Matt Maguire at Candescent Press with formatting. Sally Geeve designed and donated the beautiful cover.

Thank you all wholeheartedly.

Charles Neal, Sussex, 2014.

Contents:

INTRODUCTION

Growing up scared

A growing male child tentatively experiences thoughts and feelings, fantasies and yearnings that seem different from those he sees and hears about. Gradually he comes to know that these sensations and ideas are not allowed, frowned upon, expressly forbidden by his family and religion, his friends and social groups, his culture. Maybe he learns that such longings are against the law or may attract derision, violence or rejection. He cannot, however, find a way to stop them and he cannot talk about them to those he should trust.

Over time he does find means to hide what he thinks and feels, what he longs for; maybe he starts to experiment in secret with having what his body and spirit seems to crave, but his guilt and shame grow alongside him as he enters manhood. They contaminate his joy and freedom, to the extent of making him hate his own body and its feelings, wanting to harm or even to destroy himself. He learns in complex ways instead to pretend, to hide and to pass as being what is expected of him and not what is true. Eventually he finds escape from this in the form of a female who offers him love or friendship.

Who is this book for?

This book aims to help the reader understand the ramifications of the scenario described and the powerful effects these can have on a person's life and relationships. It is primarily aiming to reach gay and bi men or men questioning their sexuality who are, or have been, married to – or in committed partnerships with – women. It is also for therapists, counsellors, trainers and others working with men in those situations and in related areas. It is intended to be as accessible as possible to the general reader, not aimed at those with specialist knowledge. It is not primarily directed at an academic audience, though one would be welcome. The participants and I hope that we might contribute to the dialogue of our times around sexualities and relationships. It would be gratifying if the book were also of value to the heterosexual partners, children and families of the men whom it is primarily aimed to help.

We hope that these inspiring and moving life stories may also more generally engage people who are interested in other people, how they live and what makes them tick. Feedback from all readers is welcome.

"To be at peace with yourself, not to have to try to walk a line between two worlds and feel like you belong to none, that's quite a new thing..."(Nigel)

What is this book for?

In this book ten men share painful and complex life experiences as honestly as they are able. Each knew at the outset, or came to know over time, that despite having married – or being in a committed heterosexual relationship with – a woman, that he felt gay or bisexual desires and attraction. Their hope in telling their stories is to increase understanding and support for other men who are gay, bi and married and to encourage them to move towards more authentic, honest and fulfilled lives and relationships. The reasons men with same sex attraction might marry women are varied and change with time and culture as do their reasons for 'coming out' in due course – or not. We will hear, however, what a large part is played by fear and shame, self-denial and, ironically, ingrained habits of putting others first.

The goal of this work is to show that no two men, no two relationships, marriages or situations are the same and therefore, neither are the constructive solutions for one rightly to be applied to all. In some instances the heterosexual partnership remains the most important one in each partner's life; in some the project of parenting and family-making will dominate; in others sexual needs and attractions will insistently lead someone in a certain direction; in others it will recede in importance. Some marriages survive beyond the 'coming out' of a spouse. Others collapse in chaos and acrimony and others still transform into lifelong friendships. There is no inevitable next step.

In our culture there are very durable notions presuming that gay and bi male partners with heterosexual women cannot stay married or manage to make their future relationship 'work' for both people. I want to challenge those assumptions and, in this respect, the idea of 'mixed orientation marriages'[1] developing in the U.S. is helpful. While it seems true that around 60% of mixed orientation marriages end sometime after the gay or bi spouse comes out (30% soon afterwards and 30% a while later)[2] that situation is changing as our societies develop less punitive and rigid ideas about what can and cannot work in human relationships and more respectful approaches to same-sex partnerships. The number of our contributors who remained married beyond their 'coming out' reflects the 30% of mixed orientation relationships that do continue.

---

[1] Mixed orientation marriages: see the pioneering work of Joe Kort at www.joekort.com and the incredibly useful entries in the online encyclopaedia at http://www.glbtq.com

[2] The percentages cited here all come from research by the Straight Spouse Network.

"To buy into the institution of marriage in its formal and legal sense was, I now think, a foolish and unnecessary step. But I remember the excitement of doing so, for we knew we were slightly naughtily appropriating a traditional institution for our own ends. However, I see no point in being hard on either of us in retrospect." (Philip)

The vast majority of existing resources support heterosexual spouses, usually wives, in cases where their partners have come out or may come out. I acknowledge the enormous importance of these supports, information and resources for 'straight' partners of gay and bi people, especially those who had not been aware of their partner's true or changing sexuality until some revelation, exposure or 'outing'. Such spouses face highly complex issues related to marriage, parenting, identity, integrity and their belief systems as well as to sexuality. The Straight Spouse Network (SSN)[3] is one provider of peer support and research-based information to help them heal, grow and manage. Many others are listed in the 'Resources' sections at the end of this book.

Children cope according to their age, developmental stage, available support and the qualities of their relationships with parents and others. Both partners and children have been seriously overlooked until recently by the therapy and counselling worlds. Counselling with trained therapists knowledgeable about mixed-orientation marriages assists families to resolve such issues more effectively. Some of these issues are flagged up but this book keeps its focus very much on the stories of the men themselves and useful resources for other men in such situations and those working to support them.

This book is not about allocating blame: far too much of that has already contributed to the pain and distress in the situations we are

---

[3] Straight Spouse Network: see 'Resources: Organisations'.

dealing with. Some contributors acknowledge the incredible generosity and loving kindness they've experienced from – often devastated – wives and families amongst others and acknowledge their own part in badly managing such relationships so that the hurt has grown.

"I have been my own prisoner for most of my life" (Robert)

One problem in our thinking about sexuality is that we tend to regard heterosexuality and homosexuality as entirely different and separate from each other – almost as opposites – whereas, like everything to do with sex and gender, the reality is that they intersect, overlap and segue into one another. Sexualities are mental constructs that refer to our lived experiences although the rigidity of the construct often belies the complexity and subtlety of the actual experience.

In the stories told here this tendency can be detected in ideas of 'becoming gay' or being no longer 'straight' and, of course, within the relationships described this 'change' creates confusion and hurt - for spouses, children and the men themselves. It seems as if somehow the person is no longer what they were, no longer who others thought they knew. It can appear – both to the man involved and to those in relationships with him – as if he was lying, conning, pretending to be one thing but 'really' being another.

Some men with female partners are indeed hiding their known homosexual feelings from them – while living a parallel life of which they are ashamed or attempting to hide these feelings from themselves or to change them, be rid of them, by living 'as if' they weren't true. This rarely works forever. It appears that, as social attitudes towards same-sex love and relationships change for the better, fewer men are feeling the need to do this. Some of the men here, however, were hoping that their earlier experiences of same sex attraction had passed or would pass – or could be replaced by relating to a female whom they loved. Sometimes this worked for years and then no longer did.

Some sought help from people posing as skilled professionals to change their sexual orientation. This has never been known to succeed; only in the end to cause greater psychological and emotional harm to the person seeking help. (See 'Avoiding bad therapy' in the resources sections.)

Trevor was 25 when he married, loathing his own gay feelings, and 24 years later they were exposed by his wife's discovery of his internet activity. Nigel sheltered from his fear resulting from early sexual experiences within a marriage in which he led a parallel secret life. Philip told his new wife at the beginning and they lived with his sexuality together for a decade. My wife met me while I was in a gay relationship, so always knew. Chris, on the other hand, had hidden it so successfully that even he didn't know until he was a father of two and married for many years. Alex was hugely relieved to tell his new wife about his sexual connections with men in the past and have her accept this about him. Alan "knew full well" in his heart when he married at 21 but it wasn't until 23 years later that he 'came out' to his wife, who "had her suspicions". Robert has been 'found out' or 'come out' several times within marriage but has yet to deal with this openly with his wife as they enter their sixties together, while both Bruce and Dan have negotiated ways to sustain their sexualities and their marriages.

All of the men in this book grew up in times and places where there was hostility and discrimination, even violence, directed at same-sex love. They each experienced this to varying degrees whilst growing up. If they wanted a family life, respectability, acceptance, social status, safety and what others had there were only heterosexual marriages or partnerships that would provide these. Nearly everyone grew up in a family where one parent was male and one female even if they were separated: this defined 'normal'. It is impossible to overestimate the significance of the changing sociocultural climates in which these men live. Interestingly all have 'come out' in their late thirties to fifties, many once their children are themselves near to adulthood.

In the last twenty years in many European countries, including Britain, social attitudes and legal structures have undergone rapid change. 600,000 people have become Civil Partners since they were able to in the UK and in 2015 many more same-sex couples will be able to be legally married. Many gay and lesbian people now have children themselves or foster or adopt children with fewer barriers to this than ever before. Courts have softened their rigid stance on the primacy of the mother and automatically awarding her sole care and control of her child and now usually consult the child about their own future relationships with parents who are separating. All of these contribute to creating a more inclusive climate in which a range of relationships are normalised and respected.

It would be invaluable if we could now accept that sexuality is both a process and a continuum. Some people do experience their own sexuality as fixed and certain and attach that to a particular identity once and for all. It interests me when people never question this and have no inclination to investigate other possibilities for themselves, other kinds of sex and relationship, other aspects of themselves. Some people feel more fluid, ambivalent, or attracted to male and female partners and may try a range of sexual and romantic relationships and behaviours at various times of their lives. Others – and I'm pleased to see this increasing especially amongst young people – feel no need to define or fix themselves or others at all.

Who contributed?

The men who contributed their life stories were either in individual or group therapy with me at some point or came to know me through therapy. They shared their stories in the straightforward hope that others would benefit from their experience. No one was paid and some found the process too difficult and dropped out. All the men represented here have stayed with the development of the book for between one and five years and I am immensely grateful for their patience.

We used the form of a 'second therapy' or deepening dialogue between themselves and me, with me adding more questions every time and them taking time to consider their responses at whatever depth and detail they wished to engage. Some men wanted to go deeper and respond fully while others did not, or felt that they could not. Thus, readers will find occasional questions left unanswered or glossed over. Some found re-reading what they'd said earlier prompted more reflections they wished to share, others found re-reading too painful.

Most were originally written; some were recorded and then transcribed, edited and polished. I have heavily edited each story with the intention of greater clarity, focus and continuity, while retaining the originality of each voice and its story. I hope I have done my brave contributors no disservice in this process. I made all the footnotes and introductory paragraphs without consultation and they are my sole responsibility. In the spirit of honesty, openness and sharing life stories, I also decided to add my own as the last one: it still feels risky to do so, as all the 'coming outs' we have to do throughout our lives always do.

Each contributor chose the name under which they wished to write their story and for two or three it was vital to use their own name as part of their healing through honesty. Others wished to protect others they loved – or themselves – for a range of motives by using another name and altering significant specific information. All have revised their stories sensitively and removed names of partners and others involved to take account of their feelings and any unintended impact upon them.

All contributors gave freely of their time and energies through what was often a painful and difficult revisiting of their process, as well as one which most appreciated as of great value to them. They did so in order to share with others in similar situations what they have experienced and learned in their own journeys. They said they wished they'd been able to find resources of this kind when they were desperately unhappy – sometimes suicidal – or unresolved, struggling for support and information. I have encouraged each of them to pass on any contacts, sources of help or materials that have been valuable to them and have included these in the Resources sections at the end. It is due to their generosity, then, that this book exists.

"Magical solutions, magical thinking - religion, God, romance - don't work."(Alex)

So, this is also a book rooted in therapy – which is my work – as it is the means by which I have met, and had these intimate conversations with, each contributor and many have underlined the value of the therapeutic process in coming to terms with, or coming to value, their true or emergent sexuality. I hope that readers find it free of psychobabble or unnecessary jargon.

I was happily married to a woman myself for twelve years from the age of eighteen and we parented two sons. I have since lived happily as a gay man for thirty-three years, co-parenting those sons as well as my partner's younger son. We recently became grandfathers. In these and other ways, therefore, I am personally acutely aware of many of the issues that inform this book.

I have worked as a psychotherapist specialising in issues of sex, sexualities and gender diversity and led gay and bi men's therapy groups over 25 years. In this time, working with hundreds of gay and bi men has made me professionally mindful of the need for more information and resources around sexuality and marriage. I have been especially aware of a dearth of resources for men who are bi, gay or questioning of their heterosexuality and who are married to women.

As far as I know this is the first such book from a British – or even a European – perspective. Most material, as in many fields of psychology and personal development, emanates from the U.S.: much of this is useful but there are particular sociocultural contexts that are different here. Some Christian religious social systems, for example, seem less dominant on this side of the Atlantic. (Alex's story touches on some of these).

These life stories are richly varied despite sharing many overlapping themes. Each relationship is unique as is each individual within that relationship. Therefore, no two relationships can be compared. Each has been co-created by the partners and to that extent has meanings and nuances that only they can know, or of which even they may not be consciously aware. How their relationships began, developed, have been transformed or fallen away; the ways they have made new loving partnerships or not; all these derive from their individual patterns for relating which were developed within their families of origin. They have also been formed through the journeys they have made themselves and the work they have been prepared to undertake in order to grow.

Finally, I very much hope that this is an optimistic book despite the pain and sadness retold in it, as these are lives lived more and more consciously, more and more honestly and lives transformed over time with great effort. I hope that readers will be encouraged and inspired by their telling as much as I have been.

"The reality is that a lot of us are pretty damaged and, with regard to building positive attitudes towards our queer sexuality, have a lot of catching up still to do. At least it is possible now to do so more openly, unlike the experience I had of growing up." (Bruce)

Charles Neal.
www.charles-neal.com

ABOUT THE AUTHOR

Charles Neal is a UKCP registered, Spectrum trained, humanistic psychotherapist and an Advanced Sexual Diversities Therapist as well as a consultant, supervisor and trainer. After 23 years in innovative education in inner London, he founded and chaired the UK Association for Lesbian, Gay & Bisexual Psychologies. With Dominic Davies he co-edited the groundbreaking trilogy of Pink Therapy handbooks in 1996 & 2000 (details in Bibliography). He led the longest-running gay & bi men's therapy group for 23 years and three creativity groups for a decade. An Honorary Clinical Associate with Pink Therapy since its inception, he is also a consultant with the new alternative families magazine, 'We Are Family.' He is thrilled to also be a gay father, co-parent and grandfather, a writer, photographer and garden designer.

BRUCE'S STORY

Introduction to Bruce

Bruce's journey has spanned America and Europe, observant Judaism and German Jewish reconciliation, long-term heterosexual marriage and fatherhood, bi and gay explorations, work in counselling and business - all in a quest to integrate complexity and live authentically. Fear, isolation, and lack of satisfying contact have been largely replaced by a more real family life alongside wider and deeper involvements with bi and gay communities – or tribes - and a commitment to guide others as well as organising to get his own, long unrequited, needs met. His personal search for 'lost' brothers echoes the masses of lost people in Jewish consciousness.

The other vital part of Bruce's experience is that he is a bisexual[4] man. As in others of these stories, finding, recognising, developing and valuing lost, or split off, parts of his self was his most significant work and has led in time to a huge shift in values now reflected in a range of relationships not possible before. Key to Bruce's internalised oppression, early fearfulness and insecurity are binary and sexist ways of thinking[5] in our culture. Since the so-called 'Age of Reason' in

---

[4] 'Bisexual' means romantic or sexual attraction, feelings or behaviour towards a person irrespective of their gender, although the employment of 'bi' does still imply that there are just two genders. See Bi networks in Resources appendix.

[5] 'Binary': in this specific context, means viewing complex and subtle things as polarities: for example, that 'male' is opposite to 'female' in every way - from

Western thought we have been wedded to ideas of opposition: indeed, we still refer to people as being of 'opposite sex'[6]. We can only be one or the other: gay or 'straight'[7] (heterosexual), male or female, respectable married man or queer adventurer. One is held to be right or superior in every case, while one is regarded as lesser, unnatural or even immoral.

Bisexual people, of course, experience both their heterosexuality and their homosexuality[8] sometimes at once, sometimes alternately, sometimes relating to attraction for a specific person, sometimes as an internal state, sometimes changing over their lifetime or with changing circumstances. Freud claimed that a continuum of bisexual experience was basic to human sexuality.

Bisexuals have, however, been discriminated against, pilloried and made invisible since the invention of specific categories of sexuality in nineteenth century Europe[9].

Mars and Venus! - rather than the nuanced continuum of biology, sexuality and experience which truly represents the complexities of human attraction and relating. Freud suggested early on (1905) that our sexuality always lies somewhere on such a continuum. The Kinsey Reports long ago (1948 & 1953) valuably illustrated this range. I indicate some of the background on sexism in my Introduction.

[6] What is it that is opposed, or oppositional, in this term? It assumes the existence of just two distinct, 'sexes' or genders, in the face of biology, which teaches us that sex and gender are on wide-ranging continua.

[7] 'Straight': unfortunate, out of date, commonly used term for heterosexuals. Many nowadays object to its suggestion of inflexibility or rigidity. New terms are needed.

[8] I am sorry to continue using these outmoded terms, which remain in common currency.

[9] Homosexual (Latin for 'same- sex') was invented in 1869 to describe a separate category, or kind, of person in the pseudo-scientific terms of the day, when sexology was new. It is meant to define romantic or sexual attraction or

Heterosexist thinking assumes that only heterosexuality is natural or real and imagines bisexuals to be actually heterosexuals who want to experiment, while rigidly homosexist[10] people will fantasise that bisexuals are, in fact, closeted[11] homosexual people who wish to appear heterosexual or enjoy the privileges of being seen to be heterosexual. It has long been argued that you cannot be bisexual unless you are equally attracted to men and women and recent studies have completely disproved this. It is unfortunate that even sex and gender minority groups have been recruited into these outdated modes of thought and bisexuality has, at best, been tagged on to the current 'LGBT' classification as if the experience of bi people - and trans people, incidentally - were just like, or an extension of, gay experience.

And Bruce's story emphasises the powerful, disabling impact of fear, as do many of these life-stories: in Bruce's case fear of rejection by parents, of social ostracism, of violence (so much a part of Jewish and American historical experience), fear of loss of love and his family and friends if he came out - another major force in the lives told in this book.

Bruce is also one of those men who believe they have an important role to play in disseminating some of the findings from their own

---

behaviour directed towards the same sex. Heterosexual (Latin for 'other sex') was then needed (1892). Bisexuals had to wait until 1892 and, most modern of all, Trans people waited until 1949 to be discovered! Before these separate categories of people were so rigidly established, people were sexual in a range of ways, which varied between them individually.

[10] Homosexist: Just as heterosexism is the privileging of heterosexuality over all other forms of sexual experience, homosexism is its equivalent: imagining homosexuality to be the superior form of human sexual expression.

[11] 'Closeted' refers to the American metaphor of 'the closet' as the place where people must hide their true sexualities or core aspects of themselves. Thus 'coming out' of the closet.

experience to others who are just starting their journey or are held up by fear, lack of good modelling, networks, encouragement, support and information. All of the contributors to this book feel this acutely and I am extremely grateful to them for this. Bruce has worked hard with individuals, groups and men on the web, formally and informally, as a guide or mentor, alongside them on their paths.

BRUCE'S STORY

I am a member of the heterosexual tribe. That bit was easy. I want also to be a member of the gay and bi tribes. Getting there has been much more of a struggle.

I was born in 1950 on the East Coast of the USA. My parents are both deceased. My father was a German Jew who escaped at the last minute in 1938, leaving his parents and most of his family to be exterminated by the Nazis. My mother was a third generation American Jewess of Hungarian extraction. They had no other children. On reflection, my isolation, which is very much part of my homosexual experience, started with my upbringing with them. Looking back, I believe that my father married my mother so she could act as a surrogate mother to him. They lived their lives very much for themselves and as a result I felt neglected. They always presented a united front and at times I felt bullied. This was probably my first experience of being bullied, which continued to a degree throughout my childhood.

What effects do you think that being from a persecuted minority and trying to keep a low profile, or to 'pass'[12] in the new culture, had?

---

[12] To 'pass' refers to all the ways in which persecuted people from minority groups have needed to conceal their identity from others in order to seem to belong to the dominant group. This includes censoring gestures, words, dress, language, and topics of conversation, mannerisms, cultural references and so on. It has, of course, been a central part of the experience of both Jewish people and gay people in history.

I think that this was a principal source of my lack of self-esteem, fear of society and mistrust of other individuals, of the self-fear, confusion and anxiety that I have had to deal with over the course of my life. More generally, I am now aware that these feelings are not unique to myself - the contagion can spread to others and how they come to relate in disconnected and uncontactful ways. I'm particularly aware of the polarity between contact and withdrawal that I have internalised. Of course this physical and psychological threat is also a historical reality that came to pass. I often react to challenges with a worst-case scenario: i.e. that there could be a new holocaust.

I always yearned for a slightly older brother who would support and protect me. One of the reasons I was attracted to boys and men was a search for the brothers that I never had.

And has the search for a male guardian or protector continued?

Absolutely, and it still continues. However, I feel very good that the experiences that I have had have been progressively more fulfilling. An ideal male relationship for me would contain significant sharing, bonding, caring, attention, appreciation, and protection. These are central components of the masculine that I am attracted to.

What were your earliest relationships with boys like? Were you 'successful' at being a boy?

As a boy, I was unable to find these things in other men or boys. I was too afraid to search honestly because of my dread of being attracted sexually. I didn't bond successfully, didn't have a best male friend. With other boys, I was often the 'odd one out'. Other boys seemed to have been able to pair off as best friends: I felt excluded and rejected. I can see now how these feelings were planted in me and how, even now, I can still be dealing with them. That, coupled with having authoritarian parents who taught me how not to verbalise my needs, created a very difficult background. I always wanted to be part of the gay tribe of men.

Before my first birthday, we moved out West. My parents wanted to live in a more spacious environment and a place where there was better value for money. In addition, there was a good public (state) school for me to attend for free. Money was scarce and I was soon taught the values of frugality and hard work.

If money is a metaphor for your spirit, or energies, does this frugality then refer to self-inhibition, over caution, lack of expressiveness on some level, do you imagine?

Yes, it probably does. Like many things there are at least two sides of the coin. I sometimes wish I had taken more risks, particularly when younger, in terms of trying new things more readily. Out of fear, perhaps as a way of self-protection, I take time before I leap.

On the other hand, I acknowledge that I am dealing with profound issues, without the help of guides or role models so shouldn't judge myself too harshly. I am trying to accept that my pace of expression has its own volition, the speed of which should not be judged. I have internalised speed, quantity, and spending as positive values as a result of living in societies where they are respected and encouraged.

Educationally, my parents were self-made and motivated. My father completed two years of community college whilst my mother, though bright, only finished high school. I feel that one of her frustrations was that she did not go further, but in the Great Depression this was difficult. To be honest, she did not have the strength of personality to assert herself, getting this vicariously through my father.

I wonder how this authoritarian-passive dynamic has played itself out through you?

I think it has to a large degree, in that I contain significant elements of both. Though I would like to believe otherwise, I've often been given feedback that I come over in a stern way like my father, though I feel that I have an open, non-judgmental mind, I do not feel that I am successful in getting this across as much as I would like.

Concerning my own points of view or getting my own needs met, I feel I didn't adequately present my case directly and strongly, rather in a more passive, considered way. I wonder if some of this comes from my mother ... and this has meant that I have had to teach myself assertiveness skills including what I want from men. I can still sometimes feel unskilled in this endeavour.

My father was an observant Jew, though not ultra-orthodox. My mother was not terribly observant, but prepared to pander to my father's desires, including keeping a kosher home. It was expected that I attend synagogue and religious school over and above my secular commitments. Interestingly, we lived in a mixed neighbourhood away from areas of traditional Jewish residence and the secular schools I attended had few Jews. However, it was expected that any members of the opposite sex with whom I socialised would be Jewish.

How was your difference acknowledged, derided, regarded? How did you regard your Jewishness or difference yourself, and feel about it?

I felt rather uncomfortable about my Jewishness and difference but, as opposed to my gayness, at least this could be shared and understood on a more open level. Deep down I think I held resentment about being different, having more responsibilities, social limitations, but the reality is that I did not have the personal power whilst young to do anything about it, particularly in face of my parents' authoritarian beliefs. I see now that, like coming out, it took me a very long time to change my life to take into account who I really am. I have little personal interest now in the profession of religious ritual, synagogue attendance, selection of friends on the basis of religious background, but I am very interested in my Jewish historical and cultural antecedents. I recently spent a long weekend in Germany with people at a centre of German Jewish reconciliation in the town from which my father's grandparents came. I have always found that I have been drawn to voluntary and charitable organizations that support the dispossessed.

I was aware of my homosexual interests at a very early age. I recollect at age four or five lingering in the changing area of the local swimming baths to watch teenage boys and experiencing the feeling of physical attraction.

Is this a visual experience firstly, then a whole body one? Is there objectification in it or romance, envy or aesthetics, for example? How has this yearning affected you?

This is an experience that involves all of my senses. I suppose visually first; but smell, texture and touch of the body are also very important - they have a primal draw for me, a basic drive, that needs to be satisfied, enacted in some kind of bonding. There is also my desire to create something durable, emotional with men, which parallels what I have felt, and fulfilled, with women because at the same time I was interested in, and attracted to, girls.

Was this attraction in the same, or in different, ways?

Men are brothers, emotional, and sexual lovers. Women are emotional and sexual lovers and earth mothers. I can't imagine life without children. With a woman this seems so natural and easier to create. I'm open to the idea of parenting with guys but somehow it seems so much more difficult. This was immediately complex and confusing.

What was confusing exactly? Did these attractions seem oppositional?

Yes.

Had you already absorbed binary ideas?

Yes.

Were they rules about one or the other, and not both?

Yes, and towards men this was wrong and forbidden.

Did you experience conflict between these attractions yourself?

Yes, and even more confusion and fear about how to act them out in reality.

Was, or is, there in you the possibility of 'both'?

It's not a possibility: it's an existential potential and a reality for me. Some people are attracted to the opposite sex, some to their own, and some to both. So what's the big deal? It all felt so natural to me - but this was hardly the reaction from the world at large.

How did the world know about your attractions? How did the world react and to what exactly?

The world of my adolescence and youth didn't because I repressed it all, didn't disclose feelings to any great degree. I did make a few homosexual approaches to guys when I was in school but these were repulsed, subtly but firmly, with feelings of shame, diffidence, rather than out and out rejection or violence. I was aware, though, that the homophobic world could be one where significant verbal and physical violence did occur.

My heterosexual leanings, of course, were encouraged and developed without issue.

Can you say any more about how this was done in particular? It would have been culturally reinforced, too.

You already have the answer: the cards were totally stacked in favour of heterosexual experiences, which were encouraged, honoured, and valued. But the real challenge was the issue of what to do with my homosexual feelings.

The expression of homosexuality in the environment in which I grew up was frightening. So frightening that, in the main, it was taboo to even discuss the possibility openly. This taboo was present in all environments, whether it be my secular school or the synagogue. A united homophobic front seemed to be omnipresent.

Overt? Explicit? Were you ever singled out for the message or was it generalised?

Generalised. I was never personally subjected to queer bashing. As I was also involved with girls, I really don't think I was suspected of having gay leanings. Anyway, don't underestimate the power of the taboo. I have also had to deal with the personal negative effects of having heterosexual privilege - my guilt at knowing full well that I'm not heterosexual.

I knew no other homosexual or bisexual people. I knew of no clubs, places to meet or literature to read. There was only the very occasional camp figure.

Where, who and how? In the media? Locally? Known to you?

Yes, gay camp figures on television, or overtly fem, camp university students to whom I felt no attraction or identification whatsoever. As I look back, the isolation was very painful.

And how were you affected, how did you react, behave, at the time?

Frustration! I wanted to have physical contact with other boys. I wanted emotional bonding and love. I felt the awfulness of feeling all alone, believing I was the only one to hold these feelings, afraid to present who I am. I became withdrawn, moody and morose. This resulted in me having negative self-esteem and feeling confused.

What happened with these feelings: what did you do with them?

Sometimes it felt I was going to explode. More often in those early days I felt very lonely and sad.

On the one hand, I felt attracted to both men and women and it felt perfectly natural. On the other, I received no reinforcement whatsoever; it felt as if part of my very existence was denied, that the world was disallowing me recognition for who I was.

Interesting the extent to which you now feel - or then came to feel - that who you are so powerfully consists of who, or rather, which gender, you are attracted to. Any ideas about this?

This is a sensitive area as it goes straight to my existential view of myself. I have always known whom I'm attracted to, though I have dealt with it in different ways. By not acknowledging my gay side as I did my straight, I developed a negative self-image of myself as a hypocrite. Authenticity is very important to me and, as long as I rejected such a large part of myself, I couldn't possibly like myself or feel I was living a correct life. To live this life, I also needed the recognition and acknowledgement of those around me.

Contributing to this work of yours, Charles, is one important way that I give others and myself the recognition I wasn't given as to who I am, and that my sexual and emotional feelings do exist in reality. I am a human being with feelings, which I want acknowledged and validated. In other words, I want to have a world in which gay and bisexual relationships are valued as highly as heterosexual ones, a level playing field so to speak.

And then there were issues of personal security. I was very conscious of the violent nature of American society and the real possibility of being gay-bashed. I have no doubt that one of the significant reasons I delayed gay activity was the fear of being physically attacked.

Can you remember more about this climate, this knowledge and those feelings? How did you know about queer bashing but not about anywhere that gays might go or be or who these other 'queers' were?

From the media, hearsay, and homophobic remarks. It has taken years to catch up. I was very much a victim of the 'developmental lag'[13] and am still affected by it though, I am happy to realise, not nearly to the same extent.

Please say more about this experience in you today. How are you a victim? How is the lag manifest? Purely chronology? What has

---

[13] 'Developmental lag': developmental psychology posits various models for sexual development proceeding through pre-ordained phases (usually towards genital heterosexual sex!) This term was coined to describe the 'lag', which may occur when development has been skewed or halted, by repression (in this case through fear of homophobia) or trauma of other kinds (sexual assault, for example). See Davies (1996) and 'Developmental Stages in The Coming Out Process' by E. Coleman (Journal of Homosexuality, 1982)

'catch up' meant for you and how have you caught up, or are you now catching up?

In a nutshell, it meant allowing myself the gay experience I have always wanted. I was a victim in terms of how my self-imposed, and culturally imposed, repression has limited my life experience, taken so much emotional energy that might have been better spent elsewhere, spending so many days of my life feeling sad, depressed, and frustrated. I spent a lot of time catching up, trying to engage in the same level of male relationships that I achieved with women by the time I was in my twenties.

I am now happy to be aware of the progress that I have made. I feel I have a much better understanding of my needs, accepting myself and what appeals to me: i.e. discarding redundant beliefs about myself, which were rooted in childhood. I think a lot of it is about allowing experiences of different types of relationships.

My membership of the bi/gay tribe was retarded out of fear for my personal safety and also out of fear that I would jeopardise my membership of the heterosexual tribe, to which I also belong.

As I proceeded down the road of life's journey, I had significant success. I was an excellent student across the board and finished school with very high marks. I did well at the university I attended for my B.A. and successfully completed a Master's degree in a professional field. I had relationships with women as girlfriends and as platonic friends.

Where was the relationship between all this success and your 'secret' self?

At least in some important areas of my life I did not feel frustrated. And activity and time spent in those areas diverted my attention away from the gay side. But those needs remained unsatisfied and I was increasingly unsure of how I was going to meet them.

You weren't satisfied, getting needs met, emotionally soothed, and sexually fulfilled by your heterosexual self-expression?

No, these needs weren't satisfied by heterosexual success. Coupled with this, the seventies were the years of the Vietnam War.

Were you ever called up?

No. I was becoming progressively less enchanted with American politics and urban lifestyle. During University, I began to travel in Europe and Asia extensively.

Please say what you saw in these places in relation to different cultural, sexual, relational ideas and behaviours, subcultures, artefacts which may have contributed to your developing sexuality.

I sensed that Western Europe was more liberal socially, including to gays. I felt freer to explore things away from my home territory. Every trip became of a longer duration as I sought to distance myself from my country as well as my parents to avoid their domination.

Was there a rebellion going on, an anti-authority backlash in you, a cultural breaking away of some kind?

Definitely, it was rebellion that led me to break away from my parents and country of birth and upbringing.

I had, however, internalised the expectation of marriage and children and, to be honest, have no regrets about taking this course. In 1975, I married and was excited to settle down with my wife in London where she lived.

Apart from being delighted to be out of the States politically, I had also sensed the more tolerant attitude in Europe towards homosexuality. I looked forward for the first time to being in a more benevolent environment in which to express my needs.

And did you do so? You haven't yet said anything about early gay sexual contacts of any kind and how you experienced yourself in those encounters.

No, you're right, I used Europe initially to further my heterosexual experiences. But I could see the potential to realise my gay side, which I believe is easier to act on here and which I have, though it's taken longer to get around to.

But first to my marriage: after settling in, I soon went on to establish a business, which in due course was a reasonable success. My wife also worked and we raised three children, now in their thirties.

What about your relationship – sexually, emotionally, psychologically? What did you get and give, and not get and give, here?

I enjoyed my sexual and emotional relationship with my wife. I enjoyed the stability and the creation of a physical home and family. But my search for a soul mate or brother figure continued. Whether this figure would be an individual or group only experience would tell.

But for a long time I did not express my homosexual cravings, mainly out of fear of loss of my family should my wife ask for a separation or divorce.

I am interested in your language: why 'cravings', like in addiction, and not wishes or desires or wants, for example?

I say this because I was hungry for so long for gay contact. They became so strong that it felt to me stronger than ordinary desire, like a powerful hunger pain that is not assuaged.

New to the country, I had no social network of my own.

Was this as a result of repressing your true self or shyness, introversion?

It was through a combination of these factors. But I feel because I did not assert myself, I limited my power.

Why do you say that?

I did not make the decisions of whom we saw socially.

Is that a contrast with, or the same, as your mother?

There are parallels and differences here.

Frequently one person in a couple controls while the other holds more power. How has this worked between you two?

This is a very complex issue. I'm not sure that I understand or accept your statement about control and power. It may be worthwhile to consider further if you wish.

Meaning?

Like in many relationships I expect, there are periods of conflict and upset to be negotiated. I felt unsuccessful in asserting my need during these periods.

How come? What were these conflicts mainly focused around?

I'm finding these questions tough to look at emotionally, but I feel for example that they concerned different approaches in raising the children and the energy required to do so. I can understand now how this triggered off feelings of jealousy because I did not get the level of attention and credibility that I would have liked. I link this clearly to the lack of attention and being heard that I experienced from my parents.

I felt also that with most of the men I met at work and otherwise I shared little in common. To be honest, I was searching for the experience of being with queer men, but I didn't know any, didn't know where and what to look for and didn't have the courage to do anything about it. I did at times feel quite desperate about this absence.

How did you experience yourself as 'desperate', Bruce?

It felt like I was being starved of much connection that I wanted, whether it is physical or emotional. Meanwhile, I was under significant financial pressure to keep my family going and felt that little of my life was being led for myself. I felt frustrated and depressed.

This was going to change. At forty-two I met a gay man who was also unsatisfied and we had a short-term relationship. My wife found out from one of our children who had discovered some evidence concerning it. The dynamics for me have never been the same and I began to look at things in a different way.

How have they altered?

What was hidden was beginning to be explicit. My wife saw that I could be attractive to others; we had to face insecurity and threats to our relationship. We began to deal with change, instability, and the evolution of our relationship, including what was constant for us, the possibility that it might end and the energy required to start anew.

Because I was prepared to act on what I wanted, I realized that I was better able to negotiate my points of view.

In the event, the decision to stay together, I believe, illustrates a determination to try to work out things between us. And for me an acknowledgment of who I am and what I have done.

Are you able to explain this 'constant' and 'determination' from your own point of view?

I think that in essence that it is a commitment to keep the lines of communication open, to endeavour to try to look at things in an honest and sincere way.

I can see that the approaches taken can be different: I have sought professional support from yourself and others rather than being a private person who chooses to work through difficult personal issues for myself. I am consequently aware of the issues of confidentiality as I write this concerning the sensitive area of monogamy, and my desire not to "out" my wife or children.

I guarantee that nothing you share with me will ever be used without your express permission after you've considered it carefully, Bruce.

I appreciate that, Charles: that remains important to me to keep in mind. I also want, for myself, to be recognised for the contribution I am making to this study of the experience of gay and bi men in marriage.

In the ensuing years, I have considerably expanded my boundaries and activities.

Please expand on how this exploration has gone and what you've discovered.

It's good that I no longer feel deprived of expressing my human and male feelings, which might be considered primitive. I have done a lot to facilitate this, such as coming into social contact with gay and bisexual men in a variety of ways: through voluntary work in Aids charities, therapy, book, and other discussion groups, and in swimming and walking groups.

What are these human, male feelings? Why are they called primitive?

They are primitive, Charles, because they are such basic instincts or drives. I believe that, for me, emotional and physical, including gay, drives need to be satisfied, as much as eating and sleeping are, as are my needs for human touch and affection from both men and women.

How is your relationship with your children? How would you describe your relationship with each of them, past and present?

I consider my relationships with my children as loving, with period of mundaneness but also conflict, and with ongoing experience of contact and withdrawal. I feel that children find talking about their parents' sexuality and issues such as monogamy awkward and difficult. In the main, I have refrained from discussing my sexuality with them.

Say more about this sensitive issue. Do you hold a belief in monogamy while not behaving monogamously, or not really believe in its necessity, or what? Do you want your children to believe, or behave, differently to you?

I believe in negotiating authenticity and in stability in relationships and I have discovered ways to hold this, which may include the sharing that I want. I have an open mind concerning what my children might decide for themselves in their own lives.

What has been of most value to you in working through these life issues and coming to live a more satisfying life over recent years?

It is clear to me that therapy and counselling have played a very significant role in shaping my coming out experience. You and I, Charles, worked together in therapy for more than ten very productive years. Reflecting back, I can sum up the success of my therapeutic experience with you in three specific ways: being supported in coming out, being challenged and spurred into action to change my life for the better, by your use of firmness and challenge towards me while not coming across as authoritarian. Any authoritarian approach elicits my powerful resistance because of the way my parents treated me. And being helped by you to learn how to negotiate so that I could better further my needs and interests.

As part of this process, I also trained and worked for a period as a counsellor myself in the voluntary sector. This experience facilitated my further personal growth and development. After a number of years, I discontinued my formal work as a counsellor as I was aware that, in all honesty, I needed to apply my resources to my own healing process first. This had been neglected significantly for the first four decades of my life.

How has your life changed?

Enormously! I feel that I am now a fully-fledged member of the queer tribe, in my own way, with some special aspects of life experience that I can offer to share with others. The depression in the main has lifted, and self-esteem and my confidence greatly improved since coming out. Most importantly, I feel that I am more and more leading a life that feels authentic and honest. As a result, I feel much less needy, frustrated, and angry. Though of course this is all relative. I am aware of the reality that I will probably never really finish coming out: there will always be another challenge or problem tomorrow - for example, a need to decide whether to come out to each new person or situation encountered. I can sense that friends, my wife and acquaintances hold me in greater respect for what I stand for, for having the courage to go for what I want. I find that I am more ready to be open to new experiences. I feel more fulfilled and centred. I am excited and optimistic for the future.

What advice would you offer others in your situation?

Have the courage and strength to follow your convictions, be yourself as far as possible as soon as possible, be aware that taking risks can bring great rewards and not necessarily be destructive or lead to loss, as my original, fallacious, learning had taught me. Be realistic, though, and understand that your own coming out process will affect others who, in their turn, will require time and energy to process the impact of your changes on them. Be aware that you may have to deal with a wide variety of difficult emotions and challenging situations such as hurt, rejection, jealousy, frustration and anger.

Are there resources that you'd recommend to others?

Unfortunately, for many years, my isolation from my homosexuality also meant a paucity of any written resource. No organisations or cultural offerings, because it was all taboo. Only when I started coming out at the advanced age of forty did I actively seek out literature and so on. I have to admit to suffering from my own internalised homophobia. I remember clearly taking one of my children to their university at the beginning of my coming out. I wanted to buy 'Gay Times'[14] yet, such was my paranoia that I recall going to a newsagent far from the university to avoid possible recognition and when I bought the magazine my heart was pounding.

Later, many of my endeavours to find queer literature were in tandem with my counselling training. I wrote a paper on bisexuality as you will recall, and for the research I looked for every possible reference to homosexuality, and there weren't many, as you know Charles. Because of this you found the need to bring out 'Pink Therapy'.[15]

---

[14] 'Gay Times': successful UK monthly magazine for bi and gay men published by Millivres Prowler in the UK since 2007 and recently rebranded as 'GT'.

[15] 'Pink Therapy' trilogy of handbooks on therapy with lesbian, gay, bi and trans clients edited by Dominic Davies and Charles Neal, 1996 & 2000, McGraw Hill International.

There were even fewer resources with respect to bisexuality. In recent years, more have become available and more networks developed. I was greatly moved by the film adaptation of Annie Proulx's 'Brokeback Mountain'[16] and delighted to see a recent episode of 'The Street'[17] featuring a bisexual demolition worker grappling with the issue of his gayness within a heterosexual family situation.

In my view, queer, gay and bisexual men still have a great need for role models and I try to make a contribution in groups and website forums such as www.outeverywhere.com[18] The reality is that a lot of us are pretty damaged and, with regard to building positive attitudes towards our queer sexuality, have a lot of catching up still to do. At least it is possible now to do so more openly, unlike the experience I had of growing up. Yet the fact remains that I only know of a handful of men who have come out as gay or bi husbands and fathers and still remain in their marriage. I imagine that there are many, many other men out there in this situation, yet the fact remains that it is still risky to come out.

I believe strongly that the best way of coming out is to live an authentic life, married, single or whatever; a life in which you truly negotiate your relationships to try to ensure that your needs are met.

---

[16] 'Brokeback Mountain' first a short story by Annie Proulx (1997) and later an Academy Award, BAFTA and Golden Globe winning major film (2005) directed by Ang Lee, starring Heath Ledger, Jake Gyllenhaal, Anne Hathaway and Michelle Williams. It sensitively depicts the complex romantic and sexual relationship between two previously heterosexual men in the American West from the 1960s to 1980s.

[17] 'The Street' refers to a long running five times weekly British television soap opera, 'Coronation Street' (ITV) created by Tony Warren and first broadcast on 9 December 1960.

[18] www.outeverywhere.com : LGBT networking and information website. See also links in Resources Section to Bi and Jewish networks.

Crucial to this is finding a network of others who share a commonality of interests with you, engaging and sharing with them. The support, understanding, and acceptance of people, even one good friend, can make a world of difference.

ALEX'S STORY

Introduction to Alex

Alex's story says a lot about the need to belong, to connect with a variety of communities: a basic human need with tribal origins intended to support our survival as a species. This is a really important impulse with particular effects for gay and bisexual men denying their sexuality - to themselves as much as to others. Bi and gay boys naturally want to be accepted as they fully and truly are by their families, friends, peers, colleagues, children and other groups they feel affinities with. Yet most admit to having felt it necessary to conceal many aspects of just who they fully and truly are from those they most care about due to feelings of fear and shame about their emerging sexuality.

Many men, including nearly all of those who tell their stories here, set aside their true sexuality in attempting to join heterosexual - 'normal' -life, becoming husbands and fathers and hoping that marriage would either change or 'cover' them. There are plenty of benefits, after all, in joining the majority with the greatest status or power, which offer substantial rewards. Many gay and bi men genuinely yearn for a stable domestic life and for parenthood and these have seemed, indeed have been, until very recently,[19] much more possible to have within heterosexual partnerships. In fact, it is only relatively recently in our history that these ordinary aspects of

---

[19] See, for example, 'We Are Family' magazine (2013) listed in Resources section.

life were withheld from bi and gay people by law. Most men repress their multi-sexuality: only when this is openly accepted and encouraged will society become healthy.

Religious affiliation is also, of course, a vast consideration - and additional source of pressure - in the process of 'coming out' within marriage. In America, where most studies in this field have so far originated, it is even more of a formative stress as there is a tendency both for more fundamentalist Christian religious beliefs to be widely held and for people sharing those views to live and work, pray and socialise close to their families of origin and within fairly close-knit communities. Thus, the potential for rejection and loss is made more extreme. Equivalent conflicts do, however, profoundly affect Muslim, Hindu, Jewish and Catholic believers, too, in the UK today.

Gay and bisexual men often feel wholly unsupported by their church - or religious 'communion' in Christian terms - and frequently experience great pain and suffering in attempting to hold on to cherished beliefs at the same time as being aware that the their church condemns their natural sexuality or regards it as of lesser value than heterosexuality, in some cases commanding that same sex love go unexpressed. Fortunately, there are good support organisations for each religion working with believers who are gay or bi and details of support groups and information for specific religious communities are given under 'Faith' in the Resources section.

It is worth flagging up a warning for readers here. At a vulnerable time in his life, Alex became involved with what is now called 'Reparative' or 'Conversion' Counselling[20] in a desperate attempt to find a way out of his dilemma within his marriage.

Sadly, whole movements based around 'converting' people from same sex love and attractions have grown substantially since this time

---

[20] Reparative or Conversion Counselling: see Resources section 2: Avoiding bad therapy for useful links for fuller discussion of this dangerous development.

and are expanding rapidly in the UK. They often pose as counselling or psychotherapeutic organisations and keep their fundamentalist Christian mission covert, though many do not. Some belong to the 'ex-gay' movement[21], which claims to have successfully altered people's sexual desires and behaviours at their request. This has been repeatedly demonstrated to be untrue, in fact impossible, and to cause great damage emotionally and psychologically to those attempting to change in these ways. Suicide, self-harm and further mental illness is the most likely outcome for those who have tried their hardest to please therapists, counsellors, their families and, sometimes, other members of an 'ex-gay' group, with whom such a client will often live in a parody of 'rehab' for a while to make sure they don't act on their sexual feelings.

An additional huge concern for therapists such as myself, trying to develop ethical practice in this field, are the attitudes and behaviours of qualified colleagues which remain obstinately stuck in previous mind sets and comfortable with unethical practises. See for example Michael King's research at University College, London in 2009[22] showing that a lot of practising therapists and counsellors in Britain would agree to contract with a client to assist them in altering their sexuality. 'Magical thinking' indeed, to use Alex's own phrase!

Fortunately, in recent times campaigners have succeeded in getting the United Kingdom Council for Psychotherapy and the British Association for Counselling and Psychotherapy, the two major accrediting bodies in the UK, to state that these practices are unprofessional and highly dangerous, the latter after a landmark case

---

[21] Ex-gay movement. Also Resources section 2: Avoiding bad therapy..

[22] Michael King et al (2009): survey of 1,300 UK therapists, psychoanalysts and psychiatrists found that more than 200 had attempted to change at least one patient's sexual orientation, with 55 saying they were still offering such a therapy.

against a counsellor who attempted to 'cure' a gay male journalist with prayer once he had gone to see her under cover ostensibly as a client and later exposed what happened between them in a series of newspaper articles (Pilkington)[23].

However, even after publishing Codes of Ethics and Conduct including requirements for therapists to update themselves on issues affecting sex and gender minorities - as with all other minority client groups - the major psychotherapy and counselling accrediting bodies have failed to insist, in their regular re-accreditation of training programmes, that principles of equality are operated in every part of the curriculum and in October 2013 an Open Letter and petition was sent to them initiated by the campaigning group, Psychotherapists and Counsellors for Social Responsibility demanding conformity with the 2010 Equalities Act in these respects[24].

Another important aspect of Alex's background is the place and

---

[23] Pilkington judgement. In a landmark UK ruling psychotherapist Lesley Pilkington was found guilty of "treating" a patient for his homosexuality, attempting a 'gay cure'. A hearing of the British Association for Counselling and Psychotherapy– the largest professional body for therapists – unanimously concluded that the treatment she gave constituted "professional malpractice" and described her as "reckless", "disrespectful", "dogmatic" and "unprofessional". They said she showed "no empathy" towards her client. Pilkington's accreditation was suspended and she was ordered to complete extensive further professional development. If she does not satisfy the board within a year that she has complied, she will be struck off. The report concluded: "Mrs Pilkington had allowed her personal preconceived views about gay lifestyle and sexual orientation to affect her professional relationship in a way that was prejudicial."

[24] Details of PCSR Open Letter and Petition may still be on the change.org website here:http://www.change.org/petitions/ukcp-bacp-bpc-bps-counselling-psychology-other-training-orgs-end-discrimination-on-grounds-of-race-gender-and-sexual-diversity Or contact PCSR for further information at: http://pcsr-uk.ning.com

time in which he was growing up. For all of us these contexts will be formative. In Alex's youth same-sex love, sex and relationships were not only vilified but also illegal. Imagine the powerful impact of growing into your own sexuality and realising that it is regarded both as sinful and illegal by the communities in which you are developing a young self!

This impact never leaves us, even when we have worked very hard to come to a better understanding of ourselves and found ways to live authentic, satisfying lives. Most of the men who have worked so hard to 'come out' to themselves and those they care for about their sexuality in these life-stories have then also begun another journey to attempt to work through what used to be called 'IO' – which refers to the introversion of shame and guilt and low self value, sometimes to the point of self-hatred - and which I now call 'internalised oppression'[25] in each of the stories shared here.

Of course, there is a further discrimination - persecution even - with which Alex has had to deal since his earliest life and that is the prejudice directed against illness and disability in our society. This has been crucial to Alex's experiences of difference, isolation, rejection, low self-worth, anxieties and fears about bodies and sex. Sadly, this has not been lessened for anyone dealing with long-term illness or

---

[25] 'Internalised oppression', formerly called Internalised Homophobia, refers to negative stereotypes, beliefs, stigma, and prejudice about homosexuality and LGBT people that a person with same-sex attraction turns inward on themselves, whether or not they identify as LGBT. The degree depends on how much and which ideas they have consciously and subconsciously internalised. Effects include extreme repression and denial, self-hatred and self-destructive, compulsive behaviours, mental or physical ill health and relational problems. Also, forced displays of hetero-normativity, hyper-masculinity or hyper-femininity, for the purpose of appearing, or attempting to feel, 'normal' or 'acceptable'. Expressions of internalized oppression can also be extremely subtle and durable.

disability within gay and bisexual male subcultures where, as a legacy of sexism and the privileging of masculinity within Western cultures, male bodily perfection is worshipped as the gold standard and perpetuated as a kind of 'norm' in all the forms of display and communication in common use[26].

I am also interested in the distinctness and clarity of the gender divisions in the community in which Alex was forming himself. It is noticeable how the way his parents lived out extreme binary positions[27] has permeated his own marriage, ideas about what 'maleness' is and isn't, and the resulting roles which Alex has managed to occupy as a man, a husband, father, son, manager, partner and so on. A person's own historical and biographical context must always be allowed for in looking at their social, relational, sexual and psychological development, their beliefs and attitudes.

---

[26] See Shakespeare, Tom, Gillespie-Sells, Kath, and Davies, Dominic.The Sexual Politics of Disability: Untold Desires, Cassell Academic, 1997.

[27] 'Binary' used in this special sense: see Introduction and footnotes for 'Bruce's Story.'

ALEX'S STORY

I was born in a large Northern city in 1950. My father was a doctor and my mother worked as a ward sister until, following the birth of my eldest brother, she became a housewife and never took paid employment again.

The family was comfortably off but it never felt like that because we had many relatives better off than us. My parents were typically middle class in buying their home and saving for what they bought. Until I was fourteen most holidays were spent visiting grandparents and maiden great aunts, who were quite well to do, somewhat Victorian in style and well educated: teachers, bankers, scientists. They were a bit like Hinge and Bracket[28]- musical, playing bridge. They taught me lots of interesting things like that.

I had two brothers, two or three years older than me. My mother was an intelligent woman who also suffered - or, enjoyed? - poor health and was in hospital a long time after my second brother was born so he was cared for by my grandparents for about twelve months. My eldest brother was very ill as a baby and it was only the release of a new drug that helped him get better. In general I recall my mother being ill a lot, including a hysterectomy, back pain and spinal nerve damage, and my father often being the primary carer as he

---

[28] 'Hinge and Bracket': the stage personae of the musical performance and female impersonation artists George Logan and Patrick Fyffe in UK theatre, radio and television between 1972 and 2001. Dr.Evadne Hinge and Dame Hilda Bracket were two elderly, eccentric spinsters, living genteel lives celebrating their former careers on the provincial operatic stage.

looked after her as well, depending on how she was.

I was born with a hair lip and cleft palette and, as a result, hospitalised from soon after birth and had several operations before the age of three. It was not possible for my parents to visit as the hospital authorities frowned upon it then. I was baptised at three days old because there was doubt whether I would live!

Your father looked after you and your brothers?

To some extent, yes. My mother was an excellent cook and very capable with perfectionist standards regarding housework and so on. My father would often do the clothes washing - I never saw him with the iron though - and all cooking at weekends and sometimes in the evenings. He would serve dinner, help with dishes and bathe us.

He did this to ensure she would be able to cope without too much pressure and tried to protect us from emotional outbursts as children by ensuring that my mother remained stable. He did this by smoothing things over with her and looking after her. I never remember any arguments or him showing anger. I can recall only once in my life when he actively said no to her and this was when she threatened to lock the door to prevent my elder brother getting into the house because he had stayed out late, maybe 9pm. She flew in to a rage and hit him, then stormed out of the house and did not come back for quite a while - I don't recall how long. I do remember the incident vividly - even down to the colour of the coat she put on to leave.

I don't want to give the impression that my mother was not a caring woman - she was very caring and did her best, but was super sensitive and unpredictable and, for that reason, I had an unconscious fear of her.

My mother's mother died when she was four and this seemed to affect her life and general state of happiness. She left home at sixteen because she was unhappy and apparently unloved - her stepmother was strict and jealous. She went for a while to live with her aunt: also Salvation Army, teetotal (unlike her children) and more worldly: another very strong woman. She was also divorced from her husband.

My mother's parents were very straight laced. Her father was a pillar of the local community and owned a fish business. His first wife died in childbirth and he remarried a woman in the Salvation Army, in which he was a major. Enjoyment, such as cinema, was considered a corrupting influence and my mother was not permitted to go, even if it were a school outing. I thought my grandfather OK but my step grandmother odd and ridiculously old fashioned. I did not like visiting, which was thankfully rare and only for a few hours.

I saw more of my father's parents. Despite my grandmother being stern she had a good sense of humour. She was a housewife, well educated and from a family which owned a shipyard. Interestingly, her father had "run off" with another woman, a family secret not known to me when young. Their mother, who never remarried, brought up her daughters alone. I suppose this was all scandalous at the time. My grandfather worked as a railway clerk in a small town. He liked football, gardening, doing the pools and fishing: a bit of a gruff and quiet character. I was a little afraid of him but he was reliable and caring - for example, he would take us to the beach regularly and sit with his overcoat on whilst we boys played in our swimming costumes in the cold.

What do you think you learned from your relationships with your father and grandfathers about men in particular?

So far as men were concerned, I think they were occupied with bearing burdens and my relationship with my father and grandfather made me think that love was about suffering in silence. They certainly didn't speak of feelings but stoically got on with life. Doing things was more important than talking. There was a kind of power in silence. Love was providing, helping and being dutiful, whatever the circumstances. I know that is a part of loving but it is only a part: I see now that love also should have physical and emotional content.

I grew up not experiencing, understanding or knowing in my being that love is being able to express emotions - overtly sharing feelings with another (e.g. kissing, cuddling, tears, making up, saying I love you). I do not recall the men in my life, apart from my 'uncles', ever openly expressing love. It seemed to me that men did not cry, although I did, but were logical creatures who fixed things, made things and did things. I would say I saw love as a sort of Christ-like, saintly thing, about giving, not counting the cost: being a 'good' person meant to be long suffering. As a result I learned not to show emotion and found it difficult to accept love even if it was overtly offered. I knew I was loved but it was a sort of magical and intuitive knowing, which did not need verbalising. Loving was being saintly and stoical like my father.

And what did you learn from your mother and grandmothers about women and relationships?

With regard to women, I think I learned to fear rejection, and to disconnect from any part of myself which might trigger this, to be afraid of the power of my own emotions (not only expressions of love but also displays of anger, jealousy, hate and rage) and the emotions of others. I was afraid to show feelings - perhaps with the exception of self-pity. I suppose I learned to manipulate adults by being shy and quiet and encouraging pity. Expressing anger was not acceptable, as I feared this would lead to rejection and feelings of abandonment. I was both dependent upon, and fearful of, women. I also admired them in some ways.

Perhaps I didn't develop a full sense of self, repressing parts of my character that might trigger reactions in my mother. I never really felt secure and suffered feelings of anxiety and abandonment. This may have originated in my early hospitalisation but my mother's instability surely enhanced these fears. Unconsciously I knew I could use my weakness; play up to the 'poor Alex' label. I felt smothered if my mother said she loved me, which she sometimes did.

I suppose I learned that women were stronger and more powerful emotionally than men, whom they could manipulate through the use, or threat, of emotion, or by the use of words, rows. Many, if not all, the women in my life as a child (my mother, the cleaner, my great aunts and both grandmothers) seemed strong independent characters, although some could be very manipulative.

At the same time I saw women as able to be tender and communicate about relationships. I was around women far more than men growing up and would often listen intently to their conversations about problems, cooking and fashion. As a result I intuitively 'knew' women and what they wanted in life but felt cut off from men who were uncommunicative, gruff, unapproachable and physically powerful.

I think my dysfunctional family and fear created a narcissistic trait in me. I cut off from my most powerful feelings and defended myself by creating an unreal, external way of being, a fantasy world in which I was disconnected from my core being for fear of being found out as not being a real male. My relationships with both men and myself were, therefore, disconnected emotionally although I was less afraid of showing anger to males. With women I was also disconnected but able to use vulnerability and play a victim role as this seemed to be safe. I think my mother felt guilty about my face. These traits have affected, and to some extent still affect, all my relationships with both genders.

My parents were not religious in the conventional sense but I sensed they were spiritual. I did to go Sunday school but we never went to church. My dad said little about God but once told me he was Anglo Catholic: high church. My mum often talked about life after death and stuff like that. I suspect her experience with the Salvation Army put her off religion for good - as opposed to spirituality.

Childhood experience

As a child I was aware I was different. I recall an abiding sense of inner loneliness and not fitting in. This may have been because I had something wrong with my face and partly because I did not like things other boys, like my brothers, did. I'd play with the girls and they the boys. Being the youngest it was difficult for me to compete anyway. I thought my eldest brother was so clever and my other brother so confident and good at sport.

There must have been something different about me as, when I was four or five, I put on my mother's hat and coat and was found playing on a local hotel lawn! I also remember, when I was maybe six, wanting to be a ballet dancer but thinking it would never be because real boys don't do that sort of thing. Being the youngest and having a hair lip meant I was spoilt a bit, I suppose.

Do you know anything of the reaction of the children and adults around you at that time?

Not much. No one ever told me I should not be sensitive or creative: it was just something I 'knew' I should not be. I was not bullied or anything like that. I now know that my parents told my brothers they had to protect me and not say anything about how I looked. I think even today they are quite protective. They may have resented this but I don't recall anything ever being said. I was vaguely aware that my brothers might cast me into the role of helper, not leader. When playing games I'd get favourable treatment; if we were fishing or camping I'd be helped more or take on - or be given? - the role of cook, rather than hunter or fire-lighter.

My mother certainly was protective of me, yet felt guilty that I was clingy too. Sometimes she would confide in me her feelings about her childhood and my father's perceived, and no doubt sometimes real, faults. She often said he was a pessimist. My dad was protective, but distant emotionally, a caring man with a good sense of humour, who never showed any anger. He was always smoothing things over: I could never work out why. He would say things like, "Don't be like that dear" rather than state openly what he must have felt. Dad was a rather passive character: he'd moan to me about my mother sometimes behind her back. Nevertheless, they did seem to care for each other genuinely although there was an element of the victim and rescuer.

How did all this affect your own relationship with anger?

I sometimes wondered how my father put up with it all. It left me with a strong, but repressed, fear of showing anger or being assertive. I needed to control events and people as well as my own emotions, which I think were cut off. Even now I fear losing control and what might happen if I show anger. This may have affected my ability to express my sexual feelings in an uninhibited manner. I am vaguely aware of strong fear that if I got angry I would fly into a rage and do something I would regret later: might I kill someone if I let go of control?

This repressed rage came out in childhood in the form of constant low-level depression, lack of joy, irritability, being critical of others and a general gruffness. Control was also expressed through humour or playing the martyr.

If you think of 'The Drama Triangle'[29] (Persecutor/ Victim/ Rescuer/ Leveller) who played which roles most often? Which have you built in to your inner structure?

---

[29] The Drama Triangle is a model, devised by Karpmann in 1968, used in Transactional Analysis to reveal a 'game' in which there are just three positions to adopt interpersonally and intra-personally and none is healthy. They are: Victim, Persecutor and Rescuer. The healthy alternative to these relational dysfunctions is the Leveller. See, for example, Eric Berne's Games People Play' (1964, Ballantine, NY), Thomas Harris's 'I'm OK, You're OK' (1967, Harper & Row, NY) and Amy & Thomas Harris's 'Staying OK' (1985, Harper Row Int., NY).

It's difficult to say which roles are strong now although I suspect rescuer and martyr are still 'built in'. I used to play the victim, martyr and peacekeeper roles in my marriage. I also felt the need to rescue my mother sometimes by acting as her confidante or by being overly helpful and co-operative. The rescuer is still strong within me although I'm more conscious of it and more wary of rescuing people nowadays. I am now in a stable gay relationship and would say I frequently play rescuer or martyr with my partner as persecutor, though that is reversed at times. I suppose these boost my self-esteem, calm fear of rejection and make me feel needed.

My mother could switch: she could persecute my father and play victim equally well. Victim was my main role in the family; though I also knew I was 'special' to mum and my godmother. In a way my mother seduced me into an intimate emotional relationship with her which excluded my father and brothers and maybe other men. My dad was definitely a rescuer. I'm not sure what the leveller role is.

My mum seemed to manipulate and control things, often by unspoken emotional threats and constant illness. There were occasional rages which I found frightening. For example, when I was sixteen, my mother threw a bookcase down the stairs in a rage – sometimes there would just be sulky silences afterwards. Yet she could be caring and non-judgmental about others.

You included?

I did judge myself quite severely until recently, but am getting better at self-acceptance now! Maybe until thirty-five, I was judgmental and critical of people - friends, peers or others in authority who I thought superior to me or not accepting of me. Such criticisms were not expressed directly. At the same time I was less inclined to judge those I was closest to, or needed. I tend to identify with the weak or powerless and share their pain. This is probably a projective defence against my low self-worth, or repressed envy.

I learned never to push too far and became sensitive to picking up emotional atmospheres. I didn't have to be told how to behave as a child: great care was needed as an apparently small incident could set off a huge, unwarranted reaction in my mother, which once resulted in a suicide attempt in front of me with an overdose. I, of course, thought I had caused this. I found out years later that her actions probably related to problems with my father in their marriage. These may have been to do with their sexual relationship since they did not show any physical affection in public.

What do you imagine now that these problems were? What leads you to speculate that they were sexual in origin?

I have often wondered if my father may have been gay. He was not a man's man or sporty in any way, very sensitive, able to see in people what was not apparent to others and he played a rather 'feminine' role within the family. I also recall him reacting strongly to an incident on the news to do with a boy being molested by a priest, which I thought strange, as it was unlike him to react with anger. I wondered if something like that had happened to him. Also, he could camp it up a bit when being funny after a few drinks! His relationship to my mother was very similar to the one I had with my wife. My sister-in-law told me once that my mother had told her they had problems to do with impotence, lack of desire, something like that. I think my mother, like me, found any kind of rejection difficult to deal with and reacted strongly. She was super-sensitive due to the loss of her mother when very young.

We moved several times: I lived in the North East until I was four, the Midlands until seven, Yorkshire until eighteen and then London, where I have been ever since, apart from University.

This moving must have had an impact on you forming, or holding on to, relationships with other children, family, neighbours, and schools?

Yes, I suppose it did. I did not have friends in London for ages as, when we moved, I had just gone to university. I also think it means I have not kept in touch with friends I did make at school. Finally, I suppose it cut us off from our cousins and wider family quite a bit.

I passed my 11-plus, as did my brothers. Our school was quite academic with an emphasis on Oxbridge but I was not considered bright and struggled in my first years there, perhaps because I had to stay in hospital a number of times for plastic surgery.

One subject I found easy at a young age was scripture. I won a prize in junior school for my work on bible stories. At this time I had an intuitive and natural belief in God. When I reached the age of twelve or so I completely rejected the notion of God. This was, I think, partly the influence of my elder brother, who had decided it was all nonsense. Partly it was connected with my rejection of myself, not being happy in my teens because I was struggling with my sexuality and self-esteem. I remained completely opposed to religion until I was thirty-seven.

Please say a bit more about your relationship with 'God,' religion and your sexuality as a child and adolescent.

As a child I instinctively believed there was a god and liked doing scripture lessons. It offered what seemed like hope for the forlorn and abandoned, justice and compassion. I liked the idea of an all-powerful god or, maybe, father figure, who could put right the wrongs in the world. I think now this was a projective defence to my own feelings of inadequacy and regular hospitalisation. I was certainly aware that I did not like my condition and envied those who had got what I felt I should have. It seemed so unfair. When very young I'd had a powerful image of God as the great, old wise man with a flowing beard, ensconced in the clouds and having magical powers. In some ways, thinking about it now, the bible stories and pictures or images were a fantasy way of escaping my problems and the pain I felt. They provided a ray of hope that martyrs were loved and victims could be rescued.

The following stories stick in my mind:

Joseph and the coat of many colours[30] - favourite son rejected

Daniel in the lion's den[31] - magical protection of the good

David and Goliath[32] - weak boy becomes powerful man

Shadrach, Meshach, & Abednego[33] - being rescued in the fire

Ruth - meek, but inherits a protector through faith and good works

Samuel – faithful and special 'good' boy finds God big time

The prodigal son - father accepts son despite his faults

These are all Old Testament stories, Alex.

I need to think about that and what the implications are. They do reflect archetypal figures of power and weakness: God, man, father rescues the weak and helpless; faith, sacrifice wins out in the end. God in the Old Testament was BOTH caring and angry/judgemental. Given that, to my mind, my own father lacked power with my mother, maybe I projected anger and judgement I felt about them and myself onto God?

The religious hope was that God or, better still, someone else, would recognise my situation and feelings and heal me. Doctors, of course, could, and did, help - and may have reinforced the notion of

---

[30] Joseph: Genesis 37-3.

[31] Daniel: The Book of Daniel. Notable for devotion to prayer in spite of persecution.

[32] David and Goliath: Books of Samuel 1: David's battle with the giant, Goliath is seen as the victory of God's champion over enemies of god's helpless people.

[33] Shadrach, Meshach & Abednego: Book of Daniel 1-3, known for exclusive devotion to god.

all-powerful, but loving, fathers. It is difficult to put into words. I suppose the appeal was the same as watching a fantasy movie (e.g. 'Lord of the Rings' or 'Star Wars') where the good guys triumph and all turns out happily ever after. Of course life is not like that.

I never read anything about homosexuality in the bible or as a child. I was aware, however, of how boys were supposed to be. If I saw being gay as wrong I had picked up these ideas from observing 'normal' model relationships and from cultural norms. I did reject God in my very early teens and this may have been due to repressed anger when I finally realised I was gay at about the age of twelve and to my rejection of my sexuality, my self and the difficulty I felt accepting assertive male roles, which I admired in others but appeared not to possess. I've never thought about why I rejected God but I knew you had to have evidence to test a hypothesis and there was none in my experience, for God. Later, when my son died, I accepted God again, after an internal battle. I wonder now whether this wasn't more to do with fear, the need to fit into my wife's desire to go to church and the hope of redemption, rather than an intellectual choice.

In my thirties I also had a realisation - revelation? - that my earlier rejection of God was a defence against my own lack of self-worth. If I could not accept myself, why should I accept the nonsensical idea of God, an all-powerful father supposedly responsible for me? It was only too apparent that fathers were not all powerful except in fantasy. I've never been attracted to the idea of the Virgin Mary - too weak and passive, not reflecting my experience of mothers. I also found the idea of Jesus as God more difficult to accept than the idea of God the Father or the Holy Spirit. Maybe Jesus was too much of a brother or son figure. One key element of my insecurity was my unspoken sexuality of which I became increasingly aware from the age of twelve.

How did your awareness increase?

From the age of nine or ten I recall being sexually excited when my teacher was disciplining another pupil. I thought it odd that this should give me an erection but it made me think a lot about my teachers. As kids we used to play around with friends: strip poker was popular. Mostly they were boys and I realised I wanted to look at them naked, for example in showers at school. When I was about thirteen I really wanted to sleep with one older boy. I knew this would not, never could, happen.

I tried to masturbate from an early age, well before twelve, with limited success. I thought there must be something wrong with me because of this and worried about it. I knew that I was different: more sensitive, liking things most boys didn't - dancing, clothes, fashion, poetry, cooking - so felt the need to hide what I was from my peers.

I lived quite a lot through my two elder brothers and their friends, with whom I got on well and still do. We played a great deal together - board games, tree houses, cricket, the usual stuff. I don't recall playing games at home or any sport with either of my parents, although my father did take us fishing a couple of times when we were on holiday. My parents seemed wrapped up in each other. I did not have many friends of my own until after I was sixteen and these friendships were flawed, insofar as I had to hide who I really was.

Did other children see you, or treat you, get at you, as different?

I'm not sure they did. They never said anything but I was always careful not to talk about things that interested me. For example, I had started an interest in spiritual things like astrology, which I knew would be the subject of ridicule. I went along with what they wanted even if this involved being horrible and ostracising other, apparently weaker, individuals. I also hung around with my brothers' friends who were older than me so, if I was different, I could hide behind the mask of being younger. I played the clown and amused my brothers' friends so I was well liked. Maybe they sensed weakness in me: being youngest in the group, perhaps they made allowances, treated me as a favourite, I don't really know.

At school I do recall having a crush on my teachers.

Plural? Male?

Yes definitely male, there were one or two. I had a crush on one who was in his twenties and an older one, a disciplinarian. I remember wishing I could be closer to them from the age of nine or ten.

I also recall, at seven or eight, wishing I had a different father. I don't know why but I suppose my dad was not typically masculine - not sporty or strong and rather distant in many ways, although he had a good sense of fun. Conversely I perceived my mother's cousins, the 'uncles', as direct, powerful, successful, sporty, rich, strong characters.

What was your fantasy father like?

I don't think I had a definite idea, just that I would rather have someone with more masculine traits: decisive, assertive and successful, able to control others in ways my father, who loved and cared for me, did not. He wasn't powerful and was risk averse.

When I was twelve or so I'd fantasise about older boys and teachers I saw in the showers and on the playing fields. I did my best to hide this and would avoid doing anything which might suggest I was gay. For example, how I carried my books was a matter of great importance, as was avoiding strawberry ice cream or anything else which might expose my sexuality! A great deal of energy went into acting like my peers: smoking and being 'one of the lads', which I never actually felt I was.

Please say more about these fascinating rules and systems for hiding or 'passing'.[34]

---

[34] 'Passing': See also references (and footnote) in Bruce's story and Alan's.

There's not a lot more to say. I think what I did was never talk to my friends about anything sensitive (beauty, love, poetry), maybe even denigrate sensitivity; agree with comments that a particular woman was sexy (whilst I saw it was true, I felt nothing). I'd go along with homophobic comments others would make about boys at school, go to pubs and parties and force myself to drink beer, which I did not like, and act like they did. To fit in! I used to look at 'girlie' magazines with friends. I worried because I could not see the fascination but, of course, went along with the banter about big tits and so on. I feel my tendency to be critical of others in my teens was a defence against my truly low self-esteem.

What of your own relationships with girls at this stage?

From thirteen or fourteen I became part of a gang of about twenty-five girls and boys. My relationships were wholly platonic: although I did not have any girlfriends, I knew lots of them, all one to three years older than me. I tagged along to parties, meeting in the park and people's houses to listen to records, playing cards. I got on OK with them but never had a special girlfriend, platonic or otherwise. One girl, Norwegian, was physically quite large and part of this group. I was sixteen and kissed her when they turned the lights down. I felt no sexual arousal, just fear. I went to her house once and sat on the sofa, petrified to do anything. That was the end of that. I didn't go out with another girl for ten years.

Early Sexual Experiences

My first sexual experience with a man was when I was about sixteen. A man in the toilets approached me. I did not stop him as part of me wanted the attention but I was scared stiff (literally). I was so afraid that I left immediately but this confirmed what I strongly suspected, that I was homosexual. In one way this was a relief as I realised there

57

were others like me but, afterwards, I hated myself even more. Prior to this exciting and scary incident I could hope my feelings were a phase as I had read in books. On another occasion my brother climbed into bed with me and we touched one another sexually. In my late teens and early twenties I discovered cruising and started to meet men anonymously. I ceased this when I was twenty-four as I always hated myself afterwards.

When I was about eighteen I vowed that if I could not be happy like everyone else and marry, I would concentrate on being successful at work as this gave me great satisfaction and some self-esteem.

What was the work that gave you satisfaction then, Alex?

I made this vow when I was at school doing 'A levels' and continued it doing my degree. I was very lonely at university: I did not fit in for the first year and had no friends at my new home. The students were into football and sport, which I hated, and I think they thought I was snooty or posh because I lived in the south and had gone to private school. My defence was to work hard and study as best I could.

After my degree I got a job as a trainee accountant, which I quickly left, as it was just not me. I went back to college to train as a town planner between twenty-two and twenty-four. It was one of the best times ever: I loved the work and was rebellious with the lecturers sometimes - if I thought they were teaching rubbish or manipulating the students. I became the course spokesperson - a role I still sometimes adopt in groups from a repressed envy of authority.

It was during this time that I discovered cruising. I was living at home again. No one knew I was doing this. I went cruising for sex late at night after drinking with friends, now fantasising about my new lecturers as I had through University and school.

When I was about twenty-eight I told a friend I was gay, the first time I'd spoken openly about it to anyone. He suggested it was all in my mind and that women would find my sensitive, communicative side attractive - 'devastating' was his actual word. I thought a lot about this and decided to try to go out with girls. I spent time visualising what a sexual encounter with a girl would feel like and how I would react, hoping to make it easier when it happened. My experience was limited to one kiss at a party! I also vowed at this time not to pursue cruising anymore and decided that all I had to do was to force myself to relate to women sexually and face my fears.

Married life and girls

I met a nurse at a party a few months later and subsequently for a drink. Coffee at her flat seemed like the longest of my life, too scared to kiss her, petrified of what might follow. A couple of months later I met my wife-to-be. I had, in desperation, prayed for my life to change – maybe I still had some magical thinking despite my unbelief –so when it happened it seemed in some way fated, perhaps divine intervention.

She was a friend who had recently left her husband. I knew him and had attended their wedding. She treated him as a bit of a wimp and, compared to her, he was relatively uneducated and rather passive. I think there were sexual difficulties. Years later I found out he was gay. She and I talked about how difficult her life was with him and she told me she'd recently attempted suicide. This brought things to a head and he left. The fact that she'd taken this manipulative action should have set alarm bells ringing but didn't. I was sympathetic as we met to talk over her problems.

She had many similarities to your mother, which therefore were familiar to you?

Quite! I have often thought that. Both were outgoing, adventurous but controlling, both had passive husbands whom they may have despised for being weak in their eyes. My mum and wife were both intelligent, good organisers and homemakers who could be manipulative, using threats of rejection, mood swings, anger and threats of suicide. Both liked order and perfection and were really the ones in charge - superficially at least - of the relationship. Both needed love, security and sex and talked about their problems to me. I suppose I counselled them. Like my father, I tried to keep the peace, never getting angry or asserting my wishes.

I liked my wife-to-be a lot as she was vivacious and clearly liked me. We talked easily and had similar backgrounds. She had flirted with me at parties when she was married. I see now that she was unhappy, lacking self-esteem about her femininity. She also had a poor relationship with her mother.

A little later we went away together and ended up in bed. It seemed she was sexually frustrated and I felt engulfed by her need but at the time had no experience with women. I later recognised that as a feeling I had frequently in my relationship with my mother.

The sex was a bit of a disaster from my point of view but she understood, so I was happy and I was in love! The courtship was short, two months at most, and when I asked her to marry me, she said yes. We lived together for eighteen months and were married for sixteen years.

A month after asking her to marry me I told her I'd only had sex with men. I did this because I sensed it could all go horribly wrong as I felt very tense about the sexual aspect, which I thought, hoped, would improve with time. Again she seemed to accept this and was OK about it. I was very happy - for the first time in my life someone knew about my secret and nevertheless loved and accepted me unconditionally. I was overjoyed. However, the issue was never discussed again for many years, although I think it coloured our reactions to one another at an unconscious level. I remember thinking to myself that I could never have guessed that I would end up being married and very thankful.

Looking back at this whirlwind of events, what do you understand now about what was really going on in you then?

I suppose I hated myself and hoped I would change sexually with practice. At the same time the relationship fed my need to be needed and she and I were, to some degree, rescuing one another. I knew my wife had faults that made me uneasy but I'd lived with my mother's behaviour, and so much wanted to hide that I thought I could hack it. Since I'd borne so much pain it did not seem that different, apart from the sex, which I found very stressful! Both of us were in pain and recognised it in the other: we believed we could help each other.

In fact the relationship was co-dependent, each trying to fix the other. I was into astrology, psychology and tarot by now and these made me think about inner states and why people did what they did, or were the way they were. I was investigating psychology from about eighteen onwards looking for answers to myself. I was more aware that things could go heartily wrong between us: if she was, she never said so. Her need for sex seemed desperate at times, her clinging panic or worry if I was out late and anger or fear of losing me made me uneasy.

Looking back, I see my wife had huge self-esteem problems. She too feared rejection. Her first husband was also gay, from what I have gathered, and their marriage was not good for allowing her to explore her feelings and sexuality.

She knew very little about how to be feminine and I used to help her choose clothes to make her look good, show her how to decorate the house and understand the more feminine side of herself. All that time with women in my life taught me a great deal about what they liked. She thought herself unattractive, undesirable and, I suppose, I thought the same - being gay, what woman would want me? It was a case of each of us settling for something unsatisfactory because we felt there was no choice. In some ways our relationship felt fated.

We were happy at first and in love. My wife's clinging gradually turned into seeking to control aspects of my life and behaviour and our respective functions in the marriage: for example, who did gardening, who loaded the washing machine, cooked or chose the decor. I noticed my wife becoming increasingly concerned that we act out gender 'appropriate' roles of husband and wife. Later I understood that she was worried, albeit unconsciously, that others might suspect our marriage was not all it seemed and that I was not a typical male, which might reflect poorly on her.

People thought us the perfect couple as we did *everything* together and I helped around the house and with the children. After getting married I gave up my outside interests and friends and concentrated on our home life. Intellectually we got on and had similar backgrounds and we were happy to be parents. I greatly enjoyed playing with, and looking after, the children when they were young and was seen as a good father. I got on well with her parents and was accepted and loved by the wider family.

We had two children soon after we married and my wife was wrapped up in mothering and feeding. I think having children was a way of her 'becoming' more of a woman and it covered feelings of lack of femininity. She met friends who encouraged her to go to church. I was reluctant as I felt out of place. We decided to have a third child. Sadly, he was born with a heart defect and died when he was very young. The events surrounding his death were emotionally and psychically powerful and started us thinking about what was going on spiritually. The church got involved and sent a "Good News Team" to visit. I resisted and was uneasy but, because of the magical coincidences at the time, I convinced myself that there was a God after all and maybe he loved me ... as I was.

What magical coincidences please, Alex?

A couple of weeks before our son was born I suggested we call him

Joshua - for months we'd agreed on William. The birth was easy and I remember he was calm and perfect with beautiful, soulful eyes. He was born the day before Good Friday, when he was taken ill. We ended up at the local children's hospital where there was an Easter service. We were referred to a specialist hospital, where we were told he would die very soon and there was nothing they could do.

I remember looking at him in his crib thinking, 'Why is he lying in the shape of a crucifix?' We asked to have him baptised so a priest came. He asked me his name and I said Joshua. He just said, "I know that name," and I went cold, a shiver went down my spine. We took Joshua home and he died in the bed between us. It was a beautiful, though very sad, experience. The room was so quiet. He died at exactly the time the clocks went forward. I remember thinking it was as if this moment was out of space and time - eternal. It was Easter Sunday morning, I was calm and remember thinking there was a spirit of peace in the room.

A few days later, reading a book on names, I looked up 'Joshua' and discovered the name was Hebrew for Jesus. I got that shiver again and, because it was Easter, thought about the Easter story and what this experience meant.

The weather at the funeral was odd too. It was March, a sunny day and a lady sang a beautiful solo of the 23rd Psalm, which was very moving. As we walked to the grave, it began to rain while the sun was still out and the rain was lit up in golden colours. Even thinking about it now brings tears to my eyes. It looked so beautiful and I thought, 'God is crying'. It stopped when I got to the graveside, the sun went and it turned cold, windy and squally, the trees and leaves stirring in the wind. As we left the graveside (I am crying as I write this) it started to snow and the whole churchyard was white. By the time I got back to the car waiting to take us home, everything had turned white. All this happened in around ten minutes. It seemed that God was very present. I remember thinking I had seen the cycle of all four seasons in the time it took me to let go of my baby son - again eternity seemed present. My wife also sensed these things. I experienced a number of other magical coincidences, which made me think a great deal about the existence of God.

Perhaps it was all to do with my pain and the idea of sacrifice. I had no difficulty identifying with the issues: after all, I'd won a scripture prize when I was nine! I had a sort of dramatic revelation or conversion as result of synchronistic events surrounding Joshua's death but that's a complete story on its own.

Soon we wholeheartedly embraced the evangelical faith and were welcomed by the church although I did have a nagging sense that people there were not real, too concerned with appearances and being members of an exclusive club. I suppose I liked the sense of care, belonging and fellowship. Soon we were fêted as perfect Christians. We became active participants in the church, leading a home group where we began to discuss risky, but real, matters such as anger, relationships, sexuality, and masculinity and how these related to religious teaching.

One couple were into gay 'conversion therapy'[35] and had some connection with a U.S. organisation working with gay Christians. I think the husband had some sexual identity issues and was receiving help from them to change.

The Break-up

About two years after Josh died, after our fourth son was born, my wife went for counselling with a woman from the house group. She was unhappy with her relationship with her mother, whom she experienced as cold and self-centred, and still sad, maybe depressed, about Joshua's death. I think she discussed our relationship and her

---

[35] Conversion therapy: see Appendix 2: Avoiding bad therapy.

feelings about sex, my sexuality, and me.

About this time she started to see a male former colleague with whom she talked on the phone, sometimes for hours, throughout our marriage. They'd had some sort of brief sexual relationship before we married, which I knew about and did not have a problem with. She began to tell him about our problems and that she was no longer happy in the marriage. They started a brief, intense affair. It now seems that she was always in love with him though in denial earlier: they are still in a close relationship although they are not married.

You had had no extra-marital sexual contacts all this time? What had you done with your 'gay' sexuality throughout your marriage? Had you any outlets for those feelings? I imagine you might have felt horribly betrayed by this affair, having repressed so much of your own desiring?

None. I made a commitment and that was that: I was such a 'good boy' you see. I'd look at men in the street or at work and long for them, but never did anything. I just channelled all my energies into work, making a home, enjoying the children and in my caring and rescuing roles. I did think about men sometimes when having sex with my wife and used to feel incredibly guilty. Much time was spent attempting to transcend these feelings with the church work I had taken up. I wanted God to change me. I wasn't in denial about my feelings: I just refused to act on them; to do so would have been a betrayal of my marriage vows. With plenty of practice concealing my true feelings growing up, it came easily to me. I felt betrayed and angry as I had, from my viewpoint, stuck to our 'bargain' and couldn't understand what had changed. I hadn't. My wife, of course, had: she needed more from a relationship, especially sexually, and to be with an assertive man who wouldn't be 'nice' all the time.

My wife told her counsellor about this affair and was advised to give him up. She felt guilty and told me. I blamed myself. She suggested we spice up our sex but I found this hard because, if anything went wrong, she was upset and angry. It also put me under greater pressure and reinforced my sense of failure. My usual response was to try to be nicer.

Your father's traditional role?

YES, YES, YES! Just the way my father had dealt with my mother - being a saint, not rocking the boat!

Later, my wife said she felt trapped. She was struggling to give up her relationship with her lover. Her attitude became increasingly resentful towards what she called my 'martyr complex'. There is truth in her charge but, in trying to preserve the relationship if only for the sake of the children, I did not feel I had choice. The alternative would have been to leave. I found all this hard to bear. Desperate to save our marriage, I agreed to change myself as this is what she most wanted. We were very different personalities with different problems and approaches and we were both needy. I see now that the marriage would probably not have lasted even without the complication of my being gay.

We went to Relate[36] but there was a waiting list so we saw Christian marriage counsellors. As my wife only wanted to talk about my problems, not hers, we did not continue for more than a couple of sessions. We also talked to friends who tried to help.

It seems the only way in which your repressed gay sexuality was manifest was in your lack of interest in sex with your wife – and there were other factors involved in that. Is that right? You weren't 'gay' in any other ways then?

---

[36] 'Relate': Counselling organisation for people in relationships. See Resources: 'Organisations'.

Well, what is gay? I used to daydream about men but not act on them. I masturbated sometimes when my wife was out. I think my gay side expresses itself in my sensitivity, in caring for and playing with the children, in service or suffering generally. These I now see as having a strong maternal or feminine aspect. Also, my 'gay side' was expressed through my subsequent work and spirituality, the church. Maybe religion increased my sense of guilt and fear and enabled me to cope with the pain I was feeling.

I went to the doctor about my increasing lack of sexual performance at my wife's request and he sent me to a psychiatrist, then an NHS counsellor, the outcome of which was that I should come to accept myself just as I was. I later paid for several months of so-called 'psychosexual counselling' with another Christian counsellor recommended by church friends and he had links to a Christian 'conversion therapy' organisation.

I spent most of the time crying at sessions and unburdening myself about how awful things had become and the pain I was feeling at being constantly upset, criticised, ignored, undermined and rejected. The fear of loss of self and identity was overwhelming. All the while my wife became more depressed, distant, difficult and angry. In a final desperate effort to save our marriage I went on a one year Christian 'conversion course' for gay men and women. This included a trip to the U.S. evangelical home of the organisation where I was to train to do the same. I hoped that I had been changed. Sometimes you believe what you wish to despite all the facts.

Needless to say, fundamentally my sexual orientation was unchanged, but it was not all bad: I did learn a great deal about myself, about anger, lack of self-acceptance, healthy relationships, the power of feelings, co-dependency, emotional abuse, narcissism and defence mechanisms. During this time my wife finally decided she wanted a divorce. I was devastated since, so far as I was concerned, I'd done nothing wrong apart from being who I was. I had tried everything she'd asked and more but, unsurprisingly, without success. I now realise you can't change your sexuality or basic personality and that you can't make anyone love you, however compliant, obliging, pleasing or nice you are to them.

As part of the separation agreement I had to give away my house, its contents and the car and pay maintenance for all my children. It was very hard for the first few years and I was lonely and hurt at the rejection - a big issue for me anyway. However, I managed to buy a flat and my mum helped out with paying for new furniture. My children visited every other weekend for ten years although, as they reached eighteen, they no longer came.

How do you explain this?

It is difficult for me to rationalise this but I suspect some is to do with them and some me. Obviously, as children grow they need to separate themselves, have their own lives, and they assume their parents don't need them. I think my children may have resented having to leave friends and family to come to see me. For my part, the fewer shared experiences we had, the harder it was to maintain closeness. Our interests and hobbies were different and I was not present on a daily basis doing things families do: shopping, eating, homework, school runs, meeting friends, whatever. In any case, parents are not necessarily supposed to be 'friends' with their children.

I sense in them unresolved, unconscious anger, not overtly directed at its source: mother and father. It comes out in other ways: for example, not visiting or calling, being rebellious or taking silly risks. This is speculation and my reactions to them and feelings of rejection may be just as important. Maybe they and I feel a barrier because I'm gay. I'm not sure as we don't talk about it.

Although she was organised and a dutiful, loving mother, I suspect my ex-wife did not have enough time for them emotionally: being a perfect mother is difficult with a full time job and four children.

They've grown up too quickly and maybe rescued their mum. Perhaps they resent this and have employed tactics of passive resistance: not clearing up until asked, messing things up and so on. None of this is conscious with her or them, but she, too, fears losing them. The children must have been confused and angry about our separation and the loss of a conventional, supportive family arrangement. I sometimes feel I have failed them!

My wife and I decided we'd make every effort to co-operate to ensure the children were not unduly upset or their life disturbed more than necessary. On the whole this was successful and we communicated reasonably and stayed friendly. We tried to share looking after them though I accept that the bulk fell to her. At one point I suggested the youngest two come to live with me. She said she would go to court to prevent this. We agreed joint custody, however. I always shared Christmas, birthdays and other family events and took them on holiday a few times but, as they grew older, they were less bothered.

Pain, pretending and recovery.

I was in a very low state for two years following our separation, so depressed my brother worried about me. I coped at work which helped keep my mind off the pain but I gradually realised my situation was intolerable and that, if I did not embrace being gay, I'd be lonely for the rest of my life.

I had begun to accept I was gay before the marriage ended. I knew I could not change whatever the church said. Complete acceptance would have to follow, including the hard task of 'coming out'. I read all sorts of self-help books and tried various spiritual practices to see if I could lift the depression. Nothing helped.

I took up meditation and found that this was the only thing that cleared my mind and the negative emotions. I realised with complete clarity that no amount of prayer, holy water or other evangelical mumbo-jumbo would change anything to do with my sexuality. Trying to be something I was not was very unhealthy. No faith or other forms of magical thinking would move this particular - or indeed, any other - mountain. I told the church to stop praying for me and left. I have never gone back.

This decision was a good one and, from that point on, my feelings and my life have improved immensely. I am still a spiritual person but have a dim view of organised religion. I don't see life as black or white anymore and am sceptical of anyone who says they have 'the answer'. In my experience the more certain a particular group or movement is that they have the solution, the less I trust them!

I made a decision to embrace who I was and come out. I told myself that, at the end of my life, I would regret not being real. I joined an Internet group (gaydads)[37] composed of gay men who had been married or were still married and struggling. The group was very supportive: in fact maybe the most supportive experience of my life with respect to my identity. I was able to relate honestly for the first time and they really understood what I had been through. We share experiences and meet socially, go on outings or take short breaks away. This enables us to enjoy ourselves without worrying what others think.

We could experiment sexually and try out gay relationships: some guys met partners there. I made several good friends from this group and got great practical advice on legal matters and how to deal with issues such as telling the boys. I also met Christians and ex-Christians who had struggled or were struggling. Some guys work things out with their wives and stay. I am still very close to some men I met there after eight years. Thus, soon after becoming fifty, around forty years

---

[37] www.gaydads.co.uk See Resources section for other links and suggestions supporting fathers.

after I had first realised I was attracted to men, I began the coming out process. Better late than never!

First I told my brothers and their wives: they were very accepting and did not judge me. I gradually plucked up courage to tell my sons. I decided not to tell them until they were sixteen: I was afraid of their reactions and worried about how it might affect their own sense of identity. Also, as I had suffered rejection and abandonment issues all my life; I did not want any more.

How has your coming out affected your sons and your relationships?

For the most part my children's reactions have been positive - or perhaps neutral would be a better word. My eldest may have had most difficulty because our relationship may have been less strong, rather than sexuality being the issue. He does now accept how I am. The others did not react overtly and, so far as I am aware, have no issue with my sexuality now.

This is difficult for me to gauge. Although all my sons seem to accept me as I am, maybe the separation damaged them more than my being gay. Insofar as it has caused problems these are as much to do with my unexplained leaving, causing repressed anger and feelings of rejection, and having to live with their mother as primary carer at a time when she was under a great deal of pressure. With the exception of the eldest, who is dyslexic, they have done well academically. They generally seem well adapted although my youngest has had some significant periods of instability..

In retrospect, to tell them everything at the start might have helped them understand my leaving better. Who knows? However, my wife was against this and we feared they might be bullied if others found out. Interestingly, my youngest recently told me that he and his brothers - and their cousins - in fact admire me very much - now they know and understand better the difficulties I had to deal with. They appreciate how well I handled it and how hard I tried to make them as happy as I could when they were younger.

I really hope you take this in Alex.

I am trying to do this and realise my perceptions may not be accurate: at the same time I want to be truly accepted, not pitied.

What are the plusses?

There are mostly plusses as a result of coming out but it has been a painful experience getting there. I am more assertive and will not tolerate emotional abuse, no longer relating to people as a victim. I am a better listener and more integrated. I am far more independent and wary of the pitfalls of co-dependent relationships; less critical of myself and more accepting of others who are different. Generally I am happier.

I try to choose relationships now and have really close friends who accept me as I am, warts and all. I remain on reasonable terms with my ex-wife and see my children from time to time. I don't have to lie anymore and have learned a lot about how I relate. I have the respect of most people who know me. I've learned that you can survive anything and emotional pain can be overcome: you don't die from it.

The five-year relationship I had with a married man taught me that sexual, physical expressions of love are as important as duty, care and sharing things. It helped me loosen up emotionally and be more affectionate. I am able to explore sex and my own responses to it much more fully.

I have learned that being real, expressing anger, meditating and talking about problems is helpful and that magical solutions, magical thinking - religion, God, romance - don't work. I am still spiritual, loving, forgiving, wanting the best for others. I am now in a long-term relationship with a man with whom I able to be myself and better express my emotions, including anger on occasions.

Are there minuses?

I have to work at being friends with my ex-wife although, now the children are grown up, this is far less of an issue. We have a reasonable, if businesslike, relationship.

I regret not seeing my boys more when they were younger and needed me as I lost out not seeing them grow up doing everyday things in life. As a result the scope to build strong relationships with them was more difficult. Nevertheless, as I do have fair relationships with each of them, I wonder whether these problems are mainly in my head, rather than theirs.

I never told my own parents of my sexuality and don't think they would have understood. They were old and I didn't want to worry them. The separation meant I lost touch with my wife's parents, whom I liked a lot. As a result of this, Christmas will never be the same. However, this is a small price to pay. I missed my house and garden, although I now have a nice flat and nothing to complain about.

I am less trusting of people who make 'promises', and thus perhaps more realistic.

And your life now, Alex?

Of course life is not perfect now - when is it ever? I have not found all things in gay life to my liking - the gay scene and the narcissistic tendencies of some guys, for example. I don't like the overemphasis on sex. Many gay men I have met - or is it just men in general? - seem to have issues to do with self-esteem and problems with addictions to sex, over-sensitivity to criticism, cruising, porn or drugs. (I suspect many of these issues stem from lack of a sense of self-worth.) As a result commitment, expressing feelings and intimacy, can be problems and building healthy relationships difficult.

Since coming out I have continued counselling with gay

practitioners. This work has mostly been the 'talking cure' and reading self-help books and it has helped me immensely to understand my own thoughts and resolve some residual issues, such as rejection, dealing with anger, loneliness and self-esteem. I can honestly say that I am much happier now. In many ways my early life was either a big act or an illusion of happiness, with dependency and people pleasing being confused with love and acceptance.

Being real is much better! I am happy to say that I am now able to be real and happy living with my gay partner. Like any loving relationship, although we are happy together, we have occasional problems, which stem from our different characters and life experiences, but we both work at them jointly.

PHILIP'S STORY

Introduction to Philip

Philip's journey explains in some depth the attraction of being with a woman partner for many gay men at certain stages of their own life and development and hints at some important ways in which this may be reciprocal. Many women have reasons, conscious and unconscious, to feel safer, better met and cared for in relationship with a 'gay' man, whether this is overt at the start, unstated, implicit or hidden. His wife 'found out' that all Philip's previous relationships had been with men and that he was still fantasising exclusively about men, yet they were keen to be married as what they had together was 'substantial and real' for them both.

As explained in introductory chapters, there is an expanding view that same sex attraction in one or both partners to a marriage is no certain reason for the bond to fail. Philip, like several others in this book, has maintained a loving, close, continuous relationship with the woman he chose to marry and she has managed to incorporate his new partnership with T into their shared lives in warm and meaningful ways. This is important. It leads us further in challenging the idea of 'opposites'. It asks us to look at what is beneficial, gained, held between persons of different assigned genders.

Philip is clear that R's gender was "… then as now the least of it." It was the quality of their relationship that mattered most to them both and remains as true today. It may be, as Philip himself seems to conclude, that it was unnecessary to 'marry' to share these gains but as he also asks, why not? It may be that the numbers of gay and bi men and women doing so will reduce now that civil partnerships are legal and publicly approved equality in marriage just around the corner in Britain. Or else that, as we become more inclusive and less divisive about sexualities over time, more gay men and women may freely choose partners who identify mainly as heterosexual and vice versa?

Philip also raises the interesting issue of yearning for a 'brother' with whom to share life and many gay and bi men also report this as an early, sometimes lifelong, desire. This may or may not be assuaged by actual relationships with other gay men or with chosen partners. Robert's story, and Nigel's, as well as my own, also include feeling the absence of brothers whether birth brothers did exist, or were missing. 'Brothering', like 'parenting' can actually be action and experience more than designated role and gay male partnerships often include elements of 'brothering' in this new sense.

Philip's only expressed regret is having missed out on the opportunities he may have relished to be a biological parent and, of course, many of the bi and gay men who marry women do so to meet this wish, and stay married to continue to experience it in the form they most wish for. Chris is an example, as is Bruce. Philip and his wife were not able to parent in that way and he and T have not done so either. He is a little consoled by the variety of ways in which a gay man such as they can 'parent', specifically 'father', other children in their lives and gay and bi males have certainly missed out on that experience far, far too much due to social and psychological inhibitions arising from homophobia and sexism in relation to men and children generally and bi and gay men and children in particular.

I'm pleased to report, however, that this is also changing - in most European societies at least - and single men, as well as men in partnership are gradually being welcomed as parents, adoptive parents and foster carers whilst legal changes have taken, and will continue taking, place to respond to these important developments[38]. Of course, we can father other young people, adult friends, and partners as well and gay and bi men are completely disproportionately represented in all the caring and teaching professions. These special roles in our own cultures have, interestingly, always been given to, or taken by, gender and sex variant people over all of history and in all tribal societies. (See: Judy Grahn[39])

Philip is also someone for whom a considerable commitment to therapy and personal development – in a variety of forms over more than thirty years – have been hugely important, formative and rewarding, affecting his relationships with himself and others, his existential loneliness and anxieties, his worldview. Others (Trevor, Bruce and Nigel, for example) have also stressed the part that therapy and counselling have played in their journeys towards greater integrity, authenticity, clarity and choice and thereby towards increasing satisfaction with their lives. Philip particularly emphasises the special value of therapy and support groups in ameliorating that terrible, often otherwise life-long, loneliness which dulls the spirits and lives of many other gay and bi men.[40]

---

[38] See, for example, 'We Are Family' magazine (of LGBT family life) Issues 1-4, 2013 on fostering and adoption. www.wearefamilymagazine.co.uk. Also see the legal changes enacted recently in the UK: e.g. in the Fostering & Adoption Act, 2009.

[39] Judy Grahn's 'Another Mother Tongue' (1984, Beacon Press, Boston, USA) is a superb review of the history of 'queer people', their roles and functions, special contributions and values in various societies. Highly recommended.

[40] See Neal, C.: 'We Are Family – Working with Gay Men in Groups' in Neal, C. & Davies, D.: 'Issues in Therapy with Lesbian, Gay, Bisexual and Transgender Clients': Open University Press, 2000. Here I describe the first ten – of twenty two – years of the 'Coming Home' groups I ran in London for gay & bi men between 1991 & 2013 in which we focussed on all these issues amongst many others.

PHILIP'S STORY

Gay – and Married?

I aim to tell how and why it was that I came to marry a woman, what that relationship was about, how it ended and where it then led. So it is an exercise in looking back from my sixties, remembering a time more than thirty years ago, with the distance and clarity of hindsight but also the muddle of incomplete and unreliable memory. That this is worth exploring comes, I suppose, from the apparent contradiction of a man who at the time identified as gay – with at least one significant relationship with another man 'under his belt' – thinking that the right path for his own happiness and growth lay in heterosexual marriage. But that is not quite how it was…

I was the late-born only child of upwardly mobile middle-class parents and grew up in material security on the edges of the north London suburbs in the 1950s and 1960s. Photos show a smiley, fair-haired, slightly precious-looking little boy; by the time I reach adolescence I look gaunt and serious, with all the fun lost.

How had all the fun been lost by adolescence? Can you recall the process?

This process happened as I abandoned the world of play for the goals my parents had for me of educational success, being in the top class, doing well at every subject. My father wanted – generously, but in fact controllingly – to offer me the chance of the highest level of educational achievement, with all the long term career possibilities, that he could, which meant me becoming a day boy at a single sex public school. It was objectively a sensible choice and delivered the goods, as my later career showed. But I was too aware of the financial sacrifice that made it possible; the pressure to do well started a cycle of always being anxious about the next goal. Just enjoying school was not on the cards: the stakes were too high. I also had what later turned out to be a classic gay boy's fear of being different, coupled with a desperate need to fit in and not to be 'found out'. My mother, whom I adored, was less pushy than my father, though she went along with his plans for me, as she did, for a quiet life, with most of his ideas. If my father represented thrusting, purposeful activity towards goals ('doing') she represented warmth, safety and nourishment ('being').

What were the roots of your anxiety, do you think: gayness and fear of difference as well as fitting in with other boys, school, performing?

Growing up as an only child, my starting point for relationships was child-parent, which felt unbalanced and unequal. This made forming and sustaining friendships with those of my own age more difficult than if I had had siblings to practise on; my unacknowledged sexuality added a further twist. I longed for a brother, ideally a twin, who would know me as well as I did myself, without having to explain everything, and with whom I could have an intimate life secret from our parents. This dream was, of course, incapable of being fulfilled in its own terms but friends of my own age were the next best thing; I wanted them desperately though I felt unsure how to get and to keep them. I was realistic enough to know that no friend I could make would get close to being my twin brother, but I imagine my need leaked out, as if I were wearing a sweatshirt proclaiming 'Lonely Only Child Seeks Soul mate – Other Gay Boy Preferred'.

I found it easiest to make friends with other boys who shared my interest in music, which expressed and evoked emotions but did not require me to share my own, so spent many school holiday afternoons listening to records and talking about music and performances. Then as now, one-to-one seemed easier to organise and manage than being part of a larger social group; and my friends' mothers usually offered tea and cake. At school, the CCF[41] and competitive team sports were tedious and embarrassing,

What made team sports particularly embarrassing?

I felt physically unco-ordinated and unskilled in moving my body to order: cross-country running in Kenwood was tolerable as it was not competitive, even against the clock. Singing in the choir was wonderful; running the box office and front-of-house for school plays was a delight. School gave me a good start in knowing my way around literature and classical music, and my A-levels in French and German were enough to win me a place to read law at university, before which I spent six months as a filing clerk at the BBC.

You've said almost nothing about you and the other boys in all those years: can you say a bit please.

I came to sex on puberty at around fourteen, but at the start made no connection at all between masturbation and any sexual orientation. I
    hero-worshipped handsome boys at school – usually a year or two older, often hairier and deeper-voiced than I – and only realised long afterwards that there was a strong erotic charge to those feelings. When, at about seventeen, I realised I might be gay – the word then only newly minted – I thought this condemned me to misery and

---

[41] CCF: Combined Cadet Force, a Ministry of Defence sponsored youth organisation in the UK, which aims to "provide a disciplined organisation in a school so that pupils may develop powers of leadership by means of training to promote the qualities of responsibility, self reliance, resourcefulness, endurance and perseverance".

loneliness forever. I scared myself so completely that I blocked out the whole topic even from myself.

How did you block knowledge of your gayness from yourself & what had scared you especially?

Over-commitment to school, and then academic, work did a good job of keeping sex, as a disturbing subject, out of sight.

I must have picked up a picture of 'homosexuality as perversion', probably from my parents, though in my memory they hardly ever referred to or named the thing at all; I remember no other adults, at school for example, ever mentioning the topic.

I reopened this worrying box only after I'd completed a first degree, though meanwhile I'd fallen in love with a fellow student without acknowledging that either, and was a graduate student at Oxford heading for a career as a lawyer. But my erotic direction and fantasy life were and always have been towards other men, from the moment in my late teens when I owned their sexual attractiveness to me as such; and moved onwards to the much-delayed coming out stage when, to my astonishment and delight) I became aware that that sexual attraction might include me and be two-way.

As for coming out, at least in the sense of becoming sexually active with others: it could be postponed, as I chose to do, though I knew it could not be avoided. But the idea of sex with another person seemed – not at all in the medical sense – unsafe and risky, so would have to be carefully managed; my hesitations on the brink of becoming sexually active were all the greater since no version of sex between men had yet been decriminalised.

You refer to safety and sex, safety and engagement and I wonder why that's such an issue for you.

I am unsure – except by picking up, as I may have done, an

uncertainty or anxiousness about sex altogether from my father – why safety was, and remains, such an issue for me.

The 1967 Act[42] came into force just as I became twenty-one, which helped. I started the process by risking telling a few close friends that I thought I was gay – a process which went reassuringly well. In 1969 I took the rational middle-class next step by contacting the only specialist source of advice I knew, the Albany Trust[43] in London: I don't remember how I found out about it. Through the Trust's Doreen Cordell (it's a mark of the significance of that meeting that I can now recall her name), I became a member of a rather cloak-and-dagger gay men's social group, which met on occasional weekend evenings at St Katharine's Community in London's East End. I believe the group had links, perhaps an overlap, with the Gay Christian Movement, though it had no overt religious agenda. Its role was to ease the process of coming out in conditions of safety – from both the law and exploitation: for me it did both brilliantly. It had small satellite icebreaking groups in members' homes; I attended one for a while, then striking out one-to-one with friends I had made there. I met in that group the first man with whom I ever spent the night, in my single bed at home while my parents were away.

What needs would I have named that night, if he had asked me and I had had awareness enough to say? Touch, warmth, an end to

---

[42] 1967 Act: The 1967 Sexual Offences Act decriminalised homosexual acts in private between two men, both of whom had to have attained the age of 21. The Act applied only to England and Wales and did not cover the Merchant Navy or the Armed Forces.

[43] Albany Trust: a specialist counselling service promoting sexual well-being and healthy sexual relationships. Originally set up to help individuals who had nowhere to turn for expert professional help with issues of sexuality and relationships, Albany Trust has been providing that for over 60 years. Contact: http://www.albanytrust.org

physical isolation, being able to share my feelings – all higher up my list, now as then, than genital release through orgasm. My experience of sex with another person has – unusually, for most gay men I've talked to – nearly always been in the context of an intimate ongoing relationship. I therefore never properly passed through the usual experimental and promiscuous phase of adolescent sexual awakening, nor did I allow myself a delayed version of this later. The same is true in relation to my experience of alcohol and recreational drugs.

Though I am 'not the marrying kind'[44] in a conventional heterosexual sense, at a deeper level I am very much 'the marrying kind', whether with a man or a woman, as life has turned out. Harking back to the missing twin brother (the symbolism of this gains some power from the fact that my father actually was a twin, whose brother was stillborn), it's a deep connection with the other person that I'm after, in which, if all goes well, sex will be a key part: that's just how I seem to be built. It's not clear to me how and why this is so, except it must in part be to do with needing to feel safe before sex is OK and feeling safe comes from the knowledge that I don't have to perform and am OK whatever happens - which comes most easily if I know and trust the man I'm with. As I grow older, genital sex becomes more peripheral anyway: offer me a fuckfest in a backroom[45] and I will probably prefer just to kiss and hug a man I really fancy and to share through conversation.

---

[44] 'Not the marrying kind' is a phrase from before the 1967 Sexual Offences Act (op.cit.) which, like 'confirmed bachelor', was popular with obituary writers and others whose job it was to find coy substitutes for 'gay man'. You would never get the impression that these men - there was no equivalent phrase for women - had ever loved or been loved in return. Thus this book's title.

[45] 'Backroom': orig. American, the back room of a bar, sauna or cinema used for sex.

Have you got anywhere in yourself with the safety issue over time?

Well, the safety theme has receded as I've aged, though, if I fantasise about an encounter with a man I haven't met before, the anxiety about safety is often there and slaps down the pleasurable fantasies about discovery and exploration.

But it has been rare and exceptional that I have made relationships with other men complete enough to feel satisfying on both levels – emotional and sexual; though I am lucky to have been in such a loving (and erotic) living-together relationship for more than 25 years. This may be because, in the 1970s, my first significant male lover, JA, saw my existential loneliness and pushed me, gently but firmly, towards the world of humanistic psychotherapy.[46] Encounter groups[47] scared me, as I could not produce the cathartic anger most highly prized; but gestalt-based group and individual work[48] offered just what I was

---

[46] Humanistic psychotherapy: So-called 'third way' in therapy theory, emerged during the 1950s as a reaction to psychoanalysis and behaviorism, which dominated psychology at the time. Psychoanalysis was focused on understanding the unconscious motivations that drive behavior while behaviorism studied the conditioning processes that produce behavior. Humanistic psychology felt these were failing to take into account the role of personal choice, so instead focused on individual potential, stressing the importance of growth and self-actualization. The fundamental belief of humanistic psychology is that people innately have the resources (even if buried) needed to solve their problems and make rewarding lives.

[47] Encounter groups: Human relations training group or 'encounter group' is a form of group therapy where participants learn about themselves and group processes through interaction with each other, using feedback, problem solving and role play to gain insight. J. L. Moreno articulated the concept, "a meeting of two, eye to eye, face to face" in Vienna in 1914-15 in 'Invitation to an Encounter.'

[48] Gestalt therapy, another branch of Humanistic therapy, was developed by Fritz and Laura Perls & Paul Goodman in the 1940s and 1950s and is an

seeking. This gave me a language for understanding my own feelings and an ability to 'be in the here-and now' which made it easier to express what I wanted and what I felt; and to be clearer about who and what I did not want.

I have been in some form of therapy most of my life ever since. As a result almost all my closest friends and lovers have had some experience of this process, so much so that three lovers have gone on to train as therapists (did I drive them to it?). The kind of awareness encouraged by the sort of therapy I have experienced raises the threshold at the start of a relationship but, once that barrier is crossed, makes possible a deeper bond; it also supplies a framework and language for dealing with issues and for facilitating change. To be in an ongoing therapy group with other gay men, as I was for several years at various points, has been incomparably important: to share insights from my experience with others, hence to know that I am not alone. So these groups have met two basic needs, going back to my childhood and adolescence: not to be thought different, and to belong.

My first Important Relationship, mentioned above, was in the early 1970s; JA and I were both teaching at the same university and he took the initiative to seek me out; for a while he and I lived together in my house, but with notionally separate bedrooms. The time with him all felt like an experiment: trying out what it is like to be with another man, emotionally and sexually. So I made many mistakes, some no doubt coming directly from my being an only child; and the quality of the relationship and where it might lead was not clear enough for me to want, for example, to come out to my parents on the strength of it. They guessed, of course, as I found out from my father after my mother had died.

---

existential/experiential form that emphasizes personal responsibility and focuses on the individual's experience in the present moment, the therapist-client relationship, the environmental and social contexts of a person's life and the self-regulating adjustments people make as a result of their overall situation.

Please say more about your coming out, not coming out and parents 'guessing' if you can. What about your parents' - and other message givers' scripts for you about men, women, sex, sexualities and bodies?

My father's sorrow when I acknowledged that JA and I had been lovers 'in the full sense' (my father's euphemism for penetrative sex) was deep and real, though I knew I could not spare him by lying.

My parents were never communicative openly with me about sex, waiting until I was beyond puberty to give me a book which explained sex between men and women with diagrams; from their reticence, and from the fact that they slept in twin beds, I deduced that this was a complex and perhaps difficult topic for them and never pushed them on it. I also think they may have been uncomfortable with my coming into adulthood, with all the promise and energy that this carried: I remember little appreciation or encouragement to do with how I looked or moved. I was more aware of how I might be confirming some of their worst fears by how I dressed or how I disdained 'manly' pursuits in favour of music, reading or cooking.

JA was on a short-term contract, which meant he might have to go back to the USA when it ended; and had continuing links with former girlfriends, so was nominally bisexual. All this now sounds rather dodgy but he was there for me: was exotic, being Jewish, American, with a PhD from Yale and experience of seeing a 'shrink'; and we did have good times together, especially in bed. When he moved to London, our intimacy gradually came to an end. I went through two very unbalanced and inappropriate short relationships with male students, which did not come close to what I'd had with JA. I came to believe that my dreams of what I wanted with another man were simply not capable of fulfilment. – to have both love and sex with the same man and to live with him – and was in effect alone for several years as a result, my work always available to fill time and to mask the longings.

It was in this wilderness time, about 1977, that a friend invited me to his home, where I met his flat-mate R: 'Would you like a peanut butter cookie? They're home-made'. That was more-or-less her opener. She seemed sparkly, self-possessed, wise, not beyond teasing if it was called for, tall, elegant, slim and altogether special – and American.

Americans: their alternativeness, outsiderness, otherness seems significant?

American and, like JA, 'a breath of fresh air' in my terms, not a part of the English class system or of our culture of cynical understatement. And, of course, a woman, the eldest daughter of nine children – in due course providing a ready-made and astonishing set of siblings-in-law for me. But her gender was the least part of it, from that day to this: it was the quality of my relationship with her, as it developed, which mattered.

It is true, of course, that I didn't ever desire her as passionately as I might have longed for the arms – or the dick – of The Perfect Man (a cousin of Quentin Crisp's Dark Stranger[49]): but she was real and alive, and The Perfect Man – to my way of thinking – might well not exist except in my head and in fiction. It was simply fun to be with her, and I felt more fully alive when I was. But what of sex and marriage.

At that time I felt that it would do my self-esteem good if I knew that I could have sex with a woman, but not just any woman. This sounds odd now as it was in a way colluding with the dominant ideology of heterosexuality. But issues around my masculinity were there, as part of my uncertainty around sex in general: could I manage

---

[49] 'Quentin Crisp's dark stranger': Crisp (Denis Charles Pratt 1908 – 1999), a queer English writer and raconteur, famous for outraging all and sundry, describes looking for an ideal lover, the tall, dark man, and later realising no such person could exist! See: 'The Naked Civil Servant' (1968)

penetrative sex with anyone, man or woman? I really was not sure, but feared it mattered a great deal. As will be clear, I am not one of those gay men repelled by women's genitalia. There was also the possibility, in the far distance, of marriage, if I could form a nourishing relationship with R – and even the chance of becoming a father.

Suddenly a whole package of societal structures from which I had thought myself exiled, and unfairly so, might actually be within reach after all. R joined me on holiday in Crete, with sleeping together, let alone sex, not yet discussed; my courage fortified with retsina, I simply asked her to share a bed in the villa with me, which she generously agreed to do, so having sex together began.

Not long after our return from holiday, she moved in with me; shortly after that we started to talk about getting married. We decided to tell no-one in advance other than sworn co-conspirators (our two witnesses) and mailed cards telling all our friends and family once the ceremony on Midsummer Day was over. So, as marriages go, it got off to an unconventional start; and was never held together by the erotic glue which marriages are traditionally supposed to enjoy. It had more a feel of brother and sister than husband and wife; and of course I had never had either a sister or brother, except those children conceived ahead of me, who had never made it to full term, my mother having had a sequence of miscarriages before my birth.

R knew – by finding out, rather than by my clearly telling her, which I now think cowardly – that all my past sexual experience had been with men, and that if I had sexual fantasies, they were still about men: one ill-concealed copy of 'Mandate'[50] gave away a lot! In our first years together these factors seemed not to undercut our relationship fatally, for it really was R whom I wanted to live with, and she with me. There was of course some self-delusion sustaining us, for we were

---

[50] 'Mandate': monthly gay porn magazine published in the United States and distributed internationally between 1975 and 2009.

each choosing to do without something important – a relationship with a man based on strong two-way sexual attraction. But what we did have in mutual support, fun, home-making and a life together were substantial and real; and it was a great and mostly enjoyable learning experience for me.

You clearly identify R and yourself colluding, sublimating information and feeling in order to have this relationship. Why might she have done so, if you can say?

For her, I think the missing erotic experience was outweighed by the solidity of the bond we had. It was relevant to this process that she had escaped not long before from being a nun in a serious German teaching order and may have welcomed the less traditional, demanding and conventional marriage we had; we were both 'trying on' the institution for size in our own way.

I'd love to hear about your dreams of fathering, what became of them and of fathering in you?

During about the first five years we used no contraception and hoped we might have a child, though this did not happen, for no reason medical tests could pinpoint. Not long after that, we both realised with an unhappy thud that the structural weaknesses underneath our relationship should really point us in the opposite direction: not to become parents. With so many uncertainties about where we were heading, to bring a child into the world simply felt unfair and irresponsible. This in turn brought a warning that the relationship, and hence our marriage, might have no future either.

What were the 'structural weaknesses' and 'uncertainties', Philip?

The fact that I was, deep down, a gay man and she a heterosexual woman. I took these realisations much harder than she did (and still regret, but much less keenly now, never becoming a father). I hoped, sincerely but naively, that we would be together into old age and gloomily expected that, if we separated, I would be alone for ever, never finding a man with whom to be as involved as fully as I felt with R. She generously stayed with me the two or so years it took me to integrate the idea that my life would still continue meaningfully if we were no longer together; and that we could still be friends. So we parted and were divorced as soon as we could. Within about three months of that parting, reconciled to living alone for a while and feeling OK about it, I met T, whose opener was to offer a half-share in an apricot slice. He and I have lived together since 1987 and were part of the first wave of same-sex couples to become civil partnered in December 2005.

This account sheds little light on the general phenomenon, if there is one, of gay men who marry. Looking back, it is easy to see how, in my personal development, being with R (for getting married was not really the heart of it) was an essential step down the Yellow Brick Road towards a gay relationship far closer to my ideal; but hindsight can make accidents look like a causally linked and inevitable sequence of events.

Another sub-theme not yet evoked is the impact on my family and friends of getting married and then un-married. By getting married I was evidently no longer gay, perhaps had never been gay, not that this is how my father would have put it. To allow him to believe that my time with men was an aberration now definitively over was the best gift I could have offered him, by then elderly and widowed. So, eight years later, he took very hard the news that R and I were separating; and harder still the arrival quickly afterwards of T in my life, my bed and my house. By this point the balance of power in our relationship had shifted: I had become a support for my father in retirement and gradual decline into infirm old age, and was sure enough of the rightness of my life-choices to stand by them, against him if necessary.

But he too, in his way and at his own pace, came good in the end (even offering to adopt T!), though he continued to be puzzled that R, T and I could all be such good friends – which we still are. My father also continued, sweetly but misguidedly, to be protective of me in worrying – as if the 1960s had never happened – about the hostility T and I might incur by openly being a gay couple, in Brighton of all places![51] Others had less dramatic reactions and may have put my shifts of direction between men and women and back again down to the mood of the times or to the mutability of human sexual orientation.

What helped you through these life-changes?

The only person with whom I was truly open was my therapist at the time, who was wise, supportive and challenging. He took the line that whatever my relationship with R was, it was not really a marriage. At the time, I thought this rather formalist, even moralistic, but I now know what he meant: 'don't kid yourself that your heart and groin are equally involved', and 'don't be more freaked out if it ends, simply because you and R are in fact married'. Once the relationship with R was clearly ending, I started to reawaken my gay identity: my therapist saw and understood how deeply I wanted a man and was among the first to celebrate my meeting T, recognising that, this time at least, it was The Real Thing.

One of the many strengths I feel I gained from my childhood was a deep existential OK-ness, which came from being wanted and loved by my parents. This was joined by a self-sufficiency learnt from having no siblings: I knew how to amuse myself as a child and

---

[51] 'Brighton of all places': Brighton, on the Sussex coast, is generally acknowledged to be the most gay-friendly town in the UK with a large GSD population, many venues, cafés, bars and great community supports as well as a huge annual 'Pride' festival.

adolescent, and in the adult world my work has been an ever-available solace and refuge – a 'willing mistress' in fact. At best I believe that in the end I can get through any difficulty and come to happier times and – if it came to it – could manage alone. There were moments in the break-up with R when this faltered, but it always returned.

There were no guidebooks to what I went through and I don't remember any novels or films which spoke to my situation, except those few which argued that a nourishing and loving relationship was possible between two gay men, even if rather against the odds. But this was at the final stage, as I left the marriage behind and struck out on my own, not as I entered into it or lived it; the arrival of HIV in the UK polluted this shift of direction as I eagerly became closer to T. At the key earlier stages, I had to find within myself most of the resources to identify what seemed the right path, then to follow it.

Summing up the experience, I would now say that I am – as I always was – a gay man, but believe I made no mistake in choosing an intimate and living together relationship with R, in the context of my life when that relationship became possible. I do think, though, that it was unfair not to have been clearer with her at the start about my own sexual experience and aspirations. I probably feared she would have rejected me, had I been so open. To buy into the institution of marriage in its formal and legal sense was, I now think, a foolish and unnecessary step. But I remember the excitement of doing so, for we knew we were slightly naughtily appropriating a traditional institution for our own ends. However, I see no point in being hard on either of us in retrospect.

After all, as the introduction of civil partnerships showed T and me, something special and symbolic does happen when two people ask the State formally and publicly to recognise their relationship: it is a further and public kind of coming out as a couple. Other same-sex couples who have been civil partnered after many years of living together have reported the same. So it is not surprising that couples sometimes opt for this recognition, as R and I did, without quite having all the 'right' reasons. In my view, if they believe they have enough reasons, they should not be excluded or discouraged from its substantial benefits – practical, legal, fiscal, social and psychological.

A final comment: many gay men find it intriguing to discover that I have been married, so it's socially been a plus rather than a minus.

What thoughts and feelings have you about that intrigue and the positive projections of gay men who discover that you've been married?

I think they imagine I may know things that they don't, maybe even sexual tricks, from having been with a woman; on a higher level, it's unusual and hence mysterious to them. Many gay friends have enjoyed meeting R, whom I'm careful never to introduce or speak of as 'my ex-wife', and seeing in action our continuing close friendship. From experience, I too expect a depth and wisdom from another gay man who has been married, which might not necessarily otherwise be there, just as I feel personally enriched by having been through the process.

The only regret worth recording is that I have missed the opportunity of fatherhood in the narrow biological sense. To watch a child grow and become an adult: nothing could, it seems to me, quite match sharing in the development of another human being with whom I'm genetically linked, and passing on to a son or daughter what I have learned in my own life. I am aware, though, of letting my own ability to 'be a father' out from time to time – in play with others' children, in dealing with students and certainly in my relationship with T.

CHRIS'S STORY

Introduction to Chris

Chris's journey involves decades of hiding from himself, beginning with the trauma of loneliness and separation as a child, exacerbated by sexual abuse at boarding school and closing down his emotional life in favour of clever brain activity[52]. This separation, or constant distraction from feelings, is sometimes called disassociation and is common both in gay men and in people who have had their natural sexual development 'invaded', interrupted by others with more power in some respect. Chris's development was certainly delayed at that early stage and this remained evident for another thirty years in 'little boy' aspects of his personality and relationships.

When a gay person is sexually exploited early in life there is the additional danger of associating the abuse with their sexuality, as if their true sexual feelings have been caused in some sense by those experiences. In good sex-affirmative psychotherapy, it is often possible to disentangle sexual experiences that have happened too early, or been involuntary, from true sexuality, which is an individual and original part of a person. It is necessary to work through internalised shame, disgust and oppression. It also requires working to disown messages taken from outside connecting sexual exploitation of the young with same-sex attraction, these scripts still retaining currency in the face of all evidence that the vast majority of sexual

---

[52] See Resources section 2 on boarding school survivors.

abuse of children - well over ninety per cent - is heterosexual - if we call it sexual when it is more of an assertion of power over another.

Another frequent cause of shame is the experience of arousal connected with the fear, attention, or the relational dynamics associated with the abusive incidents. There's no denying that the exercise of power and control over a weaker, younger, less experienced person is frequently erotically charged, sometimes for each person involved. Sexual exploitation of younger people through false identities on social websites and the rise of cyber bullying are very recent examples of the durability and inventiveness of such behaviours.[53]

It was hugely important to Chris to be 'normal' - and to be seen as normal - for these now obvious reasons and he did all he could in life to this end through sport, success at college and in work, marriage and family life to construct powerful appearances of 'normality'. Something was always left out, however: only when Chris began his active journeying, spiritually as well as sexually (and the two are deeply connected always as elements of our 'core' self) could he both 'come out' and become fully adult. What is really striking here is the vast resource of trapped energy released in Chris once this happens. Look how creative, industrious, adventurous and, just as important, happy he can be when those natural forces are freed. Look how much more authentically available he becomes to loving and being loved. Look how the focus of his work becomes so much more meaningful, creative and constructive.

It seems almost as though, having found love for himself in himself, he has boundless reserves of it then to share with those he cares about and this even extends across the world in his charitable campaigns. Chris is both fortunate, and has worked very hard, to keep

---

[53] See Resources section 1 for information or help with recovery from sexual abuse.

his wife, daughters and good friends alongside him with a great deal of love and goodwill throughout this bumpy journey.

He is also both fortunate, and again has worked very hard, in the therapeutic experiences he has entered: his timely discovery of Mike Lew's book and workshops, finding Steve and 'Survivors UK' and working for some years in therapy with Bernard Ratigan, one of Britain's most respected psychotherapists working with sex and gender diversity. I cannot emphasise enough how important it is to find guides of this quality and experience to accompany you on a path as crucial as this. This is why I highly recommend the specialist list of therapists and counsellors who have trained in these issues to be found on the 'Find a Therapist' page at the www.pinktherapy.com website.[54]

---

[54] For more information on this issue see Resources section.

CHRIS'S STORY

"If it wasn't for the children we wouldn't be together now!" I shouted at my wife in an uncharacteristic outburst of anger and frustration. It shocked us both. I was thirty-eight and had been happily married for years, with two beautiful young daughters, a nice house and a job to die for. What more could I want?

We went to 'Relate'[55]: Jan organised it and, as was so often the case, I went along with it for the sake of peace. 'Relate' was wonderful. I loved it. For the first time in our relationship I could say how I truly felt.

How had you come to edit or limit yourself to this degree, do you now think?

Jan wasn't allowed to respond, just listen. It was amazing what came out. I shocked myself:

~ I had no friends, except my old University and school friends, now sadly all in far flung places

~ I had no personal money

~ I had no hobbies

~ I got up, did kid stuff, went to work, had a ball, came home, did kid stuff, watched telly, and went to bed, got up.........

---

[55] 'Relate': couples and relationship counselling organisation in the UK. Contact: www.relate.org.uk

~ At weekends, I got up, snuck in some work, did kid stuff, did house stuff, did kid stuff, watched telly, snuck in some work, and went to bed, got up.........

My life sounded, and felt, very empty.

Do you ascribe this lack of a life of your own, lack of self-expression to consequences of living inauthentically all those years in some major respects?

I believe that I was a hugely defensive person with a split conscious mind. One side was the little boy sitting in his emotional prison warily looking out; the other was the me everyone saw: play-acting really. I was a master at acting the 'Captain of Everything' type person.

Our counsellor asked me to say what I wanted my life to look like. It took some time to work this out, but I came out with:

~ Time for me. I wanted a night a week, a weekend a month, and two weeks a year, to do just what I wanted to do.

~ Money. I wanted my own bank account and my own credit card, plus an allowance each month, to spend on what I wanted to spend it on. And, critically, no questions asked!

Jan wanted to be desired.

Did you have any notions about what there was that you wanted to do in this time and with this space and money?

Not really, just a deep sense that I was trapped and that I wanted some freedom. And, critically, no questions asked!

And did you know why this was critical?

Yes, because if this wasn't agreed, my wife would have stuck her oar into everything I was doing. We get on brilliantly now and we have readjusted our relationship, but she still comes round to my house and asks, "What did that cost?" or "What are you doing this weekend?" I don't feel I have to let this control me now so I tell her to go away... nicely!

How did she feel undesired, did you know? What can you say about you and Jan and desire – at the beginning, over the years and at this point when you got to Relate?

I did desire her at first but five years of infertility treatment killed sex for us and, by the time we got to Relate, it was too far gone. I had really come to the point where I knew I found men more attractive.

We agreed I could have what I wanted. We agreed to think about Jan's wish to be desired.

I now realise that this was the start of a journey of self discovery that would end up in setting up house on my own, coming out as an openly gay man to the world, finding a faith, building a group of friends that mean the world to me, spending three weeks in South Africa volunteering for a charity that educates women and children in the developing world, becoming a volunteer skipper in a sail training organisation, getting the biggest job in the world, leaving my job to take a year out to research and write a couple of books, setting up a website to research the world of prayer and getting contacted three times by the BBC ... and becoming better friends with my wife than I have been for years. I love her to bits.

What an incredible amount of varied experience was waiting in you to be realised! Wow! All of this was contingent on accessing your deeper, or more, real, self somehow first.

I KNOW!! Why didn't you tell me this would happen when we first met all those years ago? It is interesting now; I have finally got to the end of my job and have nothing in my diary forever after the next week, when I am sailing. So, now I can truly be me, what will happen? Scary stuff.

What did I do? I peeled away years of defences and barriers, detoxified the past, found out who I was, then let the world in to know the real me.

And, crucially, you had to let YOU in before this. Would you be able and willing to say more about this journey and how you took these steps?

I am totally happy to do this. You told me when you helped me find a therapist that I needed an intellectual to work with as I would want to understand it. How right you were. I have included stuff on this later. I am fascinated by the process.

I now realise that I had allowed myself to become subjugated to my wife, backed into a corner. It was easier to acquiesce than to stand my ground. I therefore ended up losing so much potential for self-expression. Once I gained ground, gave myself some space and went out looking, my life blossomed.

I wouldn't put this entirely down to marriage, however, as I have always had this feeling that, if I could deal with everything in my head, I would fly. I always feared that this would mean coming out as a gay man, which was too scary to contemplate.

The Journey

So what did I do with my new resources? To start with, not a lot. To be frank, I had asked for time and money, but had no idea what I wanted to do with them!

If time and money were really simply metaphors, what would you say they had come to represent for you?

Oh, I saw them as keys: keys to I don't know what, but crucial to being able to go off and look for things. The money mounted up, and the time got left untaken.

As a child I was told I had two famous ancestors: David Livingstone and Mark Twain. I always wanted to be an explorer and a writer. I'd done a fair bit of exploring, taking a year off after my degree, but I always believed I couldn't write, wasn't creative, as this is what was ground into me at school. How wrong I learned this to be.

So, I went off exploring myself and the world. I felt free and started to explore things I had always wanted to do. I have always loved the sea, so I threw myself into volunteering for a sail-training organisation, taking groups to sea on week-long voyages. This ate into my time hugely as it involves not just the voyages, but the training and qualifications, with regular updates and renewals for all of the relevant 'badges.' I went to night classes to study psychology, then advanced psychology, and philosophy.

Why these choices Chris: what were you after?

This is a BIG question for me: I often wonder what is pulling me. I think this relates to my spiritual journey. Deep inside me is a part some people might call God. It is this part that is my real essence, that links with other people and, collectively with them, becomes God. This is the most powerful part of my subconscious mind and the real me. Over the years I have hidden it, wrapped it in defensive layers and cotton wool. Peeling these back, sitting quietly in contemplation, this is what allows the deeper me to come out. Quakers call it 'sitting in the light', listening. Franciscans get there by the way they live and spending so long in silence. Jesuits call this discernment. A more practical way of explaining it is, if I had a problem, I always used to work it out in my conscious mind, which is small and only a part of my mind. Now I let it seep through to my subconscious, maybe by sleeping on it or sitting in quiet, then the massive intellect in my subconscious gets to work and, hey presto, amazing things get sorted!

I did an Alpha course[56] and re-awakened my faith and spirituality, becoming a Quaker. I became an associate of a charity that helps women and children in the developing world. I refurbished several houses. My circle of friends grew steadily. I believe that this growth fuelled, and was fuelled by, the opening up of the real me, culminating in the journey to come out to the world.

Were the new friends different to old friends? Were the friendships of a different kind or quality, would you say?

I seem to have kept old friends, though many friendships have had to change. I don't let people treat me like their little brother any more. New ones? They all have the characteristic that we can really talk, not about the weather but about big stuff like the meaning of life. One lovely friend says I'm her only real friend. I asked her why, what is it about me, and she said that I am the most open person she knows: I just came crashing in and opened up to her and she couldn't resist.

Having just turned forty-seven, I went for a walk around a field one day with my friend Neil, who had recently walked out on his wife and was suffering from depression. He needed support and I was glad to help. That's what friends do.

Both our dogs were gallivanting around us when Neil shared with me that he was struggling with his sexuality. We walked on in silence for an age. Neil thought he had misjudged the confidence. My brain was going, 'Could I tell him about me? Would it be safe? What if I get it wrong?' Finally I told him that I was struggling with the same issues.

---

[56] Alpha course: started in Brompton, London in 1977, this course seeks to introduce basics of the Christian faith, described by organisers as "an opportunity to explore the meaning of life." Currently run in churches, homes, workplaces, prisons, universities and other locations around the world by all major Christian denominations. http://www.alpha.org

To what extent did you know this about yourself then? Had you always known, or were there ever times when you didn't? What exactly was the struggle? Not to have gay desires? Was it hidden from you as well as from your wife?

Yes, I did know I was struggling with the same issues. I have been aware of this since school. I had times when I was not struggling, like with my wife for the early years. I struggled not to have gay desires, just wanting to be 'normal': sorry about that word, but that is what I would have said to you if you had asked years ago. It wasn't hidden from me, but I had pushed it to the back of my mind.

For the first time in my entire life I had voiced a dark secret and shared it with another person. The sky didn't fall on my head. Over the next few weeks we tentatively shared our stories with each other, slowly and steadily trusting each other with the next morsel. The sky didn't fall on our heads.

Over a few more weeks I shared with Neil that my first sexual experience was with two older boys at school when I was eleven. It had gone on for most of my first year at senior boarding school. On returning the following year, they had moved up to senior school and I started to realise the enormity of what had happened, and the potential issue if anyone found out. I would be labelled a 'queer' or a 'poof' and my life would be hell. I played around with another friend but slowly started to bottle everything up once he left that school and I was on my own.

Neil asked if it had ever occurred to me that what the older boys had done with me at school was abuse. I remember that moment very clearly. It went completely quiet. I said to myself, 'You mean it wasn't my fault? You mean I can do something about this? You mean I might not be gay after all?'

That was a really strong agenda for you then – not to be gay?

As I said, I just wanted to be normal, Charles. Now I just want to be ME! At school there was a huge desire to fit in.

It was as if a steamroller came crashing through the wall of the pub and it all went black. I couldn't cope with the enormity of these thoughts and my mind closed down.

Over the next few weeks these crashes became a daily regular event. At first I called Neil and he would coax me out of the 'black holes' enough for me to keep going. Another good friend asked me what was going on, what was wrong. I said it was because Jan and I were planning to split up. He told me he didn't believe me, there must be something more and dragged it all out of me, not the whole story; I just shared with him that I had been abused at school and it was all falling out of my head. I now had a second friend to call on for help when I dropped into the black hole.

Were you planning to part from your wife then? How had this come about? There's a chunk of time and information missing between the Relate decision-making and this.

She and I decided to split up two months before Easter and stayed together for those two months. I told her about the group I joined and being abused when she took me and my stuff to Neil's at Easter.

Another good friend took me for a drink and the same conversation ensued. She said, 'I know there is something more going on so, while I am at the bar, I think you need to decide if you are able to trust me so I can help you.' When she returned with our drinks, I told her about being abused at school. I now had a third friend to call on.

I got onto the web and searched for resources to help victims of abuse. I discovered that Mike Lew, an American, was a guru on the subject and had written a book on it: 'Victims No Longer'.[57] I bought it immediately and was petrified that my wife would open the parcel, but it came and she didn't. I read it within a day.

What else did you discover then that was important for you?

The book did not have someone with my exact story in, but basically said that, if someone has been abused then there are a number of things that will be issues for him or her, like control, sex, and sexuality. Crucially, I now realise, it started to help me understand things. I began to feel that I really wasn't alone. The back of the book had a list of counsellors and organisations I could go to for help.

Would you recommend this book to others?

This book is wonderful and I heartily recommend it. I also loved Mike, a really warm, empathic person. I still chat with him by email occasionally. I started at the top and worked my way down. The numbers were all out of service or on answering machine. The last number was for Survivors UK[58] in Swindon. Steve answered. We talked for an age and he persuaded me that I should go and visit him. I couldn't possibly have gone on my own, so Neil offered to take me. By this time he had shared with me his own abuse story. He also spoke with Steve at Swindon and we agreed to both go for a session with him. The journey was endless: I was so, so nervous.

Steve knew exactly what questions to ask. There was no hiding. I told far more than I had ever intended. I cried my eyes out. It was so exhausting. I was a wreck. I agreed to come back to Steve and join his

---

[57] Mike Lew: 'Victims no Longer: the classic guide for men recovering from sexual child abuse' : Harper Collins, USA, 2004.

[58] 'Survivors UK': organisation offering support and therapy, as well as group work, for survivors of sexual abuse, rape. Contact: Tel: 0044 8451221201 (M&T 7-9.30, Th 12-2.30pm) info@survivorsuk.org

weekly group. Neil agreed also.

Steve saw both of us together just before we left. He said that he only had one concern. That is that the two of us were going through very dangerous territory and that we had to be very careful we didn't become involved with each other sexually. I promised faithfully not to. It was a very hard promise to keep at times but Steve was very wise. Neil and I are now the closest of friends and we wouldn't be if something romantic or sexual had happened between us.

Splitting up

Tell me about the process of separating and focussing on yourself, please.

As I developed my life after Relate my wife and I started to drift apart. I began to contemplate the possibility of breaking up with her, but it was too scary and I shoved it away. However, a few weeks after I started therapy with the group, she and I went for a walk around the same field in which Neil and I had shared so much. We were both unhappy and, after a tentative beginning, out poured how we both felt. It turned out that each of us had been thinking about splitting up for at least two years, but decided that we couldn't do it and would wait until the girls left home. It was obvious now that we were both ready to part.

We agreed to separate a few weeks after a big family wedding so as not to upset everyone. In reality it all spilled out at the wedding and didn't spoil it: everyone was extremely supportive.

Steve and 'Survivors'

What did you gain from working in the 'Survivors' group?

For the next few months my weeks revolved around group sessions on

Friday evenings. Neil and I would set off mid-afternoon for a long drive across the Cotswolds. The sessions were two hours long, then the long drive home. We often stopped for a pint and something to eat. We soon realised that the drive was an integral part of group work for us and we did a lot of therapy in that time.

The first session was hell. There were about eight guys present. I sat on an armchair curled up in foetal position, and left the session half way through to sit on the stairs.

The next session felt much better. The format was for us to tell the group briefly about what was going on in our lives under the headings 'trauma, trivia, joy' and then we would fall into discussion about a topic that emerged. There was no structure to the remainder of the session, just the first part.

The others had been in the group for a while so we got grilled for our stories. It was hard to talk so openly, but I learned that once something had been dragged out of me it always fell into a better place. But it always also shattered me. I learned that the more shattered I was, the bigger the mental event had been, and the better a place I then got to with it.

The focus for me to start with was the abuse at school. I learned so much about the impact of this on me. I remember thinking how strange that one of the other guys, who had similar issues to me, had been abused by an older woman, not by a guy. This really made me start to think about the 'gay thing'. I slowly began to realise that it wasn't so much about the abuse, more about what I had done in my head afterwards.

I began to really blame myself for everything I had created in my head at school. I had a period of beating myself up about this, but the group wouldn't let me do this, so I began to realise it wasn't my fault that I reacted this way: if it was anyone's fault it was my abusers'.

There was a lot of pressure to take revenge on the two guys who abused me. I couldn't work up any hate against them though. It has always struck me that, although they were definitely in a position of power over me, they were only kids themselves. The only thing that bothers me is if they had continued. If it had been masters I would definitely do something, but these guys? I reckon that the issue isn't really what they did to me when we were all so young, but what they might have done later. I have no way of knowing about this or finding out so I now think that it is not for me to deal with.

One session I was laid into in a major way for not being emotional and always play-acting. I got really upset about this. Steve said that I didn't show emotions, but play-acted them. I got cross with everyone and ended up crying, or play-acting in his view.

I went away and considered what they'd said and began to realise that maybe they were right. I didn't get my head around this overnight, but it was a clue as to where to go. If I jump way ahead, people now often tell me how open I am. I recently talked to fifty guys at the trustees meeting of my charity about an accident that happened on my boat. I got choked up when I was telling them about how the person was nearly killed. When I finished, a senior member stood up and thanked me for my courage and honesty. One of the trustees said that my conduct over the incident and in the meeting had moved my standing in the charity up substantially. Funny, I had always striven for acknowledgment, and never felt I got it fully. Now I don't need it anymore, it seems to come in abundance! This is all because I no longer play-act, but share the real me.

The great thing about the group was that they hacked into areas where I was afraid to go, and then they were there to support me. I loved the weekly trek over to them and the exhausted trip back.

Weekend workshop

Mike Lew came over to the UK to run a weekend workshop for men abused as boys. Nearly the whole group went. There were about forty guys in all. It was a truly remarkable weekend.

One of the first exercises was to get the whole group to stand in a line from a point where they had told no one about their abuse, to everyone knew. People ranged all along the line. I was flabbergasted that guys who had told no-one had the nerve to come on the weekend. All power to them.

We were all asked to prepare something out of our comfort zone for the Saturday evening entertainment. We could perform a song, read a story, dance, act. But it had to be something we felt uncomfortable doing. I decided that the most uncomfortable thing for me would be to stand, totally unprepared, and talk. I had a reputation for 'winging it' as I always prepared everything at the last minute: speeches, presentations. I had worked out that this wasn't true: it may not be written down, but everything was prepared in huge detail in my head. I was a master at having mental 'dry runs'. In fact, writing down was a chore I only did for other peoples' sakes or for comfort. No sooner had I decided this than I hit on the idea of asking them all to choose a topic and for me to make up a bedtime fairy story for them.

We sat in the Queen Anne drawing room, it was getting dark, the mist was rolling down the hill in the grounds, they chose for me to tell a story about 'the mist rolling down the garden to the house'. I was so scared, but just started and it all came tumbling out. I had forty guys sitting spellbound at their bedtime story.

Oh, and as a final twist, I told them that I always craved feedback so they weren't to give me any at all. Neil did later tell me it was magic! That was very, very, liberating. We did lots of other exercises designed to open us up and talk about the different issues we faced. I felt hugely liberated by the weekend and made some amazing connections with other guys.

My therapist, Bernard[59]

From there, you decided to work individually with a psychotherapist?

I so loved going to my individual therapist, Bernard Ratigan, every week. He is the most amazing guy.

When I first went I was surprised at a couple of things. Firstly, in my two-hour introductory session, Bernard took me back to my family and my earliest memory. I didn't see the point in this, but went there for him. Of course, I later realised that key 'drivers' for me were set up when I was tiny and desperate to be loved and noticed by my parents and older brothers. My sister being born was when I first gave up, as she was clearly the much-wanted 'star'. Interestingly, she always felt left out as she wasn't a boy and never felt like a star! I finally cemented my feelings of being unloved when I was sent to boarding school at the age of seven.

Secondly, I was expecting to have a structure to the series of sessions, but Bernard said that I needed to lead on what I was thinking about each week and that he would think alongside me. I must admit I was wondering at first if it would work. He was so right, of course: it worked amazingly. He had sensed that I was more than capable to explore my head on my own, which I proceeded to do. He often counselled caution but as ever I was on a mission.

So a pattern was set that went on for months. I would tell Bernard where I had got to with what I had started thinking about last week, and I would start to talk about the next topic that was coming along. On the way home I would always ring Neil and share the session's work with him. He would then talk with me during the week, which

---

[59] Dr. Bernard Ratigan, brilliant psychoanalytic psychotherapist and independent scholar with interests in the contested space between psychoanalysis, religious belief, (homo-) sexualities, and the arts.

helped hugely to tease out my thinking. After a few sessions I had obviously been saying, 'Neil said...' too often as Bernard teasingly referred to 'my erstwhile assistant, Neil!'

I also found that I could share stuff with other people, especially a Chinese friend I had met on the weekend group. His mind was very different and he always had a new angle on things. He would share his journey at the same time, which emphasised to me how fast I was travelling. Bernard reckoned that I got through in a week what other people might take a year to sort out.

The group fell apart not long after I started with Bernard. He was never happy with the group as he felt it seemed to be uncontrolled. I was kicked out, which hurt, but not for long. I realise that I was outgrowing it and this was causing a problem for the group leader.

Control and my wife

I loved my wife and still do: she is an amazing lady, strong willed and rather fiery. I love this in her and that I see it in my children. They are so independent and don't get pushed around by the world. I realise, however, that over the years, I'd learned to avoid explosions and conflicts with Jan and that this had the effect of me heading off to places that weren't really where I wanted to be. I had become subservient to her and the way she wanted to live her life - and mine.

Why was I attracted to someone with these characteristics? I believe I have huge issues with control. I either let people control me, or I am very controlling. In my work environment I was super controlling. At home, I had relationships with people who were very controlling, and relationships where it was more even. Looking at male friends, a theme that seems to occur often is friends who make me feel like I am their little brother. I just switch off with them and they tell me what to do.

Interestingly, I no longer do this. I want to get to a point where all my relationships are more even. I still occasionally find myself getting pushed into subservient mode by friends, male and female, and by acquaintances, but always try to stop it happening. It's still tricky sometimes.

All this work on yourself and the depth of insight and feeling you were experiencing must have had a great impact on your 'normal' life, Chris?

Head stuff

When I first realised I'd been abused, that it hadn't been my fault, I felt as if a steamroller drove through the walls of the pub and flattened me. Over the next few weeks these crashes happened several times a day. I felt as if I had dropped into the bottom of a deep, dark hole. The surrounding world seemed dim and distant. My mind was screaming at me to let go of the world and succumb to the darkness. I couldn't. I was too scared of not carrying on in the world and of everyone finding out about me and what was going on. It was such an effort to do anything, a huge effort. I just wanted Neil to give me a hug, metaphorically, and tell me it would all be ok.

He couldn't do this. He was dealing with his own issues, had always been incapable of physical contact with another guy, and couldn't do it even metaphorically. It just wasn't in his nature to give 'hugs'. What did come naturally to him, as an academic, was to ask questions: 'What caused it?' 'What does it feel like?' He was very inquisitive. This had the effect of making me climb out of the hole.

I wanted to understand what was going on but was too scared to go to anyone for help. Neil was great though, and between us we worked out that what he was doing was getting my brain going, by making me respond to questions, to kick-start my mind; we assumed it turned off when it had enormous stuff to deal with.

I couldn't get hold of Neil one day when I was in a deep hole and dire straits. What could I do? Ask questions as he would. I proceeded to analyse what had caused the current crash. Sure enough, my mind kick-started and I pulled out of the hole. Understanding those crashes was hugely powerful. I learned to spot them and get out on my own.

For example, when I was accused of not being emotional I knew this struck a chord. I felt funny inside and very tired that night. When I went looking I worked out that, at the age of seven, when I was very homesick at boarding school, I had to learn to hide my feelings and not to cry or I would be picked on. I developed all sorts of defences against this, but key was to learn to cry 'inside'.

Once I discovered this I realised that pulling down my emotional prison would help hugely, as I'd no longer have anywhere to hide from myself. But this wasn't enough. This is when I hit on the idea of writing a letter as a seven year old to my parents. How I cried! I cried even more when I read it to Bernard, Neil, my wife and, hardest, to my older brother Ken. I let my feelings flow, it was hard not to, and it was ok to do it.

Transactional Analysis[60]

I soon realised that a lot of what went on in my head could be explained using the Parent, Adult, Child model of Transactional Analysis. Basically, whenever I was feeling scared, attacked, wary or small I would retreat into my head like a lost little boy and stare out from my 'emotional prison'. This would then mean that I was operating as 'a child'. What I wanted to do was to operate as an adult. I worked out that, if I was in 'child mode' like this, I could get back to

---

[60] Transactional Analysis. School of psychotherapy founded by Eric Berne in the late 1950s. See also books: 'I'm OK, You're OK' and 'Staying OK' by Thomas A Harris: HarperCollins, 2004 & Random House 2011.

being an adult by asking adult questions of myself.

Going to see the boss at work made me feel like a boy and, although I might sit there acting as an adult, in my head I was a little, wary boy. I always had difficulty dealing with bosses! If we got past this stage we could work well together, but it invariably meant that they had to leave me well alone and gradually I would come out of my shell and start working with them as an adult. Having practiced this for some time I now find the process almost automatic, though the number of occasions that I see myself going into child mode diminishes.

An interesting recent application dealing with something that has taken me ages to get my head around is my ability to faff, to stare at a job (written or practical) and then do anything but that job. I stare into space, doodle, and daydream. I sometimes wonder how I ever get anything done. I worked out that this is a very childish thing to do. So I went looking and remembered that, at boarding school, I was made to sit in a classroom every Sunday and write a letter home. Why would I want to do that? I had been packed off unloved. So, I stared into space, doodled, daydreamed. I had ground this behaviour further into my psyche when my Mum used to sit me down in the holidays to do my homework, which I never did of course, just stared into space, doodled, day-dreamed.

Next I could work out how to become adult when I was feeling like this, by analysing what had tripped it, how childlike I felt. Hey presto! I have done more outstanding DIY jobs in the past few weeks than in the whole of the past year. I have nearly got on top of all of my written stuff. Amazing.

What do you know about your sexual development?

When I was eleven, before my first ejaculation, Tom and Frank took me into the changing rooms and took down my trousers to play with my cock. They made me play with theirs as well. It was great fun; I put up a fight, but not for long. It seemed amazing that Frank, who was Top Dog in the junior boarding house, was paying attention to me. We played around with each other for the rest of that year then, when I returned for the final year in the junior house, they had moved up to senior school.

My first ejaculation was with Tom: I didn't understand what was happening; it felt so weird, but it was funny and messy and, of course, felt great. In that final year I had two friends I messed around with, Doug and Carl. It wasn't the same as with the older boys, we didn't do much, just wanked each other a few times.

During this year it began to dawn on me, the enormity of what I had done. This could mean that I was gay, a poof, a queer. I was so scared that this was true and that I would be found out. I couldn't help being attracted to guys at school, but I was so scared of being found out.

The next year I went up to senior school. Carl and I didn't do much together sexually; it was all becoming too scary for me. I was driven to be an achiever, did really well at 'O levels', captain of everything, head boy, house captain, and swimming captain, choir senior, head sacristan. I just had to prove myself, and being a poof didn't fit.

The school was an all boys' boarding school, but girls had just started to arrive for our sixth form. I remember being desperate to have one as a girl friend. There were six girls in our year.

In physics I was paired up with Lucy: I was in seventh heaven. Surely I could get her as my girlfriend and be normal. Never happened. I don't know why, but I think I was just too scared to be forward enough to ask her out. Funny really, as thirty years on L and I are still best friends.

We had various events with local girls invited along. I met up with Rhian and we went out for a few months. Nothing happened, apart from writing to each other and me staying with her for one weekend. I was too scared to have sex; I thought that I would be found out.

After A levels, Lucy, her older cousin and I went camping in the south of France for two weeks. We had a ball. I loved her cousin and she fancied the pants off me. She made huge advances and I took the chance: we had sex and I lost my heterosexual virginity. I had made it: I was normal.

Then to University where I lodged in a vicarage. I hadn't cracked sex after all, as the nearest I got in the entire three years was with a girl I always liked but never fancied. It wasn't great; not her fault, I just was like a highly-strung violin.

Then there was Mrs Robinson! I took a year out after my degree and went sailing around the world. I was twenty-one. I spent several weeks in Hong Kong and was seduced by Kerry, a forty-two year old married woman who reminded me of Sophia Loren. I called her 'Mrs Robinson' after the seductress in 'The Graduate'[61]. She was drop dead glamorous and totally out of my league, but she was such fun to be with and just railroaded me into sex. It was glorious. We had a lot of fun and did loads of crazy things together. I loved her. It was she who taught me that I could be normal. I had finally achieved it.

There was one instant that scared me when Kerry badgered me to go to see 'Cruising'[62] with her, but I was too scared, as I thought she might suss that I was overly interested in the gay content. I didn't go and she gave me a hard time quizzing me about it and even said that if I was gay, she wouldn't mind. Boy, I was nearly rumbled!

Back in England I worked as a retail manager and got my first shop in London. I lived in a big, shared house with six other people including Jan, who really fancied me and I was sufficiently buoyed

---

[61] 'The Graduate': film, 1967 by Mike Nichols, starring Dustin Hoffman and Anne Bancroft . An older married neighbour, Mrs Robinson, seduces aimless graduate Benjamin who proceeds to fall in love with her daughter, Elaine.

[62] 'Cruising': film, 1980 psychological thriller film directed by William Friedkin and serial killer targeting gay men in New York's clubs and bars, in particular those BDSM scene.

after Kerry to risk going out with her. The first time we slept with each other we were both drunk. The first time we had a bath together I could only do it with a mountain of bubbles to hide whatever my cock might choose to do or not do. But, it was fun and I relaxed.

I feel that I'd finally managed to lock away all my fears about being found out. I knew I fancied guys, but I was able to act as a normal guy (I use the word normal with my tongue in my cheek!!) Jan and I went on to get married and I was very happy with her.

The first cracks started to appear when we wanted to have children. We couldn't. Five years of fertility treatment ruined our sex life forever. By the time we had two children sex had become such a chore, it happened once a year.

I started to ache after gay guys. It was hard with Jan so much around. I remember watching the entire series of 'Queer as Folk'[63], taping it or watching it while Jan went to bed early. It was scary in case I was caught, but oh, how it drew me in.

When we finally went to Relate and Jan said she wanted to be desired I very nearly asked to see the counsellor on my own to tell her why I no longer desired Jan, but I was much too scared.

Sex with guys was, of course, tainted by my experience of it being 'wrong' at boarding school. Free to do what I wanted having left Jan, living alone, I still felt that sex with a guy was sordid and wrong. I managed to talk this through with Bernard and realised I had to focus on finding a kind guy who would let me relax and start to enjoy sex and I met Dan. We saw each other for seven months and I did completely relax and enjoyed our sex life. It finally felt like I had come home. It felt right, so right. I loved it and I loved him.

We split up because he was much younger and hugely controlling in our relationship, so I started to go on 'Outeverywhere'[64] in earnest.

---

[63] 'Queer as Folk': hugely popular 1999 UK TV series (Channel 4) by Russell T. Davies about young gay men living in Manchester's Canal Street district.

[64] www.outeverywhere.com website for social and sexual dating for gay people.

He got cross that I went on a date and that was the end of us. It was OK; I'd had enough of being controlled. Dan gave me my ticket to freedom as an openly gay man: I will never forget that and will always be indebted to him.

I found men my own age looked and felt older than me, so not many were attractive. I went out with a thirty-four year old Somalian and was won over. We've been going out for five months now and it is great. I love going out with him. So many people look at us and I relish it! He gets coy, but it just makes me feel liberated. Unfortunately, he is having an arranged marriage soon, which grieves me as he is reversing my journey in a way. The end will happen over Christmas. I have to be there for him and move on. I now want to find a man less complicated, out and happy to be with me.

How are you considering your future now, Chris?

My new purpose? This quote says it all:

"Your vocation is about discovering who you really are and what you really should be doing.

We've got our Christian name but we've got another name called our white stone name. This comes from the book of Revelations where the angel says that your name is written on a white stone in heaven. Your vocation is to find out what your white stone name is. This is a lifelong quest.

Hold the stone, remember the story, you are trying to work out what your white stone name is, what are you really meant to be doing, who are you really meant to be." (Brother Francis. Franciscan Monk at Worth Abbey).[65]

The future is very simple. The past two years has been about 'Discovering who you really are...' and the next two about '... what you

---

[65] Brother Francis quote: The Monastery' 2005 reality television series, BBC about the lives of Benedictine monks at Worth Abbey. The moment when Brother Francis gives Tony a white stone.

really should be doing.'

I have left my job. Such a massive wrench: all those people to say cheerio to. Also, kissing goodbye to being part of an institution when I've been part of one all my life: the forces with my Dad, boarding schools, University, all the companies I've worked with.

And what am I going to do? I have worked out that I can take two years out; to find what makes my heart sing and find something that meets one of the great needs of the world.

I have four projects to focus on: management consultancy part time to keep the wolf from the door; next, a charity that produces educational materials for women and children in the third world. I plan to use my skills to help them grow.

Then there's my 'happiness project': I have taken my life from a sterile desert to a rich wonderful place and want to see if I can distil the learning from this into a book that could help others. I want to use this in talks, workshops, on the web, as a sort of life coach. It scares me, just seeing this set down: how can I possibly live up to my famous ancestor, Mark Twain?

Finally, the prayer project is an important part of the happiness project - spirituality, feeling there is more to life than just me on my own in eternity. This was hugely scary when I started it but it's amazing how suspending fear, getting on with it, gets you to that place where suddenly it all seems so obvious a thing to do. Perhaps I had a famous Bishop in my past?

Very early on in my therapy Bernard asked me a profound question:

'If you could go back to meet little Chris, just before he first went into those changing rooms, what would you say, what would you do?'

'I'd give little Chris a hug and tell him he done OK,' I cried.

'Why wouldn't you stop him? Why wouldn't you warn him?' asked Bernard.

'Because I wouldn't be me if it hadn't happened.'

There's also the little matter of my girls. How could I possibly want to change anything that would mean I didn't have my wonderful girls?

And now?

I am happy being me for the first time in my life: Chris, an openly gay man. More than that, many other possible descriptors, but being openly gay seems to be the badge I have won for now.

What would you recommend to other guys in your position?

Find someone to hold your hand (like my wonderful friend Neil). Take the leap. Get a good therapist. Know that it is amazing to find yourself. It is unbelievably amazing to be yourself.

Have you lost anything?

Nothing! Oh, yes- a deep, dark, heavy secret sitting in my head.

Dedication: I'd like to dedicate this chapter to Bernard Ratigan, my therapist, who helped me to detoxify my past, find myself, and start to explore my true potential. He did this with care, intelligence.... and a dash of humour! I will be forever grateful to him and confess I miss him deeply.

ALAN'S STORY

Introduction to Alan

Alan was brought up to be a 'good boy' by an anxious mother with ambitions for him: this is significant and parallels can be found in other stories here where close binding mothers, not particularly satisfied with their own lives and adult relationships, have needed quite a lot from - or for - their sons. It is, of course, a classic example of one of Freud's original suggestions about gay male development – over identification with the mother by a boy whose relationship with his father is much weaker. Richard I say[66] wrote an important book radically challenging and reworking earlier psychoanalytic interpretations by looking at how fathers may move away from their 'gay' sons, sometimes from very early on, through unconscious fear or embarrassment, thus exacerbating the boys' experience of rejection, isolation and vulnerability.

One effect, certainly evident in Alan's narrative, is to have become a 'good man' and, while some of this 'goodness' has manifested in desirable qualities like kindness and consideration for others, it also prevented assertion, individuation and self-definition for years. Alan, like Alex, Nigel, Bruce and Chris, sublimates his true self, desires and needs to struggle instead, over a very long period, to stay married even though it means, in Trevor's words, "… overriding any of my own

---

[66] Richard Isay: 'Being Homosexual: Gay Men and Their Development': 1989: Vintage Books. See Chapter 3 especially – on fathers and their gay sons.

desires to be happy." These patterns run deep in my experience and, even after coming out, there will be more work to do to change lifelong habits of self denial, negligence and what some call 'co-dependency'[67] in relationships.

Alan feels his upbringing was 'kindly' and indeed many well-intentioned parents can be seen to do the best they know how to help their growing child. We all have our own influences and limits, however, from our cultural, familial and personal life experiences, as well as our different abilities to challenge given ideas and reconsider moral strictures according to our own internal compass. The difficulty can arise that a child who feels quite well treated and privileged can become an adult who feels additional shame or guilt at not conforming to the wishes and ideas of kindly parents and really struggles to assert their own individuality, difference, uniqueness. Alan is constantly aware of having 'reasons to be grateful' and is having to work hard now at growing a new awareness – through his therapeutic journey – of also having 'reasons' to be angry, sad, aggrieved and motivated to change.

When one's childhood had obviously wrong, abusive or disruptive elements, it is simpler sometimes to 'form' one's own shape in contrast - or in conflict - with ones surroundings. Notice how 'dreadful' Alan still feels decades later about the possible hurt to his girlfriend of his first honest coming out as gay. The fact this was met with a resounding silence proved to be powerfully inhibiting although, at the time, Alan felt relief. It was a painful example, and set a long precedent, for not being 'heard' when Alan attempted to express his feelings, needs or wishes. He talks of having 'no outlet' for

---

[67] Co-dependency': a term taken from the work of Alcoholics Anonymous referring to relationships in which there is a high dependence on the needs of, or control of, another. It often involves placing a lower priority on one's own needs, while being excessively preoccupied with the needs of others.

his feelings and of bodies being somewhat mysterious while growing up. Alan's next attempt, when he formed such a powerful attraction for a boy, was forcibly squashed by angry parents and serves further to force the real Alan into hiding with great shame, never willingly 'rocking the boat' after that.

These 'infatuations' or crushes for unlikely or unavailable men are a classic part of the effects on boys of coming to terms with different sexual feelings than those prescribed by their society – as they are for girls experiencing their own sexual questioning. They seem to me also to be connected with the repression of expression of affection between boys in western cultures as contrasted, for instance, with those of many Far Eastern, Latin, African and Arabic societies.

Another aspect worth noting here is the effect of repressive attitudes to bodies in many families. Maybe this is decreasing nowadays: I hope so. We need to remember that before, after and alongside all the rest of life, we are bodies. Alan's early desires to expose himself and have other children, specifically boys, expose themselves is obviously metaphorical and emotional as well as deeply primal: we want to be truly seen and to truly see others. We want not to have to hide. We want to know and be known, to have our bodies, where we begin and end and which are the site of all our feelings - both sensations and emotions - accepted and celebrated.

We are instead so often made to feel ashamed, guilty, dirty even, for being interested in our own bodies and those of the rest of our family or tribe. Such a huge part of gay and bi life is then concerned with glancing, glimpsing, surreptitiously viewing, cruising, cottaging, spending time looking furtively in pools, baths, toilets, gyms, showers, magazines or online at the bodies of others. The male gaze has been the subject of enormous aesthetic and academic interest for years. Germaine Greer challenged this when she published a book about the

125

male body as the object of desire in art and culture.[68] She was looking from a heterosexual female perspective. Much more serious work needs to be done, however, in understanding this reversal of the heterosexual gaze where the male becomes, as he was in early European history, once more the object, not the objectifier.

Alan went from being a 'good' son – that is, a son who behaved in the ways his parents wished and was at pains to please them – to being a 'good' husband: pleasing to his wife, in whose friendship he can be seen to have found some shelter – and, even to a degree today, he struggles to be a more authentic – and therefore possibly not so 'good' – gay partner. Alan now regrets his behaviour towards his wife, once he felt it imperative to come out and act upon his gay desires, feeling that he treated her badly and behaved callously and insensitively. That is, in fact, one of the great problems with repression: the more something is pushed down and kept buried, the greater charge it attains until, so often, it 'comes out sideways' in what therapists call 'acting out.' This is when we can witness otherwise uncharacteristic, even almost opposite, behaviour in a person as for example where a very restrained, quiescent person rants and rages, making demands, or a sweet tempered, kindly person suddenly becomes full of foul-mouthed rage. Anger, frustration and desire are not bad in themselves, just natural human feelings, but the effects of repressing them for years can be very harmful to the person concerned or to those around them once they force themselves out in unintentional or unconsidered ways. Often the focus of therapy is to balance how to

---

[68] Germaine Greer: 'The Beautiful Boy': 2003: Rizzoli Press. The pioneering feminist generated considerable controversy because "society is not accustomed to seeing beauty in young males", Greer claims, describing her book of "pictures of 'ravishing' pre-adult boys with hairless chests, wide-apart legs and slim waists" as her attempt to "reclaim for women the right to appreciate the short-lived beauty of real boys, not simpering 30-year-olds with shaved chests."

express what needs expression and contain what needs containment: this way lies a satisfying experience of the self functioning fully.

How encouraging that what we might call Alan's spirit – his original or natural, non-adaptive self – has not been crushed by these experiences and is still battling to the surface, demanding that he be acknowledged and given expression today, sixty years on. He is still a man honouring principles of kindness and consideration for others, balancing his own wants and needs carefully with his rights and responsibilities. He is a gentle, polite, compassionate and ethical mature man. Alan's important quest today is to become more internally referenced and less compliant, more real, and thus to develop his own life more fully as a result. He shares this path with Chris, Robert, Nigel and Trevor and many of the men with whom I've been privileged to work over the years.

ALAN'S STORY

I was born in 1950. I have a younger brother, six years my junior. My mother gave birth to a stillborn daughter two years in advance of my birth.

I consider myself to have been brought up in a kindly and non-abusive way, while always feeling closer to my mother than my father, whom I found rather distant. My mother doted on me and, to a lesser extent, on my brother. Our family was essentially upper working-class, my father being a white-collar worker at a local machine tools factory. My mother came from a similar background but, unlike my father, had strong middle class aspirations. This was brought home to me in her wish for me to have elocution lessons to "smarten up" what she considered to be a lazy way of talking. She was very supportive of my education and my teachers, and I responded well to that – she was overjoyed when I passed to the local grammar school. Her support was quiet rather than overtly "pushy" but I have reason to be grateful for this support as, perhaps, without it I might have achieved rather less academically.

There was always the feeling though that she wanted, or even needed, to keep me close to her and this continued to be evident long into adult life and essentially until the end of her own life, when I was aged fifty-nine. It was clear that she spent a great deal of time, particularly after my father's early death in 1976 and the death of her male companion of ten years in 1999, worrying about the physical safety of myself and my brother whenever we were not in sight which was, of course, most of the time!

What do you put your mother's anxiety and need for closeness down to?

I don't really know. The relationship between my mother and father never seemed particularly loving in an overt sense, but may have been different in the privacy of their own space. In any case I had nothing to compare it with. Perhaps there was something lacking in my mother's personal life that caused her to be over-smothering: if there was I don't know what it was. She did have depression at times and I do know that she once had a stay in a mental hospital, although the true nature of this was kept from me. "Mummy is having a spell in hospital because she gets headaches" I was told, though I sensed, even at the time, that there was more to it than that. As was my custom, I never rocked the boat by enquiring further.

My mother probably worried less about my brother and myself – especially myself because I was her favourite – when my father was still alive and again between 1989-1999 when she saw a great deal of a boyfriend she had taken up with, a kindly widower who dearly wished to marry her. She would not do so in deference to her 'boys' even though we encouraged her. He died and she fell back to type.

At the time I left our East Anglian home town for university in London she demonstrated considerable pleasure at what she regarded as my great academic achievement, and likewise when I met the girl I was to marry there, but I guess these occasions, which meant that I would in future see less of her, were tinged with sadness for her as, being now adult, I was drifting away from her 'nest.' Partly because of my mother's concern for me, I don't think I ever became fully integrated in any grouping of boys. I think my mother's worry about me prevented me from even suggesting, for example, that I go away for a week with others on a bird-watching holiday in Scotland. In my mind, I didn't need to ask; although the answer might actually have been a grudging "yes", I didn't want to put my parents through this 'decision.'

I think I therefore left home naively equipped for life's struggles and didn't settle well to life at university. Here I was lazy in respect of my studies and I only obtained a third-class degree. Upon entering the world of work as a schoolteacher, I soon picked up again the strong work ethic that had deserted me after my school exams. I believe I have retained it to this day.

It sounds as though you started 'protecting' your parents from what you wanted early on. Did this pattern affect your free expression in other relationships too?

It appears that I subordinated many of my wishes to what I imagined reactions to those wishes might be. I certainly had no desire to upset my parents in any way or cause them to feel anxious, though not from fear of retribution. I always considered myself well treated and I was not hit in anger although I remember a couple of occasions when my father smacked me hard for some misdeed or other.

I don't really remember whether this pattern repeated itself in affecting my free expression in other relationships, although I was shy in approaching others, some would say quite painfully so. My best friend at school (I had a small circle of friends with similar interests) was the first person I told I was gay, at eighteen. This fits a pattern where I suddenly 'rebel' in a big way. He was shocked, probably more by my imparting this than by the information. He was particularly understanding and always said this was a major confidence that he was fortunate to be party to. I now think he would like to have said that he also had gay feelings but that did not enter my head at the time.

Returning to my childhood, on the whole I was a happy, if rather solitary, individual. The one unpleasant thing about our household was the arguments that took place between my parents. The content I really remember little about (only once though was the subject about a third person that my father might have been 'seeing') but they were frightening to me as a child, sitting quivering at the top of the stairs, although they stopped short of physical violence. I remember intervening at times to stop them: notions of physical violence that might lead to murder or separation and divorce loomed heavily in my thoughts.

Why, do you imagine, might fears of physical violence, as well as of separation or divorce, have been so foreground in your mind at that time?

I was never offered physical violence but was fearful that it could erupt between my mother and father, though apparently it never did. I was something of a loner with a vivid imagination. I read avidly and that included national and local newspapers that often seemed to have reports of murder trials, frequently domestic, and of suicides. I think these played a large part in my fear of something terrible happening at home.

I was aware of my mother once trying to commit suicide or, more likely, pretending to do so, by putting her head in the gas oven behind a locked kitchen door and this had a devastating effect on me for weeks.

Can you say more about the immediate – and, perhaps, lasting – effects of this on you?

It was sheer fright and a feeling that my life could change for the worse, that home would never again be the comforting place it had been. Perhaps if I had had the courage to raise the issue next morning I would have been reassured. Actually, as I write this, I think I did raise it, but was quickly fobbed off with a statement that I was mistaken and that there was nothing to worry about. Although this was never mentioned again, I continued to worry about it for weeks. I slept badly and things seemed so unreal until the feeling gradually dwindled, although future arguments tended to bring the feelings back.

Early Thoughts on Sexuality

Apart from catching glimpses of naked toddlers and small children on a beach holiday, I had little knowledge as a small child of the female body. There was no question of ever seeing my mother naked, although my father was much less inhibited, having no qualms if either my brother or myself were to come into the bathroom while he was taking a bath. I think this may have had something to do with his experience as a soldier in the War. My primary school was mixed but I remember no girls taking any particular interest in me, though I certainly recall friends and I taking some interest in the girls. As a rather quiet, shy and unexciting individual, I proceeded from primary school to an all boys grammar school and from there, without a 'gap year' – which were rare in the late Sixties – straight to university.

What would you say that you learned about males from your father and females from your mother? How have your relationships with males and females been affected by this learning?

I suppose I learned from my father that men could be rather distant, formidable and unapproachable, or at least, unapproachable by such as me; they would not want to be 'bothered' by me. I have always tended to see myself as 'small' compared with other men: more naïve, unable to compete on a level playing field. Curiously, this is exactly the sort of thing that I deduced about females even though my mother's approach to me was different from that of my father. It was that women were just as untouchable or unattainable as men.

We are talking about the 1950s and early 1960s being my formative years. Men in particular were still very stiff upper lip, with most adult men at this time having had close experience of war. Relationships with uncles and aunts did little to dispel this prevailing dynamic on my part. As time has gone on these notions of 'untouchability' have gradually waned but not gone altogether; meeting more gay men and particularly understanding women in my work place has helped them.

To say that I was interested, pre-puberty, in seeing other boys with their trousers down was an understatement! I can think of at least three boys, and there were more, whom I encouraged – and I was definitely the instigator – to show me their genitals at home or even in less safe surroundings. I was happy to reciprocate. I came to look upon this as an unusual trait that probably didn't happen elsewhere and I suppose I was mildly disgusted that I did such things. This activity continued into my early years at grammar school when I was still pre-pubescent. Although I think I was by this time aware of homosexuality as a concept, I didn't consider myself to be gay. I distinctly remember about then, however, on one occasion seeing a much older boy, perhaps 16, in the tuck-shop queue, tall and slim with a shock of red hair and imagining him, with some relish, without any clothes on.

What are some of the things that you learned at home and at school from others about bodies, sex, sexuality and gayness?

I do not remember at any time nudity being in any way encouraged at home. I don't ever recall seeing any part of my mother's body except perhaps by accident. I suppose I ascertained from them, without anything actually being said, that nakedness was not something that you flaunted and certainly there was nothing 'normal' about the naked state. I would like to think times have changed but, interestingly, my grandson asked his mother, after he'd been on holiday with me earlier this year, why I only wore underpants in bed, not pyjamas. Little does he know what my normal bedroom attire is, or isn't!

In the sex 'games' we played at school there was the unspoken idea that it was wrong. Our R.E.[69] teacher, also a priest, was VERY hot on the dangers and sinfulness of what was called 'self-abuse' – i.e. masturbation. Strangely, the concept of homosexuality as a permanent state of life never came up at school. It was scarcely, if ever, mentioned: this was all pre-1967.[70] So all I learned from school was how very attracted I was to boys and that there was no outlet to express those feelings. I discovered much later in life that my Latin teacher, of whom I saw much, having specialised in Classics at school and university, was gay. Although married and divorced with a son of his own, he had a particular affection for me, which was never expressed, and I was quite unaware of it at the time. I now feel desperately sad for this man whose life was very lonely.

There then seemed to follow a quiescent period. My coming into adulthood was in February 1965 when I was at home recovering from illness. Something happened which had caused me to ejaculate and I remember being somewhat worried by what emerged from my body: a lack of sex education apparent here! By the following year I had come to admire a boy at school who was taking part in a drama production with which I was associated. I suppose my realisation that I could be gay stemmed from that time. There followed a number of boys at school with whom I became quietly infatuated for periods of time. Apart from one, I never let my feelings for them be known: they were infatuations I kept entirely to myself but made me very unhappy and once even physically sick. I certainly anticipated ridicule if these

---

[69] R.E.: Religious Education, formerly compulsory in UK schools.

[70] 1967: Significant date. Sexual Offences Act passed in UK decriminalising male homosexuality between consenting adults in private after Lord Arran advanced a motion in the House of Lords (1965) in favour of implementing the recommendations of the Wolfenden Report of a decade earlier and Leo Abse's Bill to reform the law which resulted.

feelings were found out at a boys' school.

Were you aware of explicit prohibitions on same sex affection or sex or were these culturally implicit, as it were? Were you aware of other boys having 'crushes' or actual sex games at all?

I would say culturally implicit. It would be unrealistic to say that boys at my school did not have crushes, I'm sure they did but, at the time, I thought I was the only one and there was no place to discuss such 'unmanly' feelings with others, so I imagine others undergoing much the same torment as I was going through. Boys, within the school buildings at any rate, confined sexual activity to discreet fumblings of the genitals. I did and others did, sometimes with the overt disapproval of others: "Tut, tut, you shouldn't be doing that, you know!"

During my late teenage years I never sought a relationship with a girl. However, while working weekends at a local library, a girl became interested in me to the extent of inviting me home to meet her parents and have a meal. Both her parents and my own were very pleased with this but, partly because of the attention of her parents, I found it necessary to withdraw from the relationship which I did the cowardly way, by letter. I had definitely concluded by then that I was gay, indeed I intimated this in that final letter. I don't know what became of the girl, but imagine she had been very upset and for that I feel dreadful. This was in 1970, the year I was off to University.

There were no consequences of your semi-confession in your letter, your first attempt to come out?

There were no consequences other than a welcome silence. I never saw the girl in question again as by that time the part-time job we had both been doing had come to an end.

In my first summer vacation, back home doing a part-time job, I met a delightful boy with whom I shared an interest in natural history. We spent a lovely few weeks doing things together – nothing overtly sexual apart from some kissing and a little fondling. He seemed to enjoy my company but whether he was ready for anything more, I rather doubt. At one point I told him that I loved him, which he seemed to accept with equanimity but, after he failed to meet me a week later at a pre-arranged time, I fell immediately into depths of a despair which was easily noticeable at home. That evening it all came out to my parents who were absolutely horrified. I was instructed to bring an end to this relationship immediately and to seek out girls rather than boys for company.

What do you feel for the young man you were when you look back at this? Can you remember more about that exchange which has been so formative for you? It was the strength of painful feelings which led you to come out and I imagine this response would have sent you back into the closet.

I would hate what happened to me to happen to anyone else but I am sure it still does. I felt belittled and bad and I remember my parents' anger and horror. They were keen that I get on the 'phone to the boy and end our relationship there and then. This was difficult but I did so. I don't think he was especially upset and may have been relieved. His parents had been asking questions and in any case, as he told me, in six months' time they would all be emigrating! I felt devastated and empty for days. I was allowed a short holiday in Wales with my best friend which helped me get over the worst.

Back at university that October there was work to be done – I had to get to like the female sex, which I set about with what was a remarkable burst of enthusiasm in the circumstances. This was mostly about getting to know the new intake into my department. The early signs were not good; a fairly attractive girl whom I chased was not interested, another appeared to chase me but I didn't quite know what to do and a third, whom a male friend paired me with, found me boring. I found myself buffeted from all angles. Then along came the drama group and the woman who was to become my wife. All this time I knew full well in my heart that my gay feelings would be unlikely to ever go away

There I recognized the younger sister of the organizer as a girl I regularly saw around college: she worked in the library. I took part in a production and, during the post-production party, the young woman and I became unexpectedly amorous. This was what was supposed to happen and was the start of a relationship that led, two years later, to our marriage. Needless to say, the first meeting of my parents and my future wife and, later, our engagement, were supreme high spots in my mother's life: confirmation that her son was, in all respects, after all, normal.

In the two years between meeting my wife and the actual marriage, I had a couple of gay experiences, notably with a friend from school days, who himself went on to marry and have children, but later professed that time with me had been important in his life. Thus I entered marriage well aware of my homosexuality. During that period, I was enjoying sex with my wife-to-be, which was successful and as satisfactory as it was ever likely to be.

What was it that attracted you to this particular young woman and what would you say she was attracted to in you? Did this remain the main bond between you for the first years together? Did it change over time?

Our first encounter was a result of the heady atmosphere of a party. There was clearly a sexual chemistry between us that evening and we spent the night in each other's arms though there was no sex. I was so surprised by what happened that I wanted to pursue it, I didn't want to lose it. In any case it was in my parents' master plan! The young woman was clearly happy to go along with it. On reflection, I think there was a certain urgency in her to marry, always important in a Jewish family, although she was only twenty-four. She talked about possible marriage after six months. We saw a very great deal of each other. She found me fun to be with, kind and considerate with a sense of humour and a possible marriage partner. We had sex frequently, though not penetrative sex before marriage. She went along with this as an inevitable part of the deal.

Once married, she also went along with sex but not with any real interest or any willingness to experiment or so it seemed to me (I found it upsetting on the third day of our honeymoon when we took a bath together after which she said that she wouldn't be wanting to repeat that experience). I was attracted by her kind and gentle manner – she was not one of those 'unattainable' people. She found my 'ways' amusing and endearing and I played up to this. I think one of the strong bonds between us was a complementary sense of humour. I don't think there was much change in this over time. So, that being so, the 'coming out' was for her a great shock.

My wife and I married in December 1973. Our daughter was born in 1975 and our son in 1977. We continued to enjoy a reasonable sexual relationship during this time. I was keen, she moderately keen. We were in a period of relative contentment. Although I was aware of my homosexual urges, they did not loom large as we sought to bring up our children. I looked with admiration at men I saw in the street but that was about as far as it went. The 1980s saw few crises but, by the 1990s, my gay tendencies were starting to come to the fore with a greater urgency. I began to have infatuations that I had not had since adolescence, to feel increasingly trapped in marriage and to wonder what delights there were to sample in the gay world. Unfortunately, I am not endowed with lateral thinking: had I been, I might have sought out gay life without breaking up my marriage, in other words to lead, as many do, a double life. I tended as usual to see things in a linear progression: any gay contact must inevitably lead to a marriage breakdown and divorce.[71]

Did you and your wife have conversations about your past, about sex or desires, fantasies? With hindsight, would you say she colluded in ignoring clues you put out that you might desire men too? Or were there none? How were you managing your own same sex desire at this time: no magazines, 'cottaging,'[72] porn or fantasies about men at all?

Almost nothing was ever said about serious issues in my past. I realized soon enough that I would not get anywhere by talking about developing our sex lives and I suppose, at the same time, I would have been embarrassed to do so. The longer this situation went on, the harder it would have been to raise the subject. I accept responsibility for only rarely raising questions about sex but my wife's attitude, or silence, played its part. I do not think I intentionally put out clues about desiring men, although I can't say that she did not divine some; if she did, she did not raise them and in that sense she may have, as you say, 'colluded'.

Would you have preferred, or been able to maintain, a 'double life' do you imagine? Your strong feelings, especially over being unrequited or rejected, have made themselves readily known to others: you appear quite transparent.

---

[71] One of my goals in this book is to deconstruct ideas of the inevitability of this - or any other - trajectory. CN

[72] 'Cottaging': meeting others for sex in known places such as public toilets, or 'cottages' (sweetly called 'tearooms' in America!). Largely overtaken by the internet - grinder, tumblr, gaydar for example - making other contact, even in rural areas, more feasible nowadays.

As I have said. my gay feelings grew stronger as time went by but I don't think I ever contemplated a 'double life.' In any case I came out before that entered my mind and there followed all the upheaval connected with that. The idea of a double life holds some attraction but events, arguably brought about by my impetuosity, overtook any realisation of that.

I remember in the early 1990s, on a natural history course I led in the North of England, becoming besotted with a young man on the staff at the centre and mentioning this to my mother, whom I stopped to stay with briefly on the way home. Curiously, she did not express surprise: she knew, or thought she knew, that I would do nothing to jeopardise a perfectly satisfactory marriage. So the incident passed safely away.

Your mother's certainty seems to become almost a 'rule' transmitted to you.

Yes, I guess so. I felt some relief that I had told her about this, that I had not kept it bottled up. A few years later I became infatuated with a male student. My reticence, indeed my position as course leader, prevented me again from expressing my feelings towards him until finding an excuse to drive him home at the end of the course. It seems corny to write that I told him I had fallen in love with him, whatever that might mean, but as before, this statement was met, not with incredulity or disgust, or indeed reciprocation, but with complete non-committal equanimity!

Looking back, is there anything you can say about the surprising lack of response to you in these instances? Think more about the manner and style in which you asserted your wants with others.

I didn't find the lack of positive response in these instances surprising. At least there was no open hostility. I rather assumed I had just had another infatuation about a person who, for whatever reason – not finding me attractive or even not considering themselves gay – would not be able to reciprocate. Manner and style? I suppose these statements were just that: statements that came out of the blue; I don't remember building up to them in any sort of seductive way. I suppose they would have come as a sudden surprise and their lack of response, or equanimity of response, stemmed from that surprise.

Taking that as rejection, which I had no reason not to expect, I made my way home, feeling very low. A week later, my wife, noticing my mood, started to talk to me. This was the last day of the first half of my life. Tomorrow was to be the first day of the rest.

For better, or for worse, I CAME OUT TO MY WIFE.

She was shocked and horrified but strangely, within a few days, seemed to have accepted it about me and at this point there was no talk of ending our marriage. In some ways it almost seemed like a relief to her and she claimed, not 'to have always known it' but to have 'had her suspicions.' This brought me a sense of confidence that perhaps I could keep my marriage together and still 'see' men. I entered a period of self-indulgence and selfishness that I much regret, because I am not normally like that.

Can I just check whether you regret expressing and indulging your long repressed desires or not taking adequate account of your relationship and your wife's feelings, pace, understanding, negotiating developments fully with her?

No, I didn't regret *expressing* my long repressed desires but I do regret trying to fulfil some of those desires in the full glare of my wife, by talking about meeting gay men, and even meeting them with my wife knowing that I was doing so, although the crunch came when I admitted to having had sex with one of them. I set about answering adverts and meeting men in my wife's full knowledge. Unsurprisingly, she began to feel hostile towards me and once, when I had stayed out overnight, declared that she could no longer accept the situation, that we would have to set about divorce proceedings and that we must also tell the children, now twenty-two and nineteen, about what had transpired.

Please say something about how you managed that between you and how your children responded, both at that time and since.

My wife and I agreed on a date and time to tell the children. I would have preferred sitting down and breaking the news gently to them but my wife blurted out the words, "Your father is homosexual" before this could happen. Not surprisingly, this came as a great shock to them and for a little while it was difficult to talk to, or reason with, them about it. But it was not too long, a week or so, before they came round; with both children then less confined to home than when younger, they were able to take the implications of this with more equanimity than might otherwise have been the case. Since then my relationship with my children has been excellent. I share a similar sense of humour with them, especially my son, although they have taken a lot longer to become at ease with my new partner: really this has only developed since their mother's death in 2010. I attribute this to a sense of loyalty to their mother, especially on my son's part.

We divorced in the summer of 1998 after twenty-four years of marriage. My wife regarded our marriage as ultimately a failure but to me it was difficult to write off as such: the marriage had simply come to an end – that didn't make it a failure. There had been happy times and we'd brought up two delightful children. My sexuality had eventually got in the way of the marriage continuing until the end of time. Once divorced our relationship stabilised. There was much understanding on both sides, which even survived my wife's new-found, though married, partner meeting his death in a tragic road traffic accident, and some joyful times were spent thinking about, and being with, our two children and, latterly, two grandchildren until my ex-wife's own death through terminal illness.

Post coming-out relationships

Mother

My mother more than once expressed sympathy with homosexuality. She had a cousin in Yorkshire who was openly gay and no one in the family tried to deny this. He was just part of the furniture. Strangely, on the occasion of travelling by car to my father's funeral, she expressed empathy with gay men.

However, to have her own son of 'this persuasion' was too much. Thus her horror at my revealing the relationship with the younger boy in 1971 and her wish to set me on the straight and narrow, to 'cure' me. When divorce was mooted, she tried her best to persuade me not to go through with this and, if necessary, to keep the marriage intact, but indulge my gay tendencies quietly on the side.

Her acceptance of my new partner was very slow and incomplete at the time of her death. She blamed him for being a marriage wrecker, which is factually quite incorrect. She was unwilling to see him, which put me in some difficult situations, especially since my partner was keen to see her.

How do you feel about your mother's mixed responses to gayness and her refusal to acknowledge your male partner?

I feel quite bitter about this. I could understand it, even though it is hypocritical; anyone could have a rosy picture of it from a distance but it is different when you are faced with reality.

Ex-Wife

My ex-wife too, in spite of our good post-divorce relationship, was very unwilling to have anything to do with my partner. She was prepared to hear me talking about him and even asked after him occasionally, but seeing him was quite a different matter.

When and how did you and he connect? Was it close to the end of your marriage? How did your ex wife, mother and children learn about him – and come to meet – or not meet – him?

We met on a walk with the Gay Outdoor Club[73] at a time when my wife and I had concluded that our marriage was irretrievable and we were about to commence divorce proceedings. I told all of them that I had met a man with whom I was intending to move in in a few weeks time. It was a long time before any of them met him. None of them wanted to and I was happy to keep them apart during these early torrid days. My wife met him only twice – once when he and I were in the car and picked her up because it was raining. I hoped it might break the ice and it was only a short journey back to her home. The only other time was at my daughter's wedding. My mother met him reluctantly; we stayed occasionally with her or she stayed with us for very short periods; she displayed a certain open hostility towards him, at other times a glum silence, which I found very embarrassing. When my children met him the atmosphere was better though not great! They are more at ease with him now.

Brother

My brother was not one with whom I had a particularly close relationship though that is not to say that we were at loggerheads, for we never have been. His attitude to my gayness was remarkably similar to that of my mother, a sympathetic hearing of the news but hostility towards the implications of that – divorce, a new partner and so on.

---

[73] Gay Outdoor Club: operates throughout Britain to provide a wide range of outdoor and indoor sports and recreational activities for gay, lesbian, trans and bi women and men, more than 30 local groups and 500 events annually. Contact: www.goc.org.uk

Children

My son and my daughter were shocked by the news that I was gay but they rallied very soon and I have enjoyed relationships with them every bit as good as before they knew. My ex-wife was told, upon receiving counselling from her rabbi, that I needed to be prepared for my children to reject me for up to ten years. Fortunately, this proved well wide of the mark: they were coming round in less than ten days, and I feel very gratified by that. However, they have not found it easy to accept my partner either. In truth, he isn't the easiest character to get to know, having an unusual, but not aggressive, manner. This has been smoother since the death of my ex-wife and my partner is now welcomed to family occasions like birthdays and so on.

Grandchildren

I now have four grandchildren; my daughter's three and my son's one child. The oldest is eight and remembers his maternal grandmother; his sister, only three when she died, will not essentially remember her. The two youngest have been born since her death. It is unlikely to be in my grandson's perception that his grandmother was once married to me. He is fully aware of my male partner but not of any significance in that. We have taken him away for one short holiday together. In future he may well ask me or his own parents about his perception that granddad does not have a wife but seems to have a man for a partner, as he becomes aware of male-female relationships. We will all answer him honestly in any questions he might decide to put.

What about your partner's efforts to acknowledge, and get to know, your family? How has he behaved towards them in the years you've been together?

I have to admit that my partner's efforts to acknowledge and get to know my family have been magnanimous. He has not been put off by hostility towards him. His manner is unusual and difficult to understand at first and this hasn't helped him to integrate, but he is essentially very generous of spirit and has made every effort to be friendly. My children understand him much better now but it has taken time.

Father

Your father seems notably absent from your childhood and adolescence. Is that your experience? Has this been reproduced in relating to other men? I'm mindful, for one thing, of that lack of response elicited by your declarations of love for some when you were younger. Are you partly expecting to be withheld from, held at a distance that isn't comfortable for you?

My father died in 1976 when I was twenty-five. He was present when I came out in 1971 but appeared less horrified than my mother at the news. He rarely, if ever, spoke to me about relationships but appeared pleased when I married and had our first child. He remains to me a far more distant and detached character than my mother.

I got on well with my father but I do not remember him as someone I could talk to about serious matters. He showed pride in my achievements but was not as effusive as my mother in his expression of them. I remember well one instance of his embarrassment. In the early 1960s there was a tradition that your parent, male parent if you were a boy, would explain to you what were coyly called the 'facts of life' (i.e. basic sex education). I asked him once when he was decorating. He really found it difficult to explain and the conversation soon ended; I don't think I learned anything I didn't already know!

It would be fair, I think, to say that I partly expect to be withheld from, or held at a distance, or even disregarded altogether, although I was always hopeful at the time of some reciprocation.

Are any other issues from your life with your family of origin or that existed in your marriage, repeated as patterns in the relationship/s you have built subsequently with men? Say what you can about this, please.

My main fault surely has to be a failure to assert myself effectively in most areas of life. I don't think this applied generally in my work but it can certainly be seen as a recurring theme in other aspects of life. As a child I was always obedient and unadventurous and didn't take risks. I learned at an early stage to sublimate my desires to the general good and this was a trait my father had too. This could be seen in my desire to go along with my mother's wish that I should have good manners. I have always wanted people to make up their own minds about me; I have always had a fear of imposing myself on others. It is, I suppose, a perfectionist thing really, wanting people to want me for the right reasons. Of course it does mean that I get taken advantage of. I have been told I am too much of 'a soft touch.' I can imagine that I can come across as too quiet, unassuming and unexciting to be a viable sexual partner.

How my life has changed

It would be wrong to claim that, by giving up my marriage and living my life as openly gay, I moved from the darkness into the light. It has been far from plain sailing. I do appreciate the relief of being able to be open and honest about my sexuality and this has been accepted fully by anyone not connected to my family. I cannot say that I do not miss the settled routine of married life but, as my coming out and divorce happened about the time the children would have been leaving home anyway, things may have been different when my wife and I were thrown together on our own. My partner has a totally different personality to my ex-wife and in many ways presents more challenges to my personal comfort. A gain has been continuing to have excellent relationships with my children.

I have always tended to bottle up my true feelings, but when they have been let out it has often been dramatically and explosively. Thus, I went quickly from my marriage to the relationship with my current partner. This seems strange since I am by nature rather a solitary person, content for the most part with my own company. I have never actually lived on my own and thus been in total control of my own life. With hindsight, I would not have rushed into the second relationship following the breakdown of the first. The present relationship being what it is, and being a construct of my own making, I want to make it work.

I don't think there is much difference now in my relations with others than what was there before. I am still shy and diffident although, once I form a friendship, I cultivate it assiduously and feel that I have much to offer. I have made one or two platonic friendships among older gay men, which I think those friends appreciate and treasure. My friendships with women are probably better than they were; that may be due to the women themselves, of whom it is often said, and my experience tends to bear this out, that they can form good friendships with gay men, free from the fear of predatory heterosexual males.

Advice to others

I am gratified to exist in an environment that enables me to express my homosexuality as would scarcely have been possible before 1967, but true acceptance of gay life has taken longer and has incorporated all the years which could claim to be my 'prime of life.' I regret that I felt unable to do more to promote the homosexual side of my nature in those years.

Young gay males growing up now have great opportunities to realise their gayness in so many ways, not least the easy ability, through the Internet, to meet others. It is most important for them not to jump quickly into getting themselves tied up with partners. All the same, in spite of those opportunities, perhaps being gay can still be a lonely experience, especially if you are of a more introverted and retiring disposition. Gay culture is still in its infancy; it has not come of age, and may not even ever do so. What the gay media projects is all about nightclubs, hedonism and sex. Actually gay people much of the time lead normal lives like everyone else: they drive cars, they eat, they pay bills, and they go shopping. It is easy to get the impression, from magazines and so on, that life is one continuous round of thrill and excitement. I think it is important for young gay people to remember that and, curiously enough, not every person who is gay is flush with cash! I am sure homosexuals have been known to visit the Job Centre!

Many years ago, I read a book that probably influenced me more than I thought at the time, even though it gave me much to think about and kept me awake at night. It was the well-known novel by Radclyffe Hall 'The Well of Loneliness.'[74] It is a novel about lesbian love in a forbidding and non-understanding climate but I think gay men could equally well read it. While at times incredibly sad and heart wrenching, it gave me the impression that I was not alone out there!

Also, try the novel by Christopher Isherwood, 'A Single Man'[75] which is a sympathetic look at the problems faced by being gay, this time in the 1930s.

---

[74] 'The Well of Loneliness': ground breaking 1928 lesbian romantic novel by the British author Radclyffe Hall.

[75] Christopher Isherwood: 'A Single Man' (1964) depicts one day in the life of an English, depressed, middle-aged gay professor at a Los Angeles university. Tom Ford directed a 2009 drama film, set in 1962, based on the novel. Colin Firth won an Academy Award Best Actor award for his portrayal of George Falconer.

TREVOR'S STORY

Introduction to Trevor

Trevor tells us significant things about being a boy who 'feels different' and becomes afraid of the consequences of his own feelings and desires: afraid, for example, of being hit and ostracised. Very importantly, these fears were not neurotic or pathological but entirely realistic, based on evidence from life around him. Being bullied, beaten by peers or parents, expelled, suspended from school and so on were actual consequences of which Trevor was made aware at school and home. He was growing up with powerful – even violent - messages from his culture about the unacceptability of being 'queer.' He even made a conscious decision as a child to move schools in order to avoid becoming 'queer'.

Fear is key in this life-story too. Like many of the men whose stories we hear, he was picked on and bullied at school for being different, more sensitive, more gentle. It is unsurprising, though tragic in my view that as a result, Trevor felt compelled to suppress his natural feelings and to 'run away' from them for most of his life. Even today, he retains anxiety, fear of rejection and fear for his safety and must continually battle against this fear and the shame that underlies it. Whilst much has changed since that time, homophobic bullying has actually increased in recent years in the UK at the same time as all the legal and social advances have taken place[76].

Trevor met a woman with whom to form a romantic, emotionally-connected, relationship and then marry in his twenties. It felt like what he 'had to do' to overcome those feelings, as it did for Alan. Sex wasn't an important element in this partnership and lessened once children were born and this is not unusual. However, the feelings did not go away – they are innate - but were internalised, repressed, denied - not acted upon in his case - in order to 'pass' as heterosexual and fulfil the social demands of being a responsible married man and father. This gradually led to extreme loneliness, secrecy and isolation within his marriage and sensations of being 'hemmed in' in 'an open prison.' (cf. Robert)

Trevor regrets having become a father of a kind that wasn't consistent with his true self, being a father more like the father he had himself. This seems consistent with the repression of his 'true' self which occurred primarily on the sexual dimension but then became generalised so that he was, as it were, enacting fatherhood – passing as a father - rather than being a father and a man in the unique ways in which only he could be. Once we start lying – or passing – it's hard to stop and hard to get back to what's real anywhere in our lives. We live false selves, sometimes called adaptive selves. Trevor says, "I hadn't been living MY life for many, many years."

All the secrecy and hiding which arose from these experiences led to a parallel unconscious desire for discovery or revelation – wanting to be found out, wanting to be exposed - so that the fear and anxiety would end. It is frequently reported (by Chris, Nigel, Dan, Alex, Brian

---

[76] Homophobic and biphobic bullying: For help, advice and information on these issues see: EACH (award winning charity 'Educational Action Challenging Homophobia') http://www.eachaction.org.uk and Stonewall's 'Education for All' work to tackle bullying in schools and colleges: www.stonewall.org.uk/at_school/education_for_all/ as well as 'School's Out' who have worked for equality at school since 1974: http://www.schools-out.org.uk

and Alan, for example) that a married bi or gay man leaves material on the internet, in diaries, magazines or other places – clues about their secrets of various kinds – which his wife or others might find or they develop a sexual infection or emotional collapse which will require explanations.

Trapped and highly concerned not to do harm to those he loved, and felt responsibilities for, Trevor came very close to committing suicide. This too is a frequent experience with undisclosed married gay and bi men. Thankfully, Trevor sought professional help instead and after a necessary period or recovery on antidepressants, did more active work on himself in counselling and psychotherapy, even training to work in a job in which authenticity and openness in relationships is central!

Eventually the main thing Trevor has found helpful in developing a rich and satisfying life is the opposite of hiding; talking with others, spending time sharing with partners and communities where he feels a sense of belonging. His lifelong attraction to nakedness relates to wishing to be fully 'seen' and accepted, not judged and persecuted and not hidden any more. Discovering that he is not alone with his struggles, that there are many others who share feelings and experiences with him, who understand and empathise, who have developed strategies for coping and recovering, has been the biggest lesson of all.

How sad it is that no one was able to tell the growing boy Trevor, or the younger man Trevor, that this entire accepting world was also out there while he was struggling to grow himself. This remains a major challenge: how we facilitate children and young people in developing their authentic selves, including their authentic sexual selves. We all have a huge, as yet unmet, responsibility for the physical and psychological health and the social wellbeing, to say nothing of the lives, of children and young people from sex and gender diverse communities alongside those of their peers.

TREVOR'S STORY

I was a middle boy of three. I guess I was always the quieter one. I found it difficult fitting into the playground with other boys. I certainly didn't excel at football or anything like that. My parents were religious without going to church so we were sent to Sunday school. I suppose things just trundled along until I was about nine years old, when I first really noticed that something was different. At that time we were living in Singapore, my dad was serving in the navy and we would spend nearly every day at the swimming pool because it was so bloody hot. I remember looking at boys more than looking at girls and just knowing that somehow I was attracted to them, to boys more than to girls, knowing I couldn't do anything about it, talk to anyone about it, knowing that I shouldn't be caught looking at boys but not knowing what it was about, really not. That was my first sort of feeling that I might be different.

When I was eleven I went to a naval boarding school and there I was exposed to boys wanking each other off and things like that and I remember experimenting with that but always being petrified of being found out because, if you were, apart from being called queer and so on, you would be suspended or expelled. I remember having crushes on classmates, housemates, but never really having the confidence to do anything about that, to tell them how I felt about them. I felt sure that if I did, I would lose what contact I did have with them.

How did you 'know' at such an early age that you 'shouldn't' be looking at boys – or talking about this?

I just felt it was inappropriate and that mum and dad would not approve. I was fearful of being hit or punished for saying something that didn't meet the day-to-day life restrictions - based on past scolding and punishments from my parents.

One really painful memory was one parents' day when one of my best friends had been suspended for "queering" as we called it. Like many guys, his father had been abroad when he had been suspended. Now his dad had met up with him they were actually parked in the car next to us and his dad was screaming and shouting at him and hitting him. I could hear all of this sitting in our car and I knew then that the reaction that he was getting from his parents was just what I would get from mine if they ever found out that I was doing that sort of stuff with other boys. I really fought hard to suppress those emotions, those feelings that I had to the extent that I decided that I had to leave that school, otherwise I would turn queer. I really remember that as a conscious decision for me leaving.

You don't mention other gay boys, teenagers or young men. What about gay figures on television or in the media: what effect did these have on you?

I didn't know any other gay boys. I felt as though I was gentler and more sensitive than other boys, not as rough and tumble and not as able to play football and so on. I was picked on and bullied at primary school.

At boarding school, aged eleven to sixteen, there was a lot of 'queering' - it was spoken of disparagingly as though it was always something done by other boys. To be found out doing it would mean not only suspension or expulsion but also being picked on and bullied. I felt on the margins of acceptability by the other boys and feared being ostracised if I was discovered to be queer. I experimented with mutual masturbation at eleven with a boy of my age and at thirteen with a sixteen-year-old prefect. We had swimming lessons in the nude as well as showering with a mixed age range. I was very aware of my attraction for the naked male form but also of my need not to be seen watching and not to get aroused - being naked it was difficult to hide my interest!

Later, there were all the pop groups: David Bowie, Queen[77] and so on, real sexual beings. I really admired them and wanted to be as free as they were but felt this was impossible for me. I knew they were different, I knew their sexuality was appealing but I didn't actually know the words 'gay' or 'homosexual' or anything. I didn't know it as a legitimate way of being. I saw all the pop groups as being sexualised but I didn't see them as being gay. I was attracted to them in a strange sort of way. I left that boarding school and went to a local high school in Edinburgh and then, of course, I had crushes on guys there and still I couldn't – didn't feel I could – do anything about it.

Gay figures in the media at this time were John Inman[78] and Larry Grayson[79] and my parents would comment and make gestures about them.

---

[77] David Bowie, Queen and so on: gender bending male rock stars whose flamboyant dress and style encouraged many a young man to try make-up and flounces of lace, capes, jewels and bright colours as well as experimenting with their sexuality.

[78] John Inman: (1935 – 2007) English actor & singer from the age of 13, best known for his role as the camp Mr. Humphreys in the TV sitcom 'Are You Being Served' in the 1970s and 1980s. Also well known in the UK as a pantomime dame.

[79] Larry Grayson: (1923 – 1995) born William White: English comedian and television presenter who reached the peak of his fame in the 1970s & early 80s. Best remembered hosting BBC TV's popular series 'The Generation Game' and his high camp and music hall humour. His unique stand-up act consisted of anecdotes about imaginary friends, most famous of which were 'Everard' and 'Slack Alice'. Often cited as one of the first openly gay entertainers to have enjoyed mass appeal, although he never made direct reference to his sexuality.

What had you learned about men from your father, your mother and brothers? What did you learn from them all about women, bodies, sex?

I learned from my father, with regard to men, that there are leaders and followers of orders. My father and my brothers were followers of orders: we needed to 'know our place.' My brothers taught me that masculinity was about fighting and competition. Women were regarded as needing to be looked-after cared for and in return they were meant to run the house. From my mother I learned that men don't care: she could talk to me but not to my dad. For my mum, a woman's life was a struggle.

My father and mother believed sex was only for marriage: my mother's brothers had all 'had to marry!' My mum was very proud to wear white for her wedding, indicating that she was a virgin. Restraint was highly valued. I do not recall EVER seeing my parents naked. I was not breast-fed.

Between us brothers, nudity was not normal. I played a game of strip poker once with my brothers and some of my elder brother's male friends: I still recall the electric feeling of being naked in front of them.

Growing up gay

I was very friendly with one guy and we went on holiday to Benidorm[80] of all places. And we'd go out to sunbathe during the day and then go to the clubs and discos at night and sort of crash out afterwards. I did the 'drunk mate' thing with my hands all over him. When I was touching his body, it sort of felt electric; it felt as though

---

[80] Benidorm: Coastal town of Valencia, Spain which, until the 1960s, was a small village. One of the first targets for mass cheap 'package holiday' tourism, today it stands out for its hotel industry, beaches and skyscrapers, built as a result.

this was exactly what I wanted to do. I guess I didn't really know what he... I couldn't talk to him about it. I wanted him to feel the same way but I couldn't know for sure. I got too close for comfort for him, I think, and he jumped out of bed. We didn't really talk next day. There were all sorts of ructions. And we never, ever spoke about it. I was too ashamed to do so and pretended it never happened. It was easier to pretend that I knew nothing about it than to say what I really felt and expose myself to rejection again from him.

You and the boy you touched never spoke about it and pretended it hadn't happened. It sounds as if fear and anxiety about rejection was formative for a couple of decades in your life. Are there ways nowadays by which you try to 'run away' from your sexuality?

I suppose I've always been running away from that gay side of myself. I have found it difficult coming out to colleagues and friends - with huge fear of being rejected by them when they find out I'm gay. I've found it so unacceptable to me, how could they find it acceptable? Yet they do. I still have this anxiety today about being rejected because of my sexuality. I still feel the need to assess whether I feel safe to come out or not.

As a teenager, I was interested in boys but not able to do anything about it. When I finished university at twenty-one, I was at a party with a lot of people from my work and this guy started touching me, touching my arse as we stood around and I was really excited with one part of my mind while another part was absolutely terrified of other people seeing this, then knowing that that's what I'm like. It was very important to me that people didn't know that that was how I felt. I had to disappear from there very quickly. I saw him again but he never tried it again and never said anything: I was always worried that he might have said something to other people. I was very embarrassed around him, at work. I knew I couldn't act on those feelings, I couldn't have a relationship with a guy, I couldn't do that, couldn't face it.

How did you come to marry?

It was fairly soon after that that I started going out with J who became my wife. That seemed as though it was the right thing to do. We had what was called heavy petting in those days, but we didn't have intercourse until we were married and the marriage was not overly sexual. I suppose I didn't know that it wasn't the real thing until afterwards. Being with her felt like what I had to do, just to get married like my brothers and I guess I was fine with it for about seven or eight years. We had a really good emotional connection in our first years together.

Other girlfriends previous to the marriage were short lived and unsatisfying sexually for me; I tried but never felt that electric buzz that I'd experienced experimenting with boys at school. I felt much more at ease with girls as friends at school, university and work although I couldn't say these were really deep relationships.

Most women married to gay men say there were clues early on that were ignored by one or both partners - early insights, conversations, slip-ups. Was this true for you two in any way?

Over ten years sex became less frequent and, once I started to experiment outside the marriage, it stopped completely. I wanted to protect my wife from anything I might catch. My wife seemed to accept the changes and only ever challenged me a couple of times about not wanting sex together.

I was twenty-five when I got married and I was still looking at the guys at work, fantasising and having crushes on them, knowing there was absolutely nothing I could ever do about that. So apart from schoolboy experimentation, wanking, nothing had actually happened since then: it was all in my head. I thought that by getting married I'd be able to control my feelings and they would go away, but I sort of substituted one guy with another guy with the next guy, in terms of who I fantasised about and who I thought of when I was making love to my wife.

I knew my thoughts were wrong yet I would always check out the guy if a couple were walking towards me in the street. If there was a film or television programme, I'd admire the man rather than the woman, fantasise about kissing him, not her. When I made love, I'd imagine what it might be like to do this with a guy and I'd masturbate thinking of men.

In terms of actual contact, however, I was 'faithful' for the first seven or eight years. I would play sport at work and enjoy watching the other guys in the shower and locker room but still be fearful of being found out. I believed I could keep my sexuality under control in these ways.

One really horrible year, my brother was serving in the first Gulf war and my mother leant on me in terms of the emotional support she wasn't getting from my dad. My wife was having cancer scares left, right and centre and I felt as though I was carrying everything. When the war finished and my brother came home, I sort of collapsed. I had to take time off work. I tried speaking to my wife, saying something had to change with our marriage. I feared we were drifting apart because I knew the pull for men was getting stronger and stronger, even though I still wasn't doing much about it. She wasn't in a position to meet me or to understand what I was saying, or to support me. I felt whatever I had to do, I had to do it alone, I couldn't count on her support. This would have been early 1992.

You had two small children by then? Please say a little more about the place and significance of fatherhood for you. How does

fatherhood live in you? Has it been curative at all in relation to your experiences as your father's son?

That's right, yes. My son was about six or seven and my daughter about three. I felt quite hemmed in in terms of my responsibilities to my wife and to my children. The promise I'd made to myself and to her in our wedding vows seemed really important. I was there for them and would support my wife and children. That seemed to override any of my own desires to be happy.

I always felt I wanted to be a father, to do what my brothers were doing. I loved my children and still do – they are a very important part of me. I did struggle with the responsibility and time-consuming nature of parenting in early fatherhood. I guess I did not learn about how I had been with my parents as a child until it was too late with my own children. The relationship was not curative in that sense. My deep regret is that I acted out on my children the sort of treatment I had received from my own parents as a child. I dearly hope it has not been with the same consequences.

How was your gay sexuality pushing forward in those years?

At that stage I was picking up gay porn magazines or videos and watching those when I could. I then started putting myself into positions where I could see more guys naked or in a sauna. I didn't know gay saunas existed so they were straight saunas and I just enjoyed sitting there watching people. There wasn't anything going on but it was an electric tension as it were, seeing men, seeing the naked male form.

Next I discovered 'Gay Times'[81] and found out about gay saunas

---

[81] 'Gay Times': Leading UK gay monthly magazine published by Millivres Prowler, first appeared in 1984 as a spin-off from HIM magazine, since 2007 re-labelled 'GT'. http://www.gaytimes.co.uk

and went to those for the first time, started experimenting and every time I went really enjoyed it, but then felt incredibly guilty afterwards for having been there, having done that, been unfaithful to my wife. I'd vow I would never do this again. I'd purge the house of all magazines, DVDs and videos and a couple of months later start the whole process again, going out and buying those and saying inside, "I can't cope without them."

Then the internet came along and it was easier to find out about places to go. I started calling off at a cruising ground local to where I was. It just seemed a huge adrenaline rush to be able to do that.

The visual ("naked male form") has been important to your sexuality: is this still true? Is the internet still central to this?

Yes, the naked and semi-naked male form remains important to me today - in real life as well as on the internet. I have felt in the past that I was addicted[82] to viewing porn and to chatting to guys online about sexual fantasies. This has been a problem, with me spending long hours online.

Today I still enjoy being on Gaydar[83], exploring scenarios of being

---

[82] 'Addicted to porn': Highly contentious topic. Many report feeling addicted to porn or internet use and some psychological practitioners subscribe to ideas of such use as an illness, often employing 12 step techniques imported originally from Alcoholics Anonymous and applied to many forms of repetitive, unwanted behaviours. Other professionals disagree with descriptions of these behaviours as illness, seeing compulsions as manifestations of deeper, unresolved psychological material. See: http://www.pinktherapy.com/en-gb/knowledge/compulsiveandproblematicsex.aspx

[83] Gaydar: worldwide, profile-based dating website for gay & bi men, women and couples over 18, founded in 1999 in Cape Town by Gary Frisch & and his partner Henry Badenhorst after a friend said he was too busy to look for a new boyfriend! The Christian owners claim, somewhat disingenuously, that it is aimed at platonic networking and friendship, while millions a day use it for

naked with other guys. I'm attracted also to pictures of men naked in public places, where they ought to be dressed.[84]

There was a risk element associated with it, the risk of being caught and it was almost, 'Well, if I'm caught... ' I didn't want to be caught but I thought if I was caught, then it would be out in the open and something would happen. This went on for a long time though I realised I was getting desperately unhappy: desperately unhappy at home, at work, in everything.

So it seems part of you hoped someone else would find you out?

Yes. And that is exactly what happened. I think I must have been addicted to the internet at that point because I was on it every minute I could when I was alone in the house or even when there were people in other rooms. I guess the net was my downfall because I didn't clear up my history. That's eventually how my wife found out I was looking at those gay sites, and then she sat me down and asked me directly whether I was gay.

At that stage I thought, 'Perhaps I can get out of this, perhaps I can get out of it, I don't know.' Part of me turned round and thought, 'I am too tired of all of this. I'm totally mentally exhausted, emotionally drained from hiding who I am, what I want, what makes me feel alive.' So I said, "Yes, I am."

I think my wife half expected me to say... forgive me, then to turn around and say, 'OK, that's fine, we can continue the marriage but

---

openly sexual purposes. Play on the name of the communications system, 'radar'. Has largely replaced cruising and cottaging (op.cit) in many places and proved a vast resource for isolated men but is viewed as sometimes in danger of substituting virtual sexual contact for live person-to-person connection!

[84] Note the internalised relationship between hidden secrets and exposure – being 'caught' or 'found out', looking and being seen, while longing for discovery – both here and in other life-stories.

you can't see men, you can't go on the internet.' My feeling was that she'd opened the closet door and I'd fallen out of it and there was absolutely no way that I could go back in, so at that point I knew the marriage was over. I quickly said I wanted us to separate. It was a horrendous time. We'd been married nearly twenty-four years by then.

'I've got to leave. What do I tell people at work? What do I tell my parents?' My wife was insistent that people knew, that our parents knew that the reason that we were separating was because I was gay.

She did not want to seem to be at fault and I was struggling with my guilt over breaking my marriage vows and letting her down so badly. So she was outing me, telling me she was going to out me and I just wasn't ready for that. I know the thought of suicide entered my head at that point because I thought, 'I cannot do this, I cannot come out, I cannot be... cannot face the rejection from my parents, my brothers, my children. I cannot begin to think what my life will be like without those people in my life.' So, at that point, I did think suicide was my only option.

I was in Blackpool one weekend and I'd been drinking and the hotel where I was staying was close to the seafront. I deliberately walked towards the sea and it seemed to be the answer, to just jump over the railings into the water. I remember having to talk myself out of it, telling myself to get away. I think I came back and went to see the GP straight away. I knew I couldn't do this by myself. I had to take time off work while I sorted my head out. I got counselling from the GP's practice and further counselling through my work, and it led me into the realisation that I had been depressed for at least ten or fifteen years at this point. I seemed to be in this depth of despair and had to go on anti-depressants.

I am very moved by your crisis and near suicide, Trevor. Your wiser part led you to seek help to see you through your

'breakdown' – or breakthrough – thank goodness. So your therapeutic journey had begun?

I was on antidepressants for the first two years after coming out. Working through my issues I realised I must have been depressed for years. I also found out I'd been desperately unhappy at work and saw how useful counselling was to me. I'd been thinking about how I could get out of my job. What did I want to do? I couldn't think of a job I wanted to do. It was a bit like a light bulb: 'Oh, I could do counselling.

This is really useful to people who want the service, it can make a big difference in their lives!'

So, wisely or not, I went on an introductory counselling course, an evening course at Chester University and enjoyed it. There was lots of talk of redundancies at work and I was thinking, 'If I took voluntary redundancy, I could either do counselling or teaching.' I actually embarked on a Masters degree in counselling, which involved a real plunge into my own development and many hours of personal work. There was also group therapy in this person-centred[85] course on a weekly basis.

I had hidden my sexuality from everybody up to this point and was determined not to hide any longer. I wanted to come out and face all of those gremlins I had run away from in the past. It was a three year course, of which I am just tying up the loose ends at the moment. So, three years of exploring who I was, trying to tackle my own issues

---

[85] 'person-centred' : Another form of the humanistic strand of psychotherapy and counselling, this approach was developed by American psychologist, Carl Rogers in the 1940s and 1950s. The goal of PCT is to provide clients with an opportunity to develop a sense of self wherein they can realise how their attitudes, feelings and behaviours are being negatively affected and make an effort to find their true positive potential. It places great emphasis on the quality of relationship between therapist and client based on respect and authenticity.

with my sexuality. The strong aspect of the course - deep introspection and firm support - was a major part of my first four years of coming out.

How has your life changed since that coming out process?

I would say I'm fully recovered from my depression and I am still coming out. My dissertation on gay men from heterosexual marriages has been very important. I sometimes think I've chosen a particularly intense and strong path but one that has led me to reconstruct my perception of myself and the way I live.

I am currently in relationship with a man who was also previously married. We have been together for eighteen months and are moving in to live together. I feel strongly connected with him emotionally and physically. Our sex life is great and keeps getting better. There is an openness and honesty about our feelings that I have not had with any other person ever. I believe this is mainly due to my overcoming my past due to the counselling process. I believe our relationship would not have worked had I been the broken person of old.

Earlier you'd been unable to face rejection by those you cared about which you imagined arising from coming out. How has your actual experience of these people's reactions and attitudes towards you been?

I'm out to friends, I'm out to family, I'm out to people at work and that feels so empowering that I'm not hiding, not hiding my sexuality and I think I just keep being amazed by how accepting people are on the whole. Work colleagues refer to my boyfriend in the same way as to other partners. I'm just thinking, 'Why couldn't I be more accepting of myself? How can these people be more accepting of me than I could be accepting of me?'

I think I've had to work hard rebuilding my relationships with my children. They were seventeen and twenty-one when I came out to them so we've had to rebuild the relationship as adult to adult. And there was a fear I had that they didn't need me and wouldn't want anything to do with me. I worked hard to rebuild those relationships and they're good. I am so relieved my relationships with them have been mended and we are in frequent contact.

I still find it difficult with my parents, they're still a bit homophobic but they seem to be trying hard and I think it's hard for them. I realise I got my homophobia from them to an extent and I see they're still trying to come to terms with my sexuality. My parents have met my partner but won't allow us to stay at their house because my mother says my brother and his wife "wouldn't want to sleep in the same bed that [we've] been in." It doesn't change. People don't change their views overnight.

Would you do anything differently? What would you advise someone in a similar position to do?

I suppose the 'do differently' is an impossible thing to do: to try to come out earlier. I didn't live my life for a long time. I've likened it to an open prison. The closet I was in was an open prison and I had the keys in my pocket all the time but I just didn't dare to walk away. I was too... just petrified to do anything. It almost sounds like psychological warfare in that respect and mind games.

So the main thing I found helpful was talking to other people. I found my counselling and organisations like the Lesbian and Gay Foundation[86] in Manchester really invaluable, just being there.

Regarding that transition from living a straight life to being gay, the hard bit is actually working out what sort of 'gay' I am. I felt too

---

[86] Lesbian & Gay Foundation, Manchester, UK: details from http://www.lgf.org.uk

shy for the Canal Street[87] aspect of gay life. I met guys with acid tongues and had sex with people whose names I never discovered but it all felt too quick fix and short-term for me. That's the journey I'm still on I suspect: trying to work out where I sit in gay society.

I found a lot of support and personal development within the Edward Carpenter Community[88] and found a sort of home in the faerie community[89] as well. After my divorce, I took the plunge in 2009 and booked two weeks on an ECC event, without even having experienced one! I had few expectations, seeing it as a time for personal reflection. In fact it was a week of firsts: my first naked yoga session warmed by the log fire; the touch and hugs workshops; wearing a kilt to walk to the lakeside ceilidh; body-painting round the campfire; dressing in drag for dinner.

I felt 'at home' at Laurieston[90], at ease in the company of sixty men

---

[87] Canal Street: gay district of Manchester with many clubs and bars, nightlife etc.

[88] Edward Carpenter Community (ECC): Gay and bi men's collective, which runs events and networks, formed to honour Edward Carpenter (1844-1929) visionary socialist critic, writer, poet, vegetarian, and mystic a pioneer of many progressive causes, including women's rights and sexual reform. His radically different lifestyle became a symbol of liberation from oppressive middle class values of Victorian England and his writings were an important contribution to the development of the socialism and gay liberation. He lived at Millthorpe, Sheffield, with his lover, George Merrill (who inspired E M Forster's novel, 'Maurice') and their home became a place of pilgrimage for his many admirers. To find out more about ECC visit: www.edwardcarpentercommunity.org.uk and for more information on Carpenter's life and work visit: www.edwardcarpenter.net

[89] 'Faerie community': see footnote on next page – and contact details in Resources section.

[90] Laurieston Hall, Castle Douglas, Scotland. Co-operative of around 24 people, now into its fourth decade, living and working around a huge Edwardian house,

where being gay was taken for granted and there was no fear of judgement. It wasn't all joy: sobbing and sobbing now I felt safe to be in touch with my feelings. In the second week, later in the year, the heart circle discussion on Agape, Èros and Èrotikos[91] provided me with a language 'to understand relationships at a deeper level. What the next visit will hold doesn't matter because whatever unfolds will be what I need. I've been involved with ECC ever since and came to believe I needed to be relationship with a Laurieston man: now I am!

What sort of home have you found in the faerie community[92] Trevor?

---

with walled gardens, stables, cottages, 135 acres of beautiful woods, pastures and marshland stretching to a loch. Hosts residential gatherings, courses and holidays for LGBT groups such as those led by ECC and the 'Loving Men' group. For further information contact: evi@phonecoop.coop. 'Loving Men' provides events and resources for gay and bi men, called 'adventures in intimacy', to meet each other on a deeper level and experience a stronger sense of community, to try out new things, make connections, step outside comfort zones and learn more about who they are in a fun and respectful way. For details see: www.lovingmen.org

[91] Agape, Èros and Èrotikos: Three terms for love from ancient Greek. Agape (ἀγάπη) roughly means unconditional, selfless or, sometimes brotherly, love. Èros (ἔρως) refers to passionate love, being 'in love,' a kind of madness at times. Èrotikos more recently distinguishes sexual desire and longing, possibly simple lust.

[92] Radical Faeries: loosely affiliated, worldwide network and counter-cultural movement rejecting 'hetero-imitation' and redefining queer identity through spirituality. Launched at the 1979 Spiritual Conference for Radical Faeries by pioneering gay activists Harry Hay and John Burnside, with Don Kilhefner and Jungian therapist Mitch Walker (see bibliography) in Arizona with more than 200 men. Holds regular gatherings with hippy, pagan and eco-feminist trends in outdoor "sanctuaries close to the land". Radical Faeries today embody a wide range of genders, sexual orientations and identities. Contact: http://www.radfae.org

Faeries sounded even more fun and even less formal than ECC. I attended gatherings in Featherstone Castle[93] and Berlin. Their randomness was a real antidote to the ways I had previously lived. Dressing up for dinner in dresses, playing, exploring and fun. This too, was a safe place to cry and be vulnerable, to connect and be myself at last amongst people who are like me and understand me.

Resources I recommend[94]

I went on a complete immersion through gay history, gay culture, looking at gay films, gay-themed films, coming out stories and I found those to be very useful in terms of recognising I wasn't the only person who struggled. Here are some of my finds:

I have rented out a huge selection of gay films from 'Lovefilm'[95] – lots of coming out stories to choose from, too many to mention, but I should point out that French language films in particular really tackle the issue sensitively.

In terms of books,[96] again huge numbers[97]. One very useful book I bought early on was "Outing Yourself" by Michelangelo Signorile and I found Joe Kort's[98] books valuable.

---

[93] Featherstone Castle: Gothic style mansion, now a conference centre, in Haltwhistle, Northumberland, UK.

[94] See also Resource section with filmography and bibliography.

[95] 'Lovefilm': thousands of films, dvds, etc. rent or download from www.lovefilm.com/

[96] Undoubtedly the best UK source of new or secondhand books, films, magazines, etc., with an LGBT / GSD interest is the wonderful, historic independent bookshop at 66, Marchmont Street in London, 'Gay's the Word': www.gaystheword.co.uk/ Do support them please!

[97] I've included Trevor's favourites in the booklists in the Resources section.

[98] Joe Kort: mentioned frequently in this book and reached at: http://www.joekort.com

DAN'S STORY

Introduction to Dan

Dan's journey highlights some important new themes. Firstly, in some relationships, sex is not the glue that binds the couple: in some it never was and in others it may become of less, or no, significance over time, when set aside other aspects of their partnership. For Dan and his wife the sharing of friendship, strong support for one another over all the trials and triumphs of life and their mutual love of parenting have been of far greater importance in keeping them together than a sexual connection. This is true for many men and women, gay, bi or straight. In earlier times and other cultures these relationships may have been considered primarily romantic or affectional or have been arranged knowingly to accommodate these other needs.

It is also important to flag up here what Dan calls his lifelong 'low sex drive.' One of the most invisible and derided groups in modern Western industrial society, with its great emphasis on sex and desire, is the widely diverse grouping of asexual people, which actually forms, if true account is taken of the huge range of asexual experience, an enormous and unacknowledged population.[99] Dan doesn't identify as

---

[99] Asexuality: sometimes referred to as non-sexuality, means not experiencing sexual attraction or sexual feeling towards others or in oneself and is distinct from abstention and from celibacy, which are behaviours. Some asexual people engage in sexual activity despite lacking desire for sex or sexual attraction, for a variety of reasons, such as a desire to please partners, to have children, for

asexual though he often experiences no desire or longing for long periods, no sexual arousal or awareness of sexual needs. This is not an unhappy experience, nor is it pathological in any way. We don't know how his wife experiences her own – or their joint – sexual lives but she rarely makes demands and lack of sexual activity does not seem to be a source of conflict or misery for her either, whether this was the case before her cancer and hysterectomy or not.

Nonsexual marriages are very far from uncommon. The definition of a nonsexual marriage is often broadened to include those where sexual intimacy occurs fewer than ten times a year, in which case it seems that 20% of couples[100] would be in the category. 'Newsweek' magazine also estimates that 15% to 20% of couples are in a sexless relationship.[101] Some studies show that 10% or less of the married population below age 50 have not had sex in the past year.[102] The reasons for this, of course, are as enormously varied as those for sexual and relational connections.

At certain other times, however, Dan does feel 'gay' and has decided to lead a 'secret second life' to accommodate this. Many married – or partnered – men who have erotic or romantic feelings

---

human touch, warmth, companionship. Prevalence could be 5% of males & 10% of females according to Paula Nurius' study (1983) 'Mental Health Implications of Sexual Orientation' in the Journal of Sex Research 19 (2): pps.119–136.

See also: Olivier Cormier-Otano's research: http://www.youtube.com/watch?v=H-cI61oeOOE

Only recently has asexuality started to become accepted as a sexual orientation and a field of scientific research. Various asexual communities have formed, the best known of these is the Asexual Visibility and Education Network (AVEN), founded in 2001. http://www.asexuality.org/home/

[100] Laumann et al. (1994): The US National Health and Social Life Survey.

[101] See: http://www.today.com/id/32735936/ns/today-relationships

[102] See: http://www.kinseyinstitute.org/resources/FAQ.html#frequency

for other men lead parallel, often secret, lives alongside their heterosexual marriages – and even their same-sex partnerships. These sometimes involve fantasies or pornography, sometimes rent boys, cottaging or cruising, sometimes visiting gay or kink clubs and bars, saunas or back rooms, perhaps having 'affairs' with other men or having designated 'fuck buddies'[103] and sometimes all of these. It may be important here to acknowledge that there is a substantial population of men who identify as heterosexual and not bi or gay, and yet have sex with other men (MSM).[104]

The 'second life' running alongside, parallel or counter to, a more visible, more known or public life, has been a considerable – often a necessary –part of bisexual or queer experience from Catullus[105] in Ancient Rome to Oscar Wilde[106] in Victorian Britain and into the

---

[103] Fuckbuddies: Or 'Friends with Benefits' to use the politer, more secretive, term! These are relationships in which it is agreed explicitly that the purpose is entirely sexual and not otherwise.

[104] 'Men Who Have Sex with Men' (or MSM): Many men who have sex with other men do not - or cannot for various reasons - adopt sexual identities as homosexual or bisexual. This term was created in the 1990s by epidemiologists studying sexual health among men who have sex with men, regardless of identity. In African-American slang, called 'down low' meaning secret, covert. Prevalence is hard to establish due to this secrecy but American studies show about 16% of men who do not identify as gay or bi have had sex with men and around 3% regularly do so.

[105] Catullus: (ca. 84–54 BC) Latin, mostly erotic, poet of the late Roman Republic, much of whose work deals with the agonies and vicissitudes of his love for 'Lesbia', a married and polyamorous noblewoman, or scatological works about sex between men.

[106] Wilde: Oscar Wilde (1854 –1900) Irish writer and poet who became London's most popular playwright in the early 1890s. Today he is remembered for his witty epigrams, essays and only novel, 'The Picture of Dorian Gray' (1881) his brilliant plays, and the circumstances of his persecution, imprisonment and early

present day. For some this is simply a private life, by negotiated agreement – as Bruce, for example, has managed, while for others – often, more destructively[107] – it has been a secret one, as it was for many years for Nigel. Millions of transvestites and bisexuals have also felt compelled to lead double lives, as have millions of men who enjoy sex or romance with men while retaining a heterosexual identity or who are gay, but unable to come out – yet, or ever – for a range of reasons such as those reported throughout this book.

Sometimes this second life is not parallel but chronological, as in the cases of many women who, having been wives and mothers and brought up their children, choose female partners in the middle of their lives. It seems to be true that increasing numbers of men are also 'coming out' as gay after years of heterosexual marriage as social attitudes towards same sex love and partnerships evolve in some places. Increasing societal acknowledgement in countries where civil partnerships or marriages between same sex couples now have legal status may encourage those who feel 'trapped' or inauthentic in relationships formed before these changes.

Some men manage, by one means and another, to remain married

---

death. At the height of his fame and success, while his masterpiece, 'The Importance of Being Earnest' (1895), was on stage in London, Wilde prosecuted the Marquis of Queensberry, father of Wilde's lover, Alfred Douglas ('Bosie'). The course of this trial caused Wilde to drop charges and led to his own trial for gross indecency with other men. After two more trials he was imprisoned for two years' hard labour. In prison, he wrote 'De Profundis' (1897 – published in 1905) a long letter discussing his spiritual journey. Upon release he left immediately for France, never to return to Ireland or Britain. There he wrote his last work, 'The Ballad of Reading Goal' (1898), a long poem commemorating the harsh rhythms of prison life. He died destitute in Paris at the age of forty-six.

[107] I say this because of research showing that it is the secrecy, and not the sexual orientation, that is what partners find most shocking and hurtful if discovered and from my relationship work training & from experience working to support a range of relationships. See, for example, Goschros, op.cit.

after coming out to their wives and this is obviously of huge importance to them. We need to get used to the fact that 'mixed orientation marriages'– as they are now called in the US – have no more reason to fail than any other – heterosexual marriage, civil partnership. This is always determined by the reasons the couple have for being together and staying together; their commitment and understanding towards one another and the meanings they each give to their 'relationship', 'marriage' and 'love'.

Having worked with clients of all sexual orientations in relationships, I sincerely believe that a partnership requires the honest sharing of all relevant information in order to empower both partners equally, to treat them equitably and respectfully, and so I discourage 'secrets' though not privacy, to which I believe we are all entitled, in or out of intimate relationships. Having said that, this 'secret' is often, though certainly not always, not secret but well-known and only kept quiet by unspoken agreement. (Cf. Robert's situation.) Couples can collude in not making overt what both 'know' on a deeper level in order not to threaten the foundation of their being together. One very experienced relationship therapist I know told me that almost everyone she worked with had a 'no-go area' within their relationship which each avoided as too challenging for the status quo between them. Edward Albee's heart-rending play, 'Who's Afraid of Virginia Woolf?' dramatised what can happens when this unspoken agreement is broken.[108]

Dan and his wife, like many others, have fortunately reached a much happier accommodation which allows them to remain together,

---

[108] Edward Albee's 'Who's Afraid of Virginia Woolf?' (1962) play, won both the Tony Award & the New York Drama Critic's Circle Award of 1963 for Best Play and is frequently revived. The widely acclaimed film adaptation (1966) by Ernest Lehman, directed by Mike Nichols, starred Richard Burton, Elizabeth Taylor, George Segal and Sandy Dennis.

parenting and enjoying one another's love, warmth and friendship, without bringing to the fore painful issues of sexuality which, in this particular instance, is not seen to threaten their relationship greatly as theirs has become a nonsexual marriage and neither person is suffering. Neither complains for want of affection or companionship – they have plenty of those.

DAN'S STORY

I was born in 1962 as a desperately wanted second child. My sister was eight years older than me; my parents had been trying for a second baby for six years and had given up when I came along.

We were a very stable, ordinary middle-class family with a hard-working father and a stay-at-home mother. Their marriage may not have been the happiest, but they stuck at it. They enjoyed a golden era when my dad retired and had a very pleasant life together for a few years until my father died in 1995. My mother died just two years later. My family was quite settled and uneventful, except for my wilful sister, who was much more often in conflict with our parents than I was. Anything difficult my parents kept to themselves; nothing troublesome was discussed in front of me. My dad did have one or two affairs. I think this was because he was warm and emotional while my mother was quite cold and unemotional. They evidently decided to stay together despite these affairs.[109] Money was always tight – a relative term I know – but we never really went without much.

I was privately educated at a Catholic boy's school, hence the lack of spare money. My school days were very happy, though I was only an average achiever. This was because I was rather lazy, as I still am, and there was always more potential there than was ever tapped. I hated sport except for skiing, which I did like and was good at.

---

[109] It's interesting how these 'patterns' are often repeated through families.

What effect did being in a non-Catholic minority at a Catholic school have on you? How do you explain being always 'lazy' and having 'untapped potential'?

Being non-Catholic was never an issue really, as there were lots of us at the school. My laziness results from always liking to find the shortest, least complicated, route to anything. I always did just enough to pass exams and did not try hard at any subjects I did not like. As far as my potential goes, I have this gnawing feeling that I could do much bigger things in my life if I put my mind to it but I rather like my low-key approach. Why try hard when you can cruise and still survive and be happy?

I was brought up in a typically Anglican way, being baptized and confirmed but only going to church at Easter and Christmas. Over the last ten years I have got more involved in my local parish as a community thing, rather than a spiritual thing. I do like the ethos and structure behind traditional worship. I believe, however, that faith groups must be tolerant and inclusive.

What is the 'community thing' you are after nowadays from parish involvement? What about the ethos of the Anglican communion appeals?

I like being useful and really enjoy the gratitude extended to me over stuff I do at church. I do need others' approval and recognition. I don't like change for change's sake and the Church stays reassuringly calm and the same. My original motive for being in the church and my spirituality are both based on the wonder of humanity and immense good so many people do for others, quietly.[110]

Overall, I'd say my childhood was happy and safe. There were no

---

[110] Dan adds: "Since originally writing this, however, I have stopped doing any actual church work as I became disillusioned with it".

dramas but it was rather a narrow world. I had a pretty 'liberal' upbringing but was, in any case, a very 'good' child and teenager.

Are you at all suspicious of yourself being so 'good' as a child and teenager?

I never really wanted to be difficult and I was given a lot of freedom, which I used responsibly. I looked at the trouble my more wilful sister got into and thought, 'Well, that does not get you any further.'

Although there was nobody 'gay' that I knew of in our world, I never had any prejudice instilled in me. In fact, my father liked things smutty (Benny Hill[111] etc. on TV) and was a bit louche, while my mother was rather frosty and straight.

'Nobody gay in our world' is interesting in view of the 5-10% prevalence generally[112]? I understand that, in liberal circles, prejudice is not OK, but that doesn't preclude occurrence, only perhaps open expression. Please say more about these contrasting characteristics of your parents: 'smutty and louche' or 'frosty and straight'. How do these two play themselves out in you today?

I, too, like a bit of louche, but only with friends who I think can cope with it. So a night in a drag club is fab but only with the right people. BUT I know I am a voyeur in these places: I could never

---

[111] Benny Hill, British comedian, 1924-1992. Very popular long running TV series, ' The Benny Hill Show': In response to the accusations of sexism, defenders of Hill have said the show "used traditional comic stereotypes to reflect universal human truths in a way that was non-malicious and fundamentally harmless".

[112] "According to major studies, 2% to 10% of people have had some form of same-sex sexual contact within their lifetime." (2012:Wikipedia)

participate; I'm too straight and self-conscious. Backrooms[113] I find intoxicating and compelling; they are SO naughty by the conventional standards by which I generally run my life.

I admired my mother's sense of correctness and polite behaviour and I repeat these same things in my life, honouring the social niceties but I don't feel the need to be a rebel or outwardly offensive to society. So, yes, I do have my two sides: to the world, polite and correct and, in my secret world, I do and look at things that would disgust many of my acquaintances and, indeed, friends.

As adolescence dawned, I became aware of my feelings towards my best friend Steve becoming somewhat physical. He really loved me but was very straight and hugely popular with the girls. As I rode pillion on his moped, I would sometimes play at grabbing his crotch to hold on. He never objected but it was never taken further – I guess he understood and loved me enough to allow that little bit of physical intimacy. However, being 'gay' was never discussed. We drifted apart as he got more serious with girls at seventeen and it broke my heart.

Please expand on his breaking your heart, Dan

Steve was a very charismatic person and I loved him so deeply that to see him go off with girls - quite naturally - really hurt. I can remember saying to myself I would never fall in love again; it hurt too much. But I did fall in love again, with James.

During my teenage years, I don't think I actually thought of myself as gay: rather just as not very straight, or having a low sex drive. I did not have the same drivers as the rest of the boys did, but I did sometimes get physical urges towards some of those other boys. I just pushed them down as much too difficult to deal with. I did have a few girlfriends, too, but it never felt natural in me.

---

[113] Backrooms: a nightclub, sauna or sex club, where sexual activity can take place. When located in bars, called dark rooms or, more rarely, blackrooms.

Did you actually think of yourself as having a 'low sex drive' whilst a teenager? If so, how did you account for that? What 'drivers' did you lack? How did you sublimate 'physical' or sexual urges and what became of those?

Yes, indeed I did. I really was not particularly interested (still not). I do not account for it, just accept it about myself, like being this height. What urges I had, I just put aside as too complicated to handle. Life has been much easier without giving these their head. My sex drive was focused almost entirely on Steve and later on James and both of these, I knew, were not allowed. Not that it was wrong but just a waste of energy and emotion. Unrequited love, I guess. I moved it all into fantasyland, daydreamed and wanked to thoughts of having sex with them.

By eighteen, my big love had launched himself into my life. James was an arrogant rugby player: bright, tall and very handsome. He was in the same year as me at school but we had nothing else in common. He just turned up one night on my doorstep and then, basically, made all the effort to befriend me. Over the years we became very close indeed. He soon had his girlfriend and me as his two emotional support legs. He made me feel very loved, very appreciated and adored. He was demonstrative physically, always hugging and so on. I lusted after him big time, fantasising about having sex with him. I basically wasted my late 'teens and early twenties on that lust, to the exclusion of all others.

I am interested in how you and James developed such closeness, Dan. You say you had nothing in common, yet he got something very important from you, which he wanted.

We just shared lots of time together, whether it be simply watching

'Brideshead Revisited'[114] – we watched every episode together – walking the dogs or going to his cricket matches every Sunday. He was very verbal and physical in expressing his emotions. Reserved he was not. He wore his emotions on his sleeve so I knew how much he loved me.

By the age of twenty, I had finally dipped my toe into the gay scene just once. I went to "Heaven"[115] one night but ran out after fifteen minutes, unable to cope with it. I felt so naughty and in a very dangerous place.

What was it you found so hard to cope with at 'Heaven'? Are you able to expand on your sense of naughtiness and danger?

To my little suburban, unconfident self, it all felt too overtly sexy, not gentle enough. I was so naive and felt very exposed and not able to deal with any openly expressed sexuality. If I had gone with someone, fine, but on my own, it all felt too real for me and too challenging.

By twenty-four, I had gone off to Australia for a year, partly to distance myself from all my lovely but straight, and increasingly married, friends, and partly to allow myself to experiment. I went into

---

[114] Evelyn Waugh's (1945) novel, 'Brideshead Revisited, The Sacred & Profane Memories of Captain Charles Ryder.' In 1981 an ITV serialisation by Granada Television had a huge influence on the lives of young gay men in its telling of the unrequited romantic love of the narrator for the main aristocratic character, his male best friend. A film adaptation was released in July 2008.

[115] 'Heaven', the first of London's super clubs, opened by entrepreneur Jeremy Norman in 1979 in a huge former hotel cellars (and later roller disco) venue under railway arches at Charing Cross station, the interior designed by his partner, Derek Frost. Norman started The Embassy Club in Bond Street in 1978, which was seen as the equivalent of New York's Studio 54. Heaven quickly established itself as the centre of the understated gay London nightlife. Until Heaven, most gay clubs were small, hidden cellar-bars or pub discos. Heaven brought gay clubbing into the mainstream.

a gay house share in Sydney and again did nothing! A sixth sense was protecting me as we now know that AIDS was looming.[116] I ended up, after a whole year there, with guess what... a load more straight friends! During that year I came out by letter to my parents, who immediately phoned and were fully accepting and very supportive. Oddly, when I got back home, it was never mentioned again. They no doubt thought it was just none of their business. I was now twenty-five.

It sounds as if you went to Australia feeling a need to change the way you were relating and being and to experiment somehow. What was in the way of your realizing this once away from the UK?

Nothing at all: just my inhibitions and social conventions.

It seems odd to you that your parents never mentioned your 'coming out' again – was that characteristic? Do you have feelings or thoughts about how this silence may have affected you since?

No - that's quite expected. If I had brought up the subject, I am sure they would have engaged but I am certain that they were just respecting my privacy as a twenty-five year old and would have been perfectly willing to meet any special boy I might have brought home. Although, come to think of it, I'd been in my own home since twenty-three! However, perhaps I do feel a bit abandoned by that approach: I might have appreciated an invitation to discuss it all with them.

I had missed James enormously and that was mutual. He wrote EVERY week and phoned often too: he was keeping me on the hook!

---

[116] AIDS: Acquired immunodeficiency syndrome (HIV/AIDS) was first clinically observed in 1981 in the United States but only named as such in 1982.

I am powerfully struck by this phrase 'keeping me on the hook' and the strength of feeling I sense behind it.

James is very emotionally dependent, me not so. I guess he wanted to make sure I came back to him.

Anyway, when I got back, he seduced me! It was for one night and one night only. I suddenly got a big clue as to what all the fuss was about. I was really making love in the true sense. Finally, at twenty-five, proper sex! This was only ever mentioned in passing in years to come.

Please say something about the impact on you – your feelings, your relationship with your body, sexuality, dreams – of 'real sex' and making love with someone you cared so deeply for.

Well, it felt like the ultimate taboo, sleeping with your married best mate. Especially when you also adore his wife - and still do! But I felt so good, so grown-up and so complete: my fantasies come true! But it also felt wrong and frustrating in that there was nowhere to go with it, no continuation. I just had to put my desire back in its box and hope to distract it elsewhere. I relived that dream many times and can still remember it in great detail.

So I sat on the fence, thinking 'Someone will come along – man or woman, sooner or later.' Then at twenty-seven I met my wife, Clare and fell head over heels in love with her. Sex was fine but we know now, not exactly driven by my libido. But we had, and still have, so much besides.

We are best friends and have only really shared a sex life for the first seven of our eighteen years together so far. We have one wonderful daughter, now fourteen, who knows about my flexible sexuality. I think we have worked out that life is made up of many parts and sex is only one. Why throw out the contents of the fridge when only one vegetable has gone off? We are so lucky to be so close, open minded and mentally capable of accepting unconventional ideas about life.

Clare and I have been through a lot: cancer, bereavement, loss of pregnancy, and my second coming out …

You skip the early days and years with Clare: how did you become so close? How did you each feel, deal with, and talk about, your eventual lack of a sex life together?

We became very close very naturally, sharing much common ground, common enjoyments of friends, food and culture. The sex stuff just sort of drifted at first but then her health issues provided a very real reason to put aside our sex life anyhow.

What about your 'coming out' to your daughter: how was that for you and her?

It took a lot of courage at the time but it has never been a problem. She now, at nineteen, has a very close gay best friend too.

Are you still 'splitting off' sex from life in seeing it as so relatively unimportant?

Yes, indeed. I tended not to mention it until Clare brought the subject up and we just let it be. Then, when James's marriage fell apart, he by then alcoholic, he started to rely on me heavily. A little earlier, Clare's cancer was diagnosed and she had a big crisis, as you can imagine. As time unfolded she felt that, although I supported her very well practically, I could not support her emotional needs and she got very frustrated with me. James, meanwhile, was grateful for everything I did for him and made me feel so appreciated but he was phoning every day and I was getting very wrapped up in him. It really did come to the point when Clare asked me to choose between the two of them and I chose her without question, so I had to shut James out of my life and it really hurt, even though I knew I had to do it.

That 'without question' intrigues me somewhat: why was there never any question which person you would choose to be with?

The timescale for this was: Clare's diagnosis in August 1997; my mum died - also from breast cancer - in December 1997; Clare's crisis hit in the Spring of the following year and James's marriage imploded that summer. I cut James out of our lives in November 1998.

I fully appreciate the many crises and experiences that you and your wife have shared and supported one another through, as well as the strength of bonding which all of that can both create and demonstrate. I understand your deep feelings of good fortune, too.

Would you say that going through so much together has brought you two closer in all ways or are there ways in which you are now more distant?

I'd say that we are closer in all ways, thankfully, now that sex is completely off the agenda.

About two years ago, Clare found a gay dvd in my office and we started to talk about that and I ended up admitting I'd taken myself off to experiment with men in the previous couple of years to try to decide if I was happy staying put in our marriage from the point of view of physical fulfilment. I very quickly realised I was privileged to be as I was. Understandably, she found all this very hard to take, more the deceit than the actual sexual acts. So we went to 'Relate'[117] for some help in sorting out how we could move forward. 'Relate' were superb and we both decided we had far more to save than to lose. I also found my way to 'Pink Therapy'[118] for some individual work with you, Charles, which has been incredibly helpful.

---

[117] Relate: see 'Resources: Organisations' section.

[118] Pink Therapy: see 'Resources: Finding Good Therapy' section.

Please try to tell more specifically – for the benefit of others – just how your couple sessions at 'Relate' and our individual therapy work together were so helpful to you. What was it that was useful, please?

I think therapy gives you a neutral arena in which to explore situations and possible outcomes safely and with the support of a professional third party giving you permission to talk about very difficult issues. It feels detached from reality. It is all theoretical until you take something outside and take some action on it... or, equally... do not.

Can you elaborate further, Dan, on the experience of 'feeding your gay side?' Does it feel like a separate part of you or all the same you? What is it you want to experience and do you get this from male connection? Are you then satisfied for a while?

Yes, I connect to a part of myself that lies dormant most of the time and that does satiate me for a while; maybe for two to three months. I keep my 'gay side' fed by buying the odd DVD, visiting porn sites such as 'Youporngay"[119] and going to saunas for safer sex or to rent boys maybe three or four times a year. I keep this activity secret, as I want to keep it to myself and not have to justify it. Since Clare and I have no sex life, I don't feel that I'm completely in the wrong, as it does not compete with anything: it is a separate, unemotional, contained, small part of my life.

I am struck by what seems like defence in the phrases 'not have to justify' and 'not completely in the wrong' here. Is there a protective element in breaking your contract to let your wife

---

[119] 'Youporngay': Internet site with free gay porn videos: http://www.youporngay.com

know: keeping her from further hurt and yourself from a potential break-up?

Absolutely. I know this is a very defensive approach. On the other hand, we are now more open with a wider circle of friends about my sexuality and, funnily enough, no one has disowned me. Our life together works as long as Clare and I are both happy with the situation. Perhaps it helps that Clare had to have a hysterectomy and so has been pushed into a full menopause at a very early age and does not have those female hormones circulating any more.

What is VERY important, too, is to have a few key friends to talk with confidentially. I have an older friend, who is in exactly the same position as me – married, with kids, odd fling – and we talk occasionally to check that one another are OK. I have several other – fully out – friends, too, and they all know and love Clare but respect my confidences and never let on anything they know about my odd indiscretions.

Since coming out this time, after our sessions together, my life has definitely got so much better. I feel so much better knowing my family and key friends know and accept my odd sexuality. However, Clare and I both know we live with the danger that if either of us met someone who offered us 'the whole package' we could be tempted out of our marriage. We will just talk about it, should it occur. But if you are not looking, it is not likely to occur.

So, I advise people to be as honest as possible with those they feel safe with. True friends love you as you are: the responses of love and support I have had from close friends are overwhelming and wonderful.

I truly appreciate your emphasis here, Dan, on how crucial confidential, accepting friendships are as vital support during these complex processes.

NIGEL'S STORY

Introduction to Nigel

The first childhood experience Nigel mentions is a sense of bemused difference from others: firstly physical – as with Alex, this was due to a visible disfigurement at birth – and all the concomitant surgery, hospitalisation and trauma involved in that.[120]But gradually there was a realisation that this was not the key difference: there was another 'secret' and invisible difference that mattered far more. Maybe this even caused more pain in the end.

Nigel had brothers but, most unfortunately, his elder brother became a source of further trauma when he – and his friend – exploited Nigel sexually as a small child. Research into the impact of early sexual abuse on the developing gay boy remains confusing.[121] It does seem that more gay and bi males than those identifying later as heterosexual have been sexually abused in their early years, often within the family circle, sometimes by opportunistic adults in

---

[120] See 'Waking the Tiger: The Innate Capacity to Transform Overwhelming Experiences' by Peter Levine (1997) North Atlantic Books, Berkeley, Ca., USA for detailed discussion about the huge and often enduring impact - somatic, psychological and emotional - resulting from childhood trauma of this kind and how to work to overcome some of these.

[121] For example, see: http://lnkd.in/bZwr4DE 'Talking About Sexually Abused Boys and The Men They Become' in 'Psychology Today' online magazine 30/01/2011.

positions of responsibility or care for children, abusing that trust. Conflicting theories suggest that 'gay boys' may be additionally vulnerable to exploitation and abuse by others, usually older or more experienced males, due to their 'softer' boundaries; or that being abused by males while growing up can contribute to feeling attracted to them later or feeling that one is gay or bi oneself as a result of the experience. More research is needed and some is under way.

An unusual, further damaging, and even bizarre, aspect of Nigel's story is his own family's way of parenting: a high level of violence was present so that the children were terrified of parental displeasure[122] and conformed to their rules in their presence, making deceit, dishonesty and secret keeping habitual and necessary for safety. Interesting to notice that this led to secret activities which were in none of these children's best interests.

A related issue is Nigel's quest for safety, which he only finds in childhood by 'vanishing' inside a small, tight ball that he makes with his own body, as a shelter from his raging mother and others who invade his integrity or the unspecified threat of the three bears (see on to Nigel's story). As an adult this becomes retreating into other kinds of secret places: porn cinemas, bachelor flats away from his family, clubs and bars away from friends. Whenever he experiences threat or insecurity he withdraws into his own 'shell' and disconnects from other people.

It's also worth highlighting the frequent connection between sexual feeling and fear or anxiety: it occurs in several of the life stories. There is a clear hormonal connection between fear and excitation created by floods of adrenaline, for example, but the levels of stimulus caused by fear of being caught in something illicit, perhaps being punished, certainly one's cover as 'good' being exposed as untrue. Many BDSM 'scenes' re-enact and make creative use of these very

---

[122] An extreme form of training children to be 'good'? (Cf. Alan, Alex, Bruce)

primal overlapping feelings where safety and threat can combine.

Then there is a complete lack of boundary keeping or acceptance of full responsibility by Nigel's parents in moving their entire family abroad without him, leaving a fifteen-year-old to cope alone as a schoolboy without support.

It is hardly surprising therefore that Nigel becomes dedicated to comfort, to home, to the creation of close warm family environments and luxuries to counter the earlier neglect – and very concerned with how things will seem to other people. However, his patterns of self-neglect in many important respects, such as health care, safer sex practices, use of various drugs and alcohol, have merely reinforced earlier experiences of himself as unworthy of care. Neglected children often repeat these patterns in their adulthood when their care is in their own hands.

Nigel also becomes, as he has been trained to be, a master at keeping secrets. This harms his authentic self-development as well as affecting all of his relationships for forty years or so.

Nigel's biggest challenge today is how to live an open, honest, sharing, negotiated life; how to integrate his true sexuality with his multifaceted creative self, in all its variety of expression; how to trust that he is consistently loved for his own intrinsic and deeply person qualities and that love is not contingent on doing and being, or even seeming to be, as others wish, that he is consistently loved for his own intrinsic and deeply personal qualities. Thus he may learn to take different kinds of risks – to risk non-sexualised intimacy within deep friendships, to experiment with healthier, more nurturing behaviours, investigate his inner drives as an artist and to risk being easier in a more trustworthy and safer world.

NIGEL'S STORY

For the longest time I can remember I have had this feeling of being somehow disconnected from the world ... a sense of being other, not quite in touch with the people around me. It seems it has always been that way.

I remember conversations when I thought people were talking about one thing and it turned out to be quite something else. It is worth mentioning that I have been partially-hearing from birth: I have only one fully functioning ear. Sometimes I've managed to explain to myself that I misheard the beginning of a conversation and we were at cross-purposes, but it isn't sufficient explanation.

I remember when I was about seven or eight arriving at school late for assembly with my two brothers and my sister; we all went to the same convent school run by the Sisters of St Vincent de Paul[123].

We were always late so this seemed like just another day. Mostly the reason we were late, aside from the sheer impossibility of organising five children under ten, was my sister's hair. My sister had, still has, the most unruly mop of thick, curly and glossy black hair. My mother would never accept that it couldn't be tamed and insisted that, every day before school, it had to be tortured into pigtails, a plait or a ponytail. It was agony for my sister and agony for us boys standing

---

[123] Sisters of St. Vincent de Paul: "A congregation of women with simple vows founded in 1633 and devoted to corporal and spiritual works of mercy. Their full title is Sisters or Daughters of Charity... Servants of the Sick Poor. The term has been added to distinguish them from several communities of Sisters of Charity, animated with a similar spirit." (Wikipedia)

around waiting, satchels on our backs, caps straight on our heads, shoes brightly polished, for the daily torture to stop so we could all walk to school together.

I was always mortified at being late for anything and developed a compulsive habit of turning up early for everything to the extent that I would loiter outside the appointed place for half an hour, then entering exactly three minutes prior to the arranged time.

Today was another day we were late. We entered at the back of the dining room where school assemblies were held and I prayed we were invisible. Today wasn't a day when my prayers were heard and Mother Superior, Mary Magdalene, clearly wouldn't have been listening even if god, on this of all days, happened to be. Mother Mary Magdalene was not amused and called us all to the front, delivering a very stern lecture. She seemed very large but I guess if I met her today, I would find her of average height and more than a little overweight. She had a huge bosom that she cradled in her arms and the black apron she wore over her habit was covered in food stains. Mother Mary also had a huge voice and on this occasion used it to full effect, lashing us with her tongue, extolling the virtues of self-discipline and punctuality. I was mesmerised by the strength of feeling she managed to project and felt genuinely sorrowful and affected by her outpourings … worse for my sister, who started sobbing. "Stop that, Maria, your tears are worth nothing to me!" Mother Superior bellowed at her and, turning to me, my upturned face a picture of sorrow and remorse, "… and you, standing there like butter wouldn't melt!" and thwack, she slapped me so hard across the face that my head spun round.

I was stunned, gasping like a fish out of water. Shocked, tears welling up in my eyes, my face stinging and ears ringing, I couldn't understand this giant woman telling me I should be ashamed of my behaviour and, when I was – really, really was – accusing me of 'putting it on for effect'. What did I do wrong? Now I look at me as I was then, I still don't understand. Really, I wasn't acting, Mother Superior.

Of course it's also worth mentioning that there were many instances of humiliation and physical abuse at home. I guess this incident was particularly shocking because I thought this kind of thing only happened at home: clearly at a very early age I learned there was nowhere to be safe.

Childhood

It's difficult to be objective about my childhood, especially the part of it that deals with my developing sexuality. Hindsight colours memories and I am such a different person from the one I was last year, or three years ago or ten years ago. What I remember are seminal incidents that shaped me and my responses to the world and more, I remember the feelings I had at the time.

The very first time I remember this stirring deep in my stomach - I mean groin - a feeling of desire - was when I was no more than two years old. I know this because my sister was born when I was nearly three and we were living in a different house. My parents were struggling to bring up a family of three boys each a year apart – I'm the middle one – and to economise we shared baths. I remember one occasion when I bathed with my father.

My father had a beautiful body: he used to be a gymnast and when we were bathing he was semi-erect ... I must have asked a question about his erection because he was telling me about ships (penises) and harbours (vaginas) and docking! I asked if I could dock in the harbour and he said I only had a rowing boat, but one day it would turn into a battleship and I could dock, but not with mummy. I do believe that's the only time he ever talked to me about the 'facts of life'. The fact that I was too young to understand probably escaped him and I guess, since we never had such conversations again, he believed he had done his duty.

I had seen both of my parents naked and, of the two, had a definite preference for my father's body. The feeling went beyond 'like': I believe even then there was a sexual component although I couldn't name it at the time.

I remember another time shortly after that when I was at home with my mother, who was ironing, and my father came home for lunch. I was playing with dolls. My father was shocked to see this and that I was aping my mother's ironing and he gave her a hard time. "What's he doing?" he demanded. He was very angry as if I had done something wrong. I remember the feeling of the angry exchange. I think that's the first time I became aware of the fact that it wasn't all right to be me. Of course, as an adult, I have asked myself how it was I had dolls. How was it a surprise to my father? My mother wanted a girl.

The next time I remember feeling different was at primary school aged five. Instead of playing with the boys at playtime, I always ended up with the girls. The big thing was making little moss gardens and I loved it; I was very good at it. I do remember that my playmates found it strange that I chose to play with girls rather than kick a ball about with the boys.

Did siblings or school friends comment on your 'difference' and how?

At that first school I only remember one or two remarks. The first was when a neighbour's boy came off the football pitch and asked me why I didn't play football with the boys. I don't remember the words I used but I remember saying I preferred playing with girls. At some point later I remember being called a 'sissy.' I didn't know what it meant and had to ask my parents. My father wasn't too pleased but the funny thing is neither of them explained it to me. I think it was more of an issue at secondary school.

I used to have a recurring dream of being chased by three bears all through the house and I would run and hide in the bathroom, squatting in the space between the loo and the bath, out of breath and frightened, trying not to give away my presence. Then the three bears would burst in and find me. At that moment, this nice warm feeling would wash over me: something I now recognise as an orgasm. Years later that would become a wet dream and I'd look forward to those, but I didn't know these things at the time and, even now, I'm puzzled by the association of fear and sex.

Did an association between fear and desire, or fear and sex, remain?

That's a hard question to answer. My first experience of sex was with my older brother, who coerced me into it, then used that to coerce me into further sex acts because I was fearful he would tell someone. I wasn't really afraid of him but, thinking about it, there was the fear of being discovered by my parents: we often used to have sex with my parents still in the house.

When I began to explore my gayness and my sexuality, there was certainly no fear. Quite the opposite: it was tremendously liberating. However, recently, I have been exploring BDSM[124] and in that there is a little fear that I have found tremendously erotic.

Re-reading this section written some time ago, I have been doing more work around these memories and the feelings they evoke.

---

[124] BDSM: coined as an acronym in the 1990s to combine several communities and practices with a significant amount of crossover – bondage and discipline (B&D or B/D), dominance and submission (D&S or D/s), and sadomasochism, or sadism and masochism (S&M or S/M). BDSM – sometimes called 'kink' - is frequently used as a catchall to include a range of activities and sexual identities, forms of interpersonal relationships - some sexual and others not - and distinct subcultures. The sexual practices often involve exchanges of power, restrictions of movement, control and intense sensation. Perhaps the most well-known involve spanking and being tied-up.

The recurring dream about the three bears is based on an actual incident on a particular day when I had made my mother angry and, knowing the consequences would be that I would be beaten, I ran away. My mother had an explosive temper and there was no such thing as a quick slap. She would completely lose it and beat us with whatever lay to hand or kick or punch us, screaming with rage and calling us all sorts of names. I think her favourite for me was "fat, lazy slug". So, on this day I decided to run away. On reflection it occurs to me the reason I dared do so and succeeded is that she was heavily pregnant with my sister. In later years I found out she had broken her ankle during this pregnancy and her foot was in plaster. I was about two and a half. I remember being terrified and running upstairs... where to hide? I couldn't hide in our bedroom, the first place to look. I decided to hide in the bathroom in a small space between the toilet and the bath. I can remember the thudding sound of my heartbeat in my head: surely everyone could hear it? I remember trying to control my breathing, barely breathing at all – was this when I started holding my breath when under stress? – and trying to be as small, quiet and as invisible as anyone could be. I rolled myself up really small, holding myself in as tight and compact a shape as I could as I heard her climb the stairs, shouting my name. The first place she looked was our bedroom, then my elder brother's bedroom.

Hearing her hand on the latch of the bathroom I wet myself, squeezing my eyes tight shut between tears, willing myself to be invisible. Amazingly, she didn't see me and left. She didn't see me, my Mother didn't see me; she was looking right at me but couldn't see me! I thought it must be obvious where I was and it seemed incredible that she couldn't see me. As she shut the door and continued to shout, the relief was incredible and then this warm tingling feeling started in my groin and spread over me like a blanket of warm comfort.

It must have been some minutes before I opened my eyes and the fear of being dragged out of that space and punished abated. But nothing happened ... I waited and waited ... nothing happened. So here was a place that I could be safe... face down on the floor rolled up really tight, eyes closed, barely breathing, pushing away the world, arms and hands tightly held protecting my neck and head. Amazement isn't adequate to describe the consequences of escaping this way: there's a kind of magic, too. I learned three lessons. Firstly, there is a place I can hide and be safe. Secondly, lying about what you've done can be a way of escaping the consequences and finally, I may be rewarded – comforted by all those nice, warm, tingling bodily sensations.

For years afterwards, well into puberty, I would have this dream of the three bears from Goldilocks chasing me. Sometimes the ending of the dream would change a little and the bears would find me but never before I had that nice warm feeling! Of course once into puberty, I ejaculated, then years afterwards recognised this as a wet dream. The dreams probably stopped when I was thirteen or fourteen and I missed them, trying to force myself into the dream again to get those feelings back.

I have been to that safe place of isolation many times – pushing out the world and descending into a dark place inside my head where there is no thought, no feeling and no pain. The last time I remember going there was when I was 22, the day before I made a rather serious attempt to kill myself.

Back to the BDSM and an explanation that my role is Dominant participant: so I am no longer the powerless child but the powerful child.

There is another link with the feeling of powerlessness and this particular period in my life. I was born with only one fully functioning ear (Microtia-anotia[125]) and had only the lobe of the left ear.

---

[125] Microtia-anotia: a congenital condition where the ear is underdeveloped (microtia) or even entirely absent (anotia). There may be some residual hearing

My mother said it was a result of taking Thalidomide[126], something that, as a young adult, I found difficult to understand because surely I would be more deformed than I was? I have subsequently discovered that this condition has been linked to the prescribing of medication during pregnancy for the treatment of genital warts. I know now that my parents never used contraception and my father was frequently unfaithful and passed on his STI to my mother.

However it was at about this time that I started to go through a process of reconstructive surgery. From two and a half until I was sixteen – and had the right to choose – I went to hospital for between two and four weeks every year for surgery, sometimes twice a year – about 14 operations in all. Somewhere in my mind there must be an association between these events: I was being sent away to a place of punishment, pain and isolation because I was bad.

At the same time I learned that I had no control over my own body. At the time reconstructive surgery was a developing discipline and many students visited: I was wheeled out and exhibited, prodded and poked whilst they examined me as if I didn't exist. All procedures involved complex and painful skin grafts – my body is covered with scars from these – so I have more than a few body image issues. Another factor was that my mother always insisted I had a private room and wasn't mixed up with the other children in the main ward,

---

or none. Microtia can be unilateral (one side) or bilateral (both) and occurs in 1 out of about 8,000–10,000 births. Usually treated by reconstructive surgery to make a new ear, functioning as well as possible, using the person's own cartilage from elsewhere. Today many alternative treatments exist or are under development.

[126] Thalidomide: Drug invented in 1957 in W. Germany as a sedative or hypnotic, which claimed to cure "anxiety, insomnia, gastritis and tension', Widely used against nausea & morning sickness pregnant women, and available without prescription from 1960: 5,000 - 7,000 infants were born with malformation of the limbs as a result: only 40% of these children survived.

so compounding the issues I already had: feeling incredible isolation and "aloneness".

I was the fat, lazy, slug who wasn't good enough and needed to be fixed in order to be acceptable, isolated from other children ... different. It's now easier for me to understand: when I began to have feelings for boys not girls, I was discovering another profound difference and experienced a primal fear of being sent back to places of isolation, darkness, separation and pain because of this new difference.

Charles, as you know, my mother recently passed away and the adult me – in spite of the very real physical and emotional abuse she inflicted on us as children – understands that her trying to fix me with these painful surgeries wasn't punishment. I believe she felt guilty that drugs she had taken during pregnancy resulted in my deformity and reconstruction was a way of expiating her guilt. The isolation in a side ward wasn't intended as a punishment but a way of making me special. I never had the opportunity to have these important conversations with her but my understanding allows me to have enough compassion to forgive her.

How did you experience the sex acts and games you describe? Were you in pain, curious, enduring, excited?

I suppose I need to explain the beginning. I was about ten, naïve and very much conditioned by the environment I was brought up in, including the school run by the Sisters. I was an altar boy, my head filled with an otherworldly kind of spiritualism. Other world? I mean, with hindsight, that I hadn't a clue how the world worked; I was still in a state where I trusted that everything worked for good for those who trust in the Lord. I still believed in saints and miracles.

It was the year Robert Kennedy was assassinated.[127] He was my

---

[127] Kennedy assassination: 6 June 1968.

hero because the nuns used to tell me what a great man he was: it didn't hurt that he was so handsome! 'The Times' published a memorial edition that I treasured. Why? Nobody knows. There was this day when I was ten and went into my brother's bedroom. He and my sister – she was seven and he eleven – were both naked. He took my special paper and said, unless I joined in, he would tear it up. I don't remember much though I do know that my sister and I both sucked his cock. I can't remember more than that.

My brother was always in trouble and spent time away in Approved schools or borstal[128]. When he came back these 'sex games' would continue and, obviously as he got older, became more advanced. I think the first time he actually fucked me was when I was about twelve and these incidents carried on until my father kicked him out of the house when he was sixteen.

Soon afterwards my brother 'passed me on' to one of his school friends for sex, he by that time being in borstal. I say 'passed on' only because this guy 'courted' me and I'm sure my brother must have said something to him. I remember this 'friend' inviting me for tea and almost straight away the sex games started. How did he know? I was certainly coerced into sex but not through fear.

'Groomed' would you say?

Groomed? I can't say, he was my brother's friend. When he was thirteen my brother started a relationship with a lawyer who was

---

[128] 'Approved schools': between 1933 & 1969 residential institutions with harsh disciplinarian regimes to which young people could be sent by a court, usually for committing offences but sometimes because they were deemed to be beyond parental control. 'Borstal': run the UK Prison Service to reform delinquent young people, originally under 21, but in the 1930s the age increased to under 23. The Criminal Justice Act 1982 abolished them, introducing youth custody centres.

subsequently convicted of paedophilia and this went on for several years. Did he learn from this man? Whatever. This guy and I had nothing in common apart from my brother and the guy was two years older than me. I was invited for tea: thinking I was suddenly popular, I went along after school. In his bedroom it wasn't long before he asked me to wank him off; actually his mother walked in to announce that tea was ready. I can't believe she didn't see anything, but we all acted like she hadn't. After tea she suggested we play outside: I mean very strongly suggested, as in 'Don't you go up to your room again!' We went down the Chine[129] into the thick profusion of rhododendrons where he offered to initiate me into a secret club: all I had to do to earn membership was to suck his cock. What was I feeling through all this?

I didn't have friends. Wanting to be accepted, I went along with it. I can't say I liked it but I do remember the smell of his salty cock and liking the taste and feel of it and the look of his body. His pubic hair fascinated me. I resented being manoeuvred into this situation, however, and while such 'games' might have continued, I had a fight with him in the playground, threw him over my shoulder and a wall that had a six-foot drop the other side. I hurt him and he never bothered me again. He had used some name to describe me; I don't remember exactly what it was. I just saw red and reacted. It was probably something like, "You're my bitch".

You weren't the only one groomed for sex, were you?

Nope: all my brothers apart from the youngest, who was eighteen months old, and my sister played these games, we even drew in friends. One horrendous summer my female cousin came to stay and she and my brother started a sexual relationship. He and I shared a bedroom so when they wanted to get it on, I used to have to go next

---

[129] 'Chine': steep-sided river valley.

door. I climbed into bed with my sister and played sex games with her. One night my parents woke up and caught us. All hell broke loose. Being asked by my father if I had ejaculated: what the hell was that? I didn't know what it meant! Did I have an erection? What the hell was that? All these things I'd never heard about. I was twelve and barely knew what wanking was: I'd never heard it called masturbation.

You said that your 'difference' was more of an issue at secondary school: please expand.

I wasn't on the 'team' of any kind, I spent playtimes reading, walking around on my own, until Dominic that is. We were similar outcasts and spent about two years as lunchtime friends wandering around school talking about history, art, and life. I thought he might be 'like me' but we never discussed it: I don't think I fancied him but I loved him and missed him when we left school and moved on.

There were a number of other occasions, three or four, when I would strike up a friendship with some boy at school and be invited for tea. I remember having a good time and couldn't understand why I was never invited back. With hindsight I realise they were always attractive boys that I probably had a crush on, if I could have used those words. Did I betray myself in some way? I don't know; I was never invited back and the friendship faded rapidly. Was I considered weird? I don't know.

My siblings never made any remarks. I was always the quiet, sensitive one and I was already different as I was born with only one ear. Obviously my difference to them was due to that.

I left home at fifteen or, rather, home left me. My parents and siblings moved abroad and left me to live on my own in a flat above a shop. During that time I did have a girlfriend; it was quite short lived, about three months I think. Why did it break up? Probably because I wanted sex and she wasn't ready. Aside from a couple of incidents when I was in my early twenties I didn't really have much other experience of sex until I was twenty-eight and I met my future wife.

***There's a five to ten year gap here: latency? What was your life
like then? What relationships of any sort did you make?***

At nineteen I had a brief affair with A, my brother's ex-girlfriend, who
was both a friend and an ex baby-sitter of ours. I became the shoulder
to cry on: we spent a lot of time together and, as I listened to her
problems, I fell in love with her. We went to my sister's wedding and,
with my brother present, she kissed me. I was already in love with her:
knees jelly, heart fit to burst and all that stuff. I was convinced she was
in love with me but she was just trying to make my brother jealous.
We were at a disco later when another, older, cousin came on to me.
Weirdly, I subsequently discovered she was having an affair with my
father! A., deciding to stake her territory, took me to bed which, I
have to say, was a disappointment and an embarrassment for us both.
Later, at her sister's, she and an old friend thought it would be OK if
they went upstairs for sex whilst I sat there watching David
Attenborough[130] as if I didn't know what was going on. Even after all
these years, I still can't believe the situation: I was heart broken.

There were a couple of drunken fucks with girls, quite a lot of
snogging. No other action until about twenty-one at a housewarming
for a guy and his male partner - the only gay person I'd ever
knowingly met. I was terrified: I was in the midst of a bunch of people
that I knew about and didn't want to know about. I got trashed and
stood with my back to the wall most of the night: I mean literally! As
the party ended I took it into my head to seduce the host. His
boyfriend, sitting opposite, eventually left in disgust. In bed I even
suggesting he call his boyfriend for a threesome, though I don't think
I'd ever heard that term. I knew I wanted to be fucked and he duly

---

[130] David Attenborough: English broadcaster and naturalist, whose career as the
main presenter of televised natural history programmes has endured for sixty
years.

obliged. Afterwards in the shower, in spite of the hot water, all I could do was shiver … fuck, fuck, fuck, fuck: I'm queer!

I remember leaving next day in white jeans, high-heeled cowboy boots and a sheepskin jacket, thinking that this must never ever happen again. My cousin spoke to me about it and I wrote it off as a one off experiment, and told him if he ever told anyone I'd slit his throat.

And that was it. No partners of any kind until my future wife when I was twenty-eight. The first time we had sex was there fear? I don't think so. Once she made her intentions clear, hormones and sex deprivation took over. I suppose there was a little performance anxiety. I came very quickly the first three times: by the fifth I'd got the hang of it!

What did you know at this time about 'queers' and their lives? Where did you get this? Did this scare you?

All I knew about poofs is that they were dirty old men in raincoats who got sent to prison for molesting young boys. Because that's what my parents told me. Fear certainly stopped me exploring my sexuality: the fear of being different and being discovered … being caught out as a poof. I knew of course, at some level, that I was gay.

At what 'level'? What does that mean?

For so much of my life I had feelings I didn't have a name for. Words used to describe homosexuals when I was growing up were 'queer', 'poof', 'bender', 'shirt-lifter' and 'fudge-packer.' I didn't want to be labelled that way. There wasn't a way I could describe what I felt when I was twelve or fourteen standing next to a boy in the school urinals. Any thoughts I had were associated with all of those pejorative terms, so of course I couldn't own those feelings. I pushed them down, suppressed them, and forgot them.

How did you first meet your wife and what attracted to you to one another?

I first met U when I was at University. She was in a relationship with a guy on my course. I've always been able to form close relationships with women and it was like that with U. A group of us used to go to her house and I would cook for everyone or she'd join us at various parties. At all of these I was the caterer and we, as the older ones, would end up in the kitchen talking about life, the universe and everything.

Things changed in my final year: at the graduation ball, I remember taking a long walk around the grounds while U poured out her troubles – the issues she was having with her partner, the history of their relationship and the history of her divorce. Her partner wanted to move on; he'd finally graduated and wanted to find his own life without being tied down to U and her children. I wasn't attracted to her and didn't have a clue that she was attracted to me; I was just a sympathetic friend. To this day I'm not sure whether she was attracted to me at this time.

Over the course of that summer she pursued me, dropping notes at the house where I was staying alone. We went for dinner or she would come over and I would cook. I wondered whether she was attracted to me, but pushed it out of my mind as silly: who could be interested in me? I spent much time alone, all my friends having graduated and left University. I was starting my Ph.D., working part time for a software company. I supported her when she asked G to leave; we went to an Italian restaurant to celebrate her first job and I paid, even though I could barely scrape two pennies together: my intentions were nothing but platonic.

The relationship became sexual one Sunday – I still have the date in my diary – when she invited me for lunch. The children were with their father and she had definitely set out to seduce me, gone to a lot of trouble. We sat down to view photo albums, her so close that I shuffled up the sofa; she'd move closer again and so on, until there was nowhere else to go. I said something like, "What's going on?" and she replied something like, "Just shut up and kiss me." The rest of the afternoon was spent in passionate and intense sex. Afterwards I was completely exhilarated. I remember one distinct thought: 'Hallelujah, I'm not queer after all!'

Was U your first 'real love'?

No, A had been the first person I fell head over heels, hopelessly and uncontrollably, in love with: that feeling when you kiss someone and drown in them, your legs turn to jelly and there is nothing except that moment when you look at someone and your heart beats faster, you can't breathe and you think you might actually faint because you've never seen anything more beautiful. It took me a long time to find that again. As luck would have it, I get that every day now!

Please say more about the development of your relationship with U.

Our relationship continued in the same vein over the summer, but summers end and we had to get back to work. I began to get cold feet as the relationship intensified and U wanted to know where it was going. I wasn't ready to commit although I was happy to have sex with her. We decided to split up and she joined a dating agency. We remained friends and spoke a lot on the 'phone, even about the men she met, some of whom she had sex with, which we spoke about too. She told me how much she missed me and we agreed to have a shag for old times' sake. I was clear that it was just sex and she appeared to be OK with that. Judging by the underwear she was wearing, it was clear she knew how to turn me on.

A few weeks later we met at a party and again she was dressed with the intent of pursuing me. It wasn't difficult: she had a great figure, could be very sexy and was a great kisser. Snogging in the kitchen, I was properly wound up with sexual tension, when she asked what I wanted to do. I wanted to make her breakfast in the morning and ended up going home with her.

For the rest of the year at weekends, the children being with their father, we would be together and during the week, while her daughter was at play school, we would have really passionate sex. We did other things - picnics, trips out. One memorable evening, the first occasion she introduced me to her friends, we were driving home when I started singing Nat King Cole's 'When I fall in love, it will be forever.' Her response was to swerve off the road and say, "If you're asking me what I think you're asking me; then the answer is yes".

And were you? Was that in your mind by now?

I don't think it was. I was too much in the romance of the moment to think what I was saying; yet it all seemed perfectly right. U didn't force me into a proposal: it was a moment in time when I was completely and utterly happy. We had just spent a perfect evening together. I felt completely at home and in love with her. So, whilst the answer may have been to a different question, it was the right answer, if that makes sense. I enjoyed her company, we laughed a lot, we had things to talk about, and she was the first person that I had ever met who was genuinely interested in me. I was in love.

At the same time I was uneasy. The only thing I could hang my uneasiness on was religion. I was a Christian and she was an atheist. She started reading the bible, trying to understand my objections: much later she told me that she'd started praying, 'God, give me this man and I'll believe in you.'

There was another objection in my subconscious that I couldn't even name which was simply that I was, am, and will always be, homosexual. At some visceral, rather than conscious, level I knew this, even though there appeared nothing wrong with the sex U and I were having. I wasn't pretending: I lusted after her; she could really turn me on. There was, however, always a sense of something lacking, I couldn't in any way shape the thought into identifying what it was. I was genuinely puzzled. I decided I needed to leave the University and the area and get a job. U was very supportive, driving me to interviews. Eventually I got a job in the South and stayed with her cousin and her husband who, years later, once I had come out, told me he'd always suspected I was gay.

Did the cousin's husband elaborate?

The closest he came was, "It's the way you stand." though I think that is more a reflection of his stereotypes than a comment on my behaviour.

I found a house share and started my new job. At some point we stopped seeing each other for a few months, although we often spoke on the 'phone.

How come you stopped?

U wanted our relationship to move on: after all, I had proposed and then withdrawn the proposal. Since I wouldn't commit, the only alternative was for us to part company.

It was during this time, I saw an ad for a gay bar nearby and I decided to try to find it. I remember pacing up and down the street where it was supposed to be, my heart pounding. I actually couldn't find it and I wonder what would have happened if I had. What prompted that? What feelings? Was that fear? Much later, in my mid-thirties, I remember going into sex shops and having that feeling. What was I thinking? I have no idea or even a memory: it was an autonomic impulse that didn't need thought. I never found that bar nor indeed did I follow it up by exploring other avenues.

I think that it was for my birthday that U sent me a parcel containing a ring and a note. I don't remember what the note said except that it was a proposal that I accepted. This time I promised myself – and her – there was no backing out, no changing my mind.

She travelled from the Midlands to where I worked almost every weekend, bringing her daughter, who had by now had decided not to see her father when her siblings did. I was beginning to have what I'd always wanted: a relationship and a stable family. We made plans for the wedding and somewhere to live. She was prepared to move South with the children to be with me, but we couldn't afford anything there for a family of five, so I decided to commute from the Midlands. It was the height of the property boom so I sold my flat at a profit quickly and moved into U's house. A month later, we got married.

My wedding day was the best day of my life up to that point, captured beautifully in one particular photograph by a best friend. U and I are in a cloud of confetti, me laughing with my head thrown back, truly happy. It's a memory that I treasure today. Every moment of unconfined joy in my life since then is compared to that moment.

The honeymoon on the other hand was not great: it wasn't all bad but there were days where I was angry and tied up in knots, like a pressure cooker about to explode yet I didn't know why. Nor did U but that's when, I believe, she adopted a strategy to hang on to me at any cost. The feelings in me weren't all down to my struggle with my sexuality. At times she would ask me to do things, sounding so much like my controlling mother that it grated on me. It's taken many years, and an understanding of transference[131], to realise that I wasn't really in relationship with U at those times, but listening to the echoes of past relationships, not seeing her or reacting to her as she was, but as I expected her to be, based on what went before.

We got over the honeymoon and I was perfectly content with our

---

[131] 'Transference': a term from psychoanalysis for a phenomenon first described by Freud. The unconscious redirects feelings and desires that were important in a person's childhood towards a new person, who represents an original person with whom the present person can become unconsciously confused.

life for the next seven years. I do mean perfectly content. I had everything I had ever wanted. Yes, there were tensions, but I never thought about anyone else or looked at anyone else of either sex. She was my world. I think I was hers.

I'm interested in when, how and why your gay feelings became foreground: were they dormant or sparked off by beautiful men, film or television, dreams or fantasies? Did you know other gay men at that time?

Stirrings

I've just re-read that last paragraph after quite a gap[132] and realise that it's not entirely true. It's a romanticised memory of a time in my life that was pretty special.

From about the age of fifteen I'd indulged from time to time in anal masturbation. From the early Nineties I worked abroad and became a Monday to Friday commuter. Masturbation has always been a source of comfort for me. Maybe that goes back to the three bears? Anal masturbation produces a particularly intense orgasm, but there came a time when I wanted more than just a finger to play with.

I was working in Germany where, on the route back to my hotel, there was a gay sex shop. I was curious, more than curious. I'd walk past that shop trying not to look but my heart would beat faster as I'd imagine what might be inside. For months I did nothing about those feelings. The culture of the project was to work hard and then, as a group, go out to dinner and, more often than not, end up in the hotel bar until late at night.

---

[132] Nigel's story and one or two others, were reconsidered and expanded over quite some time as our dialogue gradually deepened. See Introduction for genesis of the life-stories.

Eventually, curiosity and excited anticipation got the better of me and I really needed to see inside the shop, which had a cinema too. Really late one night, early morning, I left the hotel to check the shop out. I had to be sure none of my colleagues could see me. I walked up and down the street chain-smoking, trying to make sure that no one I knew would see me, and checked out the opening times of the shop.

Weeks later I excused myself from a dinner, waited half an hour after everyone had left the hotel and for pedestrian traffic to die down, for the right moment to dive in. By the time I'd crossed that threshold I was trembling so much I almost dropped the money when I went to buy a ticket, trying to present an image of confident insouciance.

The cinema was a very dark video room with thirty chairs and sofas. There were about half a dozen men, eyes glued to the screen. I sat as far as possible from anyone and started watching. I remember it: an American video, three very muscular blonde guys by a pool doing things to each other I hadn't even dreamed of! I saw cocks on film fully erect for the first time. I'd seen some of my Dad's soft-core porn but never seen a fully erect cock or guys sucking or fucking each other. The film was overwhelming my senses. I became aware that a number of patrons had unzipped and were wanking to the action.

Twenty years later I still remember that mix of fear and excitement: the excitement of seeing everything happening on screen and the reality of the very palpable flesh of the men in the room. At some point a guy sat in the same row as me, in spite of the fact that most of the room was empty and at that point fear took over – I had to leave, but this was probably about three hours later.

I returned to the shop that evening and left with a couple of gay magazines and a dildo. Some weeks later they ended up in a bin at the train station. It was too dangerous to have such things: they might be discovered: I might be discovered.

Some time later I visited another gay sex shop which mostly sold books and videos and remember being amazed seeing two men fucking on TV behind the till while a number of men in the shop were browsing the books like it was W.H.Smith on a Saturday morning, all so normal.

Eighteen months later my project moved to the Netherlands. Initially I lived in a shared house, then I eventually got a house of my own in the suburbs. Many weekends, instead of me going home, U and her daughter would come and stay. That was the only other time for years that I tried any exploration. I found an ad for a gay chat line in a newspaper and dialled it. After many false starts I agreed to meet a guy at the train station. He never showed and I never repeated the experience.

That was it – all thought, all feeling, all ideas were pushed down, confined, locked and bound.

You haven't told us yet about 'coming out', the end of your marriage and forming a gay identity.

Coming out was a very slow process. IT consultants travel to where clients are: that meant commuting daily from the Midlands to London when I was first married. When I returned to live in the Midlands I would still have to travel to clients. It became a rhythm: Monday mornings I would catch a train to London, Newcastle or some other city and return Friday evening.

I was then head-hunted by a large firm which involved travelling to London weekly and staying in company housing. I started to explore my sexuality more. In fact I remember the time it all changed and I realised I'd just been hiding what I had known in my innermost self for a long time.

Mobile 'phones were not widely used then so, after work, I'd use a public call box to 'phone home each night. Working away was a cause of much friction in the marriage but I told myself and U that we were building a future for the family. Two of the children were now at university and we'd bought a much bigger house and I needed to earn money at that level to pay for our lifestyle. It was very stressful for us both. I remember one evening having the daily 'phone call and getting into an argument – probably about money – I was so angry at the outcome I decided I was going to act out my feelings. In the phone box, amongst many adverts for call girls, was a card advertising a rent boy and I decided to find out what it would be like. I remember the internal debate about how, if I went down this path, there was no going back, that it would lead to the end of my marriage and everything I'd built up so carefully.

Nevertheless I went ahead and called the number; the guy's flat was a few streets from the place I was living. I arranged to meet him ... not a nice area near Paddington and the flat grubby. I was led into a curtained off area with a single bed and asked to undress. My heart was pounding so hard it almost deafened me. I was more aroused than I had ever been as he started to undress too and guide me to the bed. He gave me a blow job, the first since I was a child and all those familiar buttons were pressed – I hadn't had an orgasm like it for a long, long time and the feeling of being touched by, and touching, a man was connecting in me feelings that had been suppressed for years. Afterwards I left the flat having paid £60 for the 30 minutes spent there. I was both exhilarated and then ashamed of what I'd just done but over and above that I knew, just knew, that I had never felt more alive.

Sharing a flat with a colleague, it was difficult to explore this side of my nature. I wanted to know more about sex between men and started to visit a porn shop, buying videos, magazines and sex toys. That was satisfactory for a few months but there was an inner desire to touch a real man again – without stating the obvious, men feel different to women: harder, more muscular and in my experience they behave differently. Though they can be tender and loving they can also be aggressive and energetic.

Shortly after this I started to cruise small ads looking for an escort and found a suitable guy. The sex wasn't terrific but the feelings were profound; all my eroticism connecting with my body in a way that I'd not experienced.

As a senior manager, I could have my own apartment and, once installed, I took full advantage of chat lines to meet as many men as possible and experience as much as possible. Over 18 months I met different men for sex on average twice a week. I was intoxicated by my discovery that sex could be so great, fun and fulfilling. It wasn't that U and I didn't have sex … far from it. We had more sex than most married couples of our acquaintance but our sex lives were compressed into Friday, Saturday and Sunday. I'm not complaining about the sex we had either: I not only wanted, but knew how, to please her, but my own pleasure was never a large part of it.

The stress of keeping these secrets began to tell and I knew I had to do something about this situation. I hated the deceit. One time I found out I'd caught crabs[133] too late to prevent U catching them. When she discovered them, I pretended I'd been with a female prostitute after a drunken night out. Though hurt, upset and angry, she believed my explanation.

Later that same year on holiday in Greece, I felt compelled to tell the truth. Throughout the holiday I'd been in a foul mood, snappy and completely withdrawn from the family. I honestly thought they'd eventually arrive at a point where they'd want me to leave, U would ask for a divorce and my secrets would be safe. That was preferable to telling the truth.

One evening I drank a lot of wine and sat on the terrace of the villa smoking, drinking more. It was a cloudless, star-filled night sky and the cicadas were deafening. After her bath, U came behind me, placing her hands on my shoulders and just said: "What's wrong? This isn't you." It was one of those moments when I felt like I'd lost control of my body. I remember feeling I was standing outside of myself,

---

[133] 'crabs': Pubic louse, a parasitic insect that feeds on human blood. The main symptom of an infestation is itching in the pubic hair, sometimes also eyelashes, resulting from sensitivity to louse saliva, which can become stronger over two or more weeks following initial infestation.

watching myself say, "I'm gay." Her first response was, "How do you know?" so I told her and then she said, "Oh my god, I'm so sorry that I trapped you into this marriage." I sobbed like a baby at the relief as she held me tight.

The following morning we talked about what we should do – and that I might not actually be gay but perhaps bisexual. After all that night had ended with us making love ... to comfort each other ... if I could have sex with her, how could I be gay? I agreed to start working with a therapist to try to understand why I felt the need to have sex with men. Perhaps there was a clue in my childhood traumas, which I had told her about.

But that was also the start of a slow disintegration of our relationship as I made promise after promise not to have sex with others and repeatedly broke those promises. We stayed together for another ten drama-filled years.

Those were years where we both hurt each other by trying to maintain the fiction we had built of a happy, chocolate box life with roses around the door. We had a beautiful house, a very active social life, the children growing up, thankfully happy, healthy and well adjusted. But they were years where she cried every day because of her sense of isolation and betrayal and I couldn't come to terms with my own internalised shame and homophobia and admit that I was gay even to myself. You remember, Charles, when I first started working with you, that U enthusiastically supported me reading about homosexuality and the development of gay identity, reading the same books: even at some point forcing me to say the words, "I'm glad to be gay," when I certainly didn't feel it. Eventually the lies and deceit became too much and U decided to end the marriage.

After separating I could start accepting myself and my new life as a single gay man. U texted me a couple of years later with the following wish for me:

"I hope your building work is going well and that you're enjoying your new life. Take care.

P. S. I don't have nightmares now but I sometimes dream we're still together and wake up alone."

So I wrote back:

"As for enjoying life... to be at peace with oneself, not to have to try to walk a line between two worlds and feel like you belong to none, that's quite a new thing. Like your nightmares, mine have stopped. But I still do dream of us, not sometimes but often and they're for the most part happy dreams, and I wake up and I miss you too."

And she wrote back:

"SO YOU'RE NOT SORRY THAT I ENDED IT? EVEN THOUGH IT WAS INCREDIBLY PAINFUL FOR US BOTH. I FIND IT HARD TO WATCH 'ANTIQUES ROADSHOW' ON A SUNDAY EVENING NOW."

And then, shortly afterwards in the middle of lots of stress and turmoil at work, I received a text:

"Came 2 c the bluebells at the woods. They r breathtaking this year!"

The woods and bluebells had special meaning for us. It was a kind of resolution.

Say something, please, about building a loving gay partnership and how your life has changed since then, Nigel.

I met a wonderful man about three months after I separated from U. K is younger than I by about 17 years – this generational gap isn't so much of an issue but he comes from a different cultural and religious background. Dealing with K's own internalised and cultural homophobia has not been easy and it has been hard to build a relationship. My issues around working out a way to be with myself as a gay man were covering up unresolved childhood traumas that made

217

it difficult for me to trust anyone so that presently there is new therapeutic work for me to do to tackle the fundamentals.

K and I have been together for more than eight years and I now know what it feels like to love someone physically, emotionally and erotically all at the same time. My present life is less compartmentalised than it was. I don't pretend to be anything other than I am, a man who likes men and women, but has a strong and perfectly natural sexual attraction to men that has been there since before I could name it. Having said that, it's not all plain sailing: I still have very many fundamental issues to deal with that do intrude into our relationship.

I'd also appreciate you sharing what has been most helpful to you in this process and what you recommend to other men in similar circumstances.

First of all I had some difficulty in finding a therapist who understood any of the issues around men marrying and later in life identifying as gay. I was lucky in that I lived and worked in London, because my experience of living in the provinces and trying to get help wasn't a happy one. I did see one or two experienced psychotherapists who weren't prepared to take me on as a client.

I was fortunate enough to be referred by a GP working at a London based sexual health clinic, to you, Charles and we've been working together for seventeen years ... so I'd say one resource one needs is patience!

After about two years of working together you suggested that I participate in a gay men's group which you have run in London almost forever.[134] I think that I was in this group for about five years.

---

[134] I have written at length about the great value to men of working within gay and bi groups when possible and the wide range of issues which arise: see 'We Are Family' (Chapter 7) in Neal, C. & Davies, D. (eds): Pink Therapy Volume 3:

It was certainly an experience that helped me greatly in dealing with my own internalised homophobia. I met gay men in a non-sexualised context for the first time and have come to know many of them very well: we are still in contact, even though many eventually left the group as did I. They are my family of adoption.

When I first gave in to (but not accepted) my gayness I went on a spree of self-indulgent hedonism and every meeting with a man, whatever the intention, ended - or even began - with sex. I was searching for an expression of myself that was complete and felt "authentic" but the combination of deception muddied the waters and made it difficult for me to think of men outside of a sexual context.

Part of my journey to normalising my relationship with my sexuality and myself was to meet a man outside of any sexual context. I sought out a man with a similar situation: a married gay father. We used to meet for dinner and talk about ordinary things: how difficult it is to bring up teenagers, transitioning out of our existing relationships, sharing our histories and our discoveries of our own sexualities, talking about the emotions. We tried to help each other to figure out what a future might look like, given the imprints we carried of what a conventional, acceptable relationship would look like. I recall that neither of us was optimistic at the time about finding a satisfying, intimate, dependable relationship. Part of that was from cultural scripts – the notion that all gay men were promiscuous, unreliable, etc. Part was about experience: meeting men with whom we had developed deep emotional attachments where these feelings weren't returned. These are exactly the experiences most teenagers naturally go through as they develop intimate relationships: it's just that we were doing this in our 40s and 50s. More than ten years on, we're still friends.

'Issues in Therapy with Lesbian, Gay, Bisexual and Transgender Clients' , 2000, Open University Press.

I found Ted Gideonse's book, 'From Boys to Men'[135] really helpful in identifying what the feeling of being "other" from a young age is like. Identifying and understanding queerness as a distinct part of my identity is a challenge - don't know if you noticed but I've always had trouble with that. I found it useful because most of the stories don't focus on first sexual encounters but descriptions of what it was like to experience feelings of being different, the awareness that this was in some way dangerous and the things we do in order to 'pass' as being the same, long before we understand feelings of sexual attraction. Gay boys aren't the same as others and their experience of life isn't the same as straight boys (surprise!) I guess I always knew that but didn't have ways to describe it. Whilst it is very much about growing up in the US, I think the feelings are universal. The essays in the book reminded me of parts of my life that I had forgotten.

I remember that when I was in the group I was always rather optimistic about the way that society is changing and becoming more accepting of 'otherness' in spite of a recent history of appalling homophobic crimes. I've also had this feeling that there are many gay men who have a tendency to ghettoise their experiences; of course I understand from my own history why that is so, but I have a hope that this is also a world that is passing.

I've been reading "Love in a Dark Time" by Colm Tóibín,[136] which is a wonderful survey of some of the greatest and gayest artists of the 19th and 20th centuries and the way social conditions affected the

---

[135] Ted Gideonse (Editor) :'From Boys to Men: Gay Men Write About Growing Up': 2006: Da Capo Press, Cambridge., Mass., USA. A really stunning collection of essays, not coming out stories exactly, but about what it is like to be different, aware of that difference from the earliest of ages and the magical variety of such differences.

[136] Colm Tóibín: 'Love In a Dark Time: Gay Lives from Wilde to Almodóvar': 2002: Picador. An important collection of essays on a wide range of gay creative lives.

ways they worked and the content of this work because of their homosexuality. Tóibín provides an intensely sympathetic description and highly sensitive interpretations of the biographies of these people from Oscar Wilde to Pedro Almadóvar.

Then I see programmes such as these (below) and realise that there is some progress in people's attitudes. I still have this optimism that we are, and in particular the young are, becoming more tolerant and accepting both of ourselves and of others.

www.channel4.com/programmes/father-ray-comes-out/4od[137]

www.channel4.com/programmes/coming-out-to-class/4od[138]

www.channel4.com/programmes/the-joy-of-teen-sex/4od[139]

---

[137] 'Father Ray Comes Out' Channel 4 British TV programme, in which Father Ray, a warm, gregarious vicar, has transformed his parish, building a community in central London, where many struggle with feelings of anonymity. Now Ray is prepared to jeopardise all his work for the truth, and share a very personal secret with them: he is gay. He's decided that in order to be a good minister he must be honest with his parish.

[138] 'Coming Out to Class': Channel 4 British TV programme in which QBoy, the UK's first openly gay rapper, meets young gay teens, teachers, and others to explore why 62% of gay teenagers are choosing to 'come out' to school - why?

[139] 'The Joy of Teen Sex' Channel 4 British TV programme. Dr Anita Sturnham, counsellor Emma Kenny, and sex expert Sam Roddick offer honest advice and support to confused, curious teens in the Sex Advice Shop.

ROBERT'S STORY

Introduction to Robert

Robert's story is full of pointers to the difficulties so many males have when they are mothered in an unsatisfying way. Like several other men in this book, for example, Alex and Alan, his relationship with his mother is somewhat inappropriately close while he is distanced from his father. Gender relations changed in the nineteenth and twentieth centuries with male work patterns profoundly altered by the dominance of industrialisation and women's by their enforced centrality in home keeping and parenting. These, however, don't apply to Robert's particular history so much as both his parents were at home, although neither was available in ways that met his childhood needs.

His mother, like some other parents represented in these stories, was evidently struggling with stresses in her marriage - deeply affected by her husband's alcoholism and needing to escape the awfulness of home life. This often proves a burden for a child who can come to feel responsible for their parent's unhappiness.

Then there's the 'distance' between Robert and his two heterosexual brothers and their interests and activities. Above all there is the devastating experience of the sudden dislocation from all his familiar certainties at home to be sent away to boarding school in early childhood. This is almost always accompanied by messages of privilege, specialness and gratitude, yet experienced so frequently as agonising separation.

A lot of valuable work has been done in recent years on the damaging effects of being separated from home, family and familiarity to attend boarding school for many children - and some of this has especially focused on these effects in relation to gay children. This has clearly demonstrated the damaging effects of boarding school life on intimacy and relationship skills, secrecy, difficulties with closeness and the inhibition of self expression, all of which Robert's story also illustrates. See, for example, the campaigning, information and therapy, as well as the Boarding School Survivors' groups run by Nick Duffell and Marcus Gottlieb[140] in the UK. Boarding school was a formative negative experience for Chris, too (Chapter 4).

Most marked of all, perhaps, is the enduring experience of loneliness and isolation that Robert has carried from his first home, through schools, college and early adulthood into living within a marriage as a parent. This is a defining characteristic of the stories told in this book, whether for early years, through adulthood or within marriage and families: this intense loneliness and isolation. It is, as I say in the Introduction, the major motive for putting this book together and a clearly expressed drive for contributors now sharing their lives with others in this way. It moves me greatly that many men, maybe especially those struggling with their identity or sexuality, have had to endure life with an absence of comradeship, openness, intimacy skills and effective communications and the presence instead of requirements to be male, or masculine, in certain inhibiting ways. 'Men's work', to which I refer elsewhere[141], has been predicated on

---

[140] Boarding School Survivors Groups: Nick Duffell's book 'The Making Of Them' (Lone Arrow Press, 2000) Nick's groups for boarding school survivors and his campaigning and education base are at www.boardingschoolsurvivors.co.uk See also 'Resources: Organisations' section. Gottlieb's useful introductory article on boarding issues: http://marcusgottlieb.com/

[141] Men's work: see footnote explanation in Charles's story, chapter (10).

counteracting these patterns.

The loneliness will only be reinforced further when living alongside a wife and sons with whom one fears to be one's true self, one's full self, to be real. So much cannot be shared or said or done together when this is the case.

All through his life, not just within his marriage, Robert has repressed not only his sexuality but also his personality more generally – and, of course, these are connected. Our sexuality – our sexual feelings and behaviours, not our sexual identity only – is a core part of who we truly are, not a 'bolt on' aspect of our lives. It is one of the ways in which our selfhood expresses itself, makes a form from innermost sensibilities. In the gay and bi men's groups I have led, we have spent a lot of time considering the many ways in which our sexualities are expressed apart from, or as well as, simply through sexual contact with others.

Being 'gay' or 'bi' – or 'straight' or any other sexual identity – amounts to so much more than merely sexual actions. It's such a waste, it seems to me, that the subtleties and richness of the personalities of most of the men who tell their stories here have been denied, closed down and repressed, had lids put over them, often for decades.

Robert is still in the process of his 'coming out' journey within his marriage and family and, although he and his wife have had to look several times at the facts of their lives together face-to-face they have, as we have seen elsewhere, chosen each time to retreat from confronting these further. How far Robert will manage to make the changes he wishes for towards authenticity, openness and richer companionship, we cannot tell. Being sixty presents many further challenges for a couple married for so many years with sons now leaving home.

Thank goodness Robert found satisfying creative outlets through making art as well as greater expression of his core spirit and aspects of his personality being recently expressed through his work in the drama group. He seems, as many of us are, chastened and motivated by turning sixty, into a stronger determination 'not to stagnate' and I wish him well with all my heart in undertaking the rewarding transformations he seeks.

ROBERT'S STORY:

Please tell me what you can about your home life and growing up with your parents.

My father was what might be described as a gentleman farmer – he didn't actually work on his farm, he had a steward to look after the day-to-day running of it. My dad would do some office work in the morning then, after lunch, would settle in front of the television to watch horse racing. The curtains would be closed in the 'snug' and all the sporting papers laid out on the floor. No one dared to disturb him. My mother didn't work. She never had a paid job. She did some charity work to get her away from home.

My mother's and my father's parents were all fairly wealthy. Mother's father was a farmer and my father's dad had a woollen mill in the Scottish Borders.

I never knew either grandfather as both died just before I was born. This is something I only discovered recently. On 11th February, 1952 my paternal grandfather died. Nine days later my mum's father died. I was born on 5th March. I cannot imagine how my parents must have felt, both grieving just as I was born. I was amazed to discover this as neither parent had ever mentioned it. I wish I had talked to them about this period before they died.

I adored my maternal granny. She had a lovely house and garden and I loved staying with her. She seemed to have time to sit and talk with me, unlike my parents. Her house was the opposite of my other grandmother's house, which was dark, gloomy and quite scary.

I never stayed there, nor did I want to. I had a very formal relationship with her. We used to play cards whenever we went for tea. My dad never came so I never witnessed my father with his mother. So the two grannies were opposites: one warm, gentle and very friendly, the other slightly cold, formal and distant.

Until I was sent away to boarding school at eight, most of my time was spent at home on the farm. It was a fairly isolated existence. Playing with friends involved car journeys and planning. There was no 'street life'. Consequently I became very adept at entertaining myself, especially as both my parents were absent a lot of the time, my father through his drinking - he was an alcoholic - and my mother through her love of hunting.

During the winter, she would often be out all day on her horse following the hounds, leaving me alone with my dad, whom I never saw. For one year I was at home alone because my brothers had already gone to boarding school. I often retreated up to my room, or the box room, where the dressing up clothes were. I also spent a great deal of the time under the stairs, looking at old family photo albums and school reports.

What were you trying to find, or gain from these, do you now imagine?

The photos were for company maybe? I was alone so often in the house. I think I was looking for connection: if I couldn't have it with the real person, then I could have it with the person in the photograph. Or perhaps searching for photographs I'd never seen before which would shed some light on my mother or father. Going through the things in my mum's desk was similar: seeing what she liked to keep, discovering her cheque book, working out how much money she had, wanting to know more about her.

I can remember many of my clothes from an early age in great detail. If someone offered to knit me a jumper, I chose the yarn. I can recall so many of my mother's clothes, the colours, the prints, and her jewellery box. I used to sit at her dressing table and put on make up. I loved to explore all the shelves, drawers and what they contained. All this was done in secret of course. I spent a lot of my childhood dressing up in her clothes, her cast-offs.

Once she found me standing in front of a full length mirror in her bedroom wearing a huge headscarf wrapped around me, perhaps a bit of jewellery: I was naked underneath. She very tactfully said, "That'll make a nice fancy dress outfit." How kind of her to say that. She knew I adored fancy dress. I lived for any excuse to dress up, which I guess was an escape for me. I also loved the feeling of delicate fabrics, such as chiffon or silk, against my skin.

Although I had two brothers, I spent most of my childhood alone. As well as dressing up, I loved to put on puppet shows and plays. I wrote the script, played all the parts and made the costumes.

Please say more about your relationships with your brothers and why you were so lonely.

My two brothers were older than me. We were each two years apart. I never had a particularly close relationship with either of them. We were all sent to the same prep school and were there together for one year. We only really saw each other when we passed on the twice weekly letter from my mother which was addressed to all three of us – one letter to be shared between three: we had to share this little bit of love.

At school we were known by our surname followed by 1, 2 and 3 to differentiate between us. I was given the number 19 to put on my locker, shoes and so on. Everything was highly depersonalised. Of course, we saw each other during the holidays. My middle brother and I both rode so I saw more of him when we went to Pony Club events together. My eldest brother was into mechanics and electronics, which were far removed from what I was interested in – dressing up, art, and puppets.

Being sent away to school at the age of eight, I was desperately homesick and starved of love. At times it was unbearable but somehow I learnt to survive - at a cost, I guess.

Can you say more about learning those survival techniques at boarding school and what they have cost you, please?

There was no discussion about going there: it was a *fait accompli*, the done thing in my parents' generation and class. I had been so happy in primary school that the trauma of being sent away was enormous: leaving my home, my mother, my cats and my pony. I was separated from everything familiar and everything that I loved.

I learned very quickly to hide my emotions at school, which meant never to be seen crying or showing any homesickness. The only time I allowed myself to cry was in secret, under my bedclothes after lights out and, even then, it had to be quiet as there was only a chair between each bed in the dormitory; there was no privacy at all.

I learned to survive through gardening – we could apply for our own or shared little gardens – and writing plays for me and my friends, getting involved with the school puppet theatre and trying to be involved with any aspect of every drama production. I wanted to find vehicles to escape from reality.

If there was a play being put on, I desperately tried to get a part. Sometimes I was overlooked and that was hard to deal with. Plays took me away from the awfulness of boarding school.

Masturbating was another escape and still is. I recall very vividly my initiation into wanking. At some point I was made captain of a dormitory and all captains had their baths after the other boys had gone to bed. I was instructed what to do with my penis and so became part of the nightly ritual of group masturbation. We seemed completely OK about jerking off in front of each other.

With hindsight, public school was a worse experience than prep. The school was very games-oriented and I loathed games.

What was loathsome to you?

There was a huge emphasis on games and yet all I ever wanted to do was to spend time in the Art Department. I was scared of getting physically hurt, especially in rugby. I couldn't tackle anyone for love or money. I also associated games with being out in cold and wet. At prep school we'd read for an hour after lunch, then the games master would announce the teams for the afternoon. I so hated that moment: I didn't even like playing cricket because I couldn't throw the ball and didn't want to be hit with it. I did enjoy tennis but there was little on offer: it wasn't considered a 'proper' sport! My brother H, who was later killed in a car crash, was very good at games, therefore it was expected that I would be. What a disappointment I must have been!

What about affection, love, crushes, comfort?

There was a lot of mutual masturbation and sleeping in other boys' beds but no anal intercourse as far as I know.

At prep school I often picked flowers from my garden for the junior matron, Miss McN - trying to buy some affection or love I suppose. Being a 'good little boy' was the best way to survive both at home and at school. I definitely had a 'crush' on her.

Many years later, I used to have sexual fantasies about various male masters there while I masturbated. I imagined them walking through the dorms at night with very little, or no, clothes on, imagining all the boys were asleep: but I was not! I used to fantasise about them showering after swimming with the boys and then, when they were on their own, taking their trunks off only to be disturbed by the headmaster, who stood admiring their beautiful, lithe, muscular, tanned bodies and genitals.

Going to art school was a relief after boarding school but I was very lonely again to begin with. I didn't know a soul in London and lived in a rather grim bedsit. It was incredibly similar to my first nights at prep school. On the other hand, I no longer had the restrictions and confinements I was used to, my day was no longer regimented.

So, your isolation, begun at home, continued all through school and even afterwards when you went from school to art school in London – is that right?

Yes, I went straight from boarding school to art school and living alone in London, another great contrast like going from my warm little rural primary school to the harshness of boarding school. The only people I knew were my mother's sister and her husband, near Guildford, whom I saw occasionally.

The theme of isolation has run all through my life from early childhood to now. Also, the skills I developed to deal with my isolation were an integral part of this. What seems extraordinary to me is that all during my years at art school – six years in total – I never had a girlfriend or slept with a girl or boy. All my contemporaries were shagging non-stop and I was still a virgin!

I hated parties: I always ended up standing in the kitchen at parties as the famous song line goes. Although I loved the work at college, I found the social life very difficult. Looking back now I think that I realise that the reason I had no sexual relations with girls at this stage was because I was unsure of my sexuality. Yet I wasn't aware of any gay people all through my student life. I was just seen as an oddball.

I used to go to the cinema on my own at the weekend, as I had no TV in my bedsit. I still do this quite often to escape reality. I phoned home on Sunday nights from a call box. It took a long time to build any social relationships. I experienced strong feelings of isolation and low self-confidence

What relationships were important to you in these years – with teachers, fellow students, and family?

Some of my closest friends at college were from outside. One was at drama school and I met her again recently after many years.

When I left the Royal College in 1976, I took a trip to America to sell textile designs. I had a contact in New York, a relation of a friend. He was the first man I went to bed with. The whole experience was so exciting – being in NYC, my first sexual encounter with another man, it was just so liberating.

When I returned to London, the lid came back down and I continued where I'd left off, with very little social life and no sex life at all.

How did the lid come down?

'Bringing the lid back down' meant repressing my gay side again. Returning to the UK meant I had to conform. Being abroad had given me permission, as it were, to act on my sexuality. I did tell a few people about my sexual encounter. I guess this was my first attempt at 'coming out.'

For years I lived for the occasional visit from my friend in New York. He would stay at my flat and the sex was fantastic. Gradually these visits phased out but up until a year or so ago he would keep in touch by telephone. There was always something electric about him. He constantly challenged me in a way that enthralled me.

Can you say how he did so?

In retrospect, he definitely seduced me, although I recall that I was first to make physical contact. I touched his legs, which I thought were amazing. I'd never done this before and wasn't judging myself. I yearned for this closeness, body to body.

He used to tease me, which I responded to. He provoked me in ways in which no one else had, brought out a side of me which was always closed: a fun part of me, a playful part. When I think of him the first word to come to mind is 'outrageous'!

During this period I went to see a Jungian analyst and around this time first had sex with a female. It wasn't a pleasant experience. There were three of us in the bed, two males and one female, all having had too much to drink. I had no idea what I was doing or indeed where and how to have sex with a girl! It was all very disturbing. Afterwards she said I had been very aggressive.

What was the ostensible reason for you to see a Jungian analyst?

I started Jungian analysis because I was desperate to try to change my life. I was drinking heavily and very unhappy. A good friend's boyfriend was training to be an analyst and gave me a recommendation.

What do you now make of the young woman's accusation of aggression?

The three in a bed incident occurred after much drinking and wasn't a good manner in which to have my first sexual encounter with a female. There was almost no communication and I had no idea how to penetrate: I was completely out of my depth. Later, the girl used to come to my flat for sex at lunchtime. I was never 100% sure whether I wanted this or not but guess I was flattered that she wanted me as she had quite a reputation with the boys.

Still living alone at this time, I went on to have my first 'proper' girlfriend with whom I had great sex, until she decided to return to her former boyfriend. I was devastated and felt totally abandoned. Years went by with no girlfriend or any encounters with guys.

Not long after I returned from New York I shared a house with two gay guys and an actress. I recall two key things. One Saturday night my housemate was entertaining a friend in the sitting room and I felt awkward, as I was the only other housemate remaining in, so I drove to the 'King William' gay pub in Hampstead for a drink. I was picked up by a taxi-driver who suggested we went to his house, so I followed his taxi. We went to bed and he attempted anal intercourse, but was unable to penetrate me despite encouraging me to sniff Amyl Nitrate. I remember having a very sore bum next day: not a good experience.

Also at this time one of the guys in the house began to 'court' me, which I felt very uncomfortable about. He used to buy me presents and wine and dine me. It never really led to anything serious but I was never able to tell him to back off despite feeling so uncomfortable about what he was doing. So, during my stay in the shared house the question of my sexuality was very much to the fore.

This seems crucial: an important choice point. What do you make of your discomfort? Here is your emergent sexuality. Is this when you brought 'the lid back down'? Why?

I realise I've never grown up sexually. I never experimented with girls or boys whilst at art college. I did at school with one boy who used to jerk me off in the library: the risks we used to take! I used to lie in other boy's beds but we never had sex. While masturbating I always fantasised about men, never, as far as I remember, about women. I hated being on my own all those years. In a strange way nothing's changed really; though I now have a family I still very often feel on my own.

I was eventually introduced into an organisation, which came under the umbrella of personal growth, with lots of cathartic experiences: screaming, shouting, anger release and so on. It was on this course that I met my wife-to-be. I had been on my own for so long, it was a good feeling to finally have a companion.

How did you come to marry?

To begin with, sex was great and the relationship good. After about a year, she suggested we get married and I remember just going along with it, although I was uncomfortable about it. In retrospect, I should have said, 'Hang on, I need to think more about this.'

Were you flattered by being asked by a woman, do you think?

Yes, a bit. I have tried most of my life to be untraditional so wasn't that keen on the idea of marriage. The whole organisation of it was very acrimonious, with her parents doing what they wanted. I didn't have a best man or anything. The whole thing was taken away from me and I would have wanted something much more alternative, not so traditional a wedding.

Was your wife-to-be much more traditional? I'm thinking that lots of young people didn't support marriage at that time.

In hindsight, I think she took me by surprise there. I didn't think that she would go along with the whole traditional approach that seemed to be coming from her family. She was the last of four sisters to get married and I think she probably chose to model her marriage on what had gone before. Basically there should have been a lot more communication and discussion around this time. Where I could add a more personal, untraditional touch was through my artwork. I did a drawing for the front of the invitation as well as making little painted cardboard figures to put around the base of the cake.

Was it really, then, more of a contract about parenting?

No, because not long afterwards she told me she didn't want children and I was really shocked, as I did. When we decided to go for it nothing happened and we had an awful period of going to the hospital, having to time sex, and so on. It was a big killer of sexual feeling, not at all erotic.

It was having children that killed our marriage and our sex life.

After our first child was born we had sex once, not an enjoyable experience, then the second child came along. That was nearly twenty years ago and we haven't had sex since. How our marriage has survived, God only knows. We have slept in separate beds for at least ten years now. Of course, there have been some very rocky times, hitting each other, verbal abuse, but we somehow have survived it all and now, with two boys gone to University, we are still together, alone in our house once more.

What I've done with my sexual feelings all these years, I don't know. I guess I've buried them, denied myself them, until recently.

Can you say more about your experience of yourself through this period of denial?

Coming Out 1

I think W first began to be aware of my sexuality when we went to see a Marriage Guidance counsellor when the boys were young. Reference was made to my relationship with the man from New York, but the subject was never properly explored. Many years later we went to see a Child and Family Therapist about C's behaviour, which was causing problems for all of us. We used to see this lady on a regular basis and our meetings were helpful.

One day at the end of our session she, quite unexpectedly, asked W if it would be all right to see me individually next session. Little did I know that I was to spend the whole hour talking about my sexuality. The psychiatrist had sussed me out!

Wow! How did that feel?

I liked and respected the therapist enormously and, though initially shocked when she 'sussed' me, felt greatly relieved to unburden myself. I remember feeling liberated that I could talk to someone so candidly about my sexuality. She was very supportive and completely non-judgmental. She suggested I'd be a lot happier if I found some gay friends and went out more. She assured me that she wouldn't bring up the contents of this session at our next one all together and that it was entirely up to me to raise the subject when I felt like it.

I wasn't going to divulge anything and don't recall clearly how that session went but it all came out towards the end, which was also the end of our work with the therapist. W found it extremely difficult, feeling understandably betrayed, shocked and outraged. I think she also felt ambushed. Well, the shit hit the fan the next morning. (W has this habit of sitting on things for 24 hours).

We were going on a family holiday a few days later and everything was booked. W came into the kitchen and exclaimed that we couldn't possibly go now and she needed time to reconsider everything. I remember pleading with her and asking her to reconsider cancelling the holiday. All I could think of was how disappointed the boys would be. It was a very tense and awkward exchange. The whole situation between us seemed to have changed dramatically in a very short space of time. I feared our marriage was over.

Were you both in shock?

As is her way, after a whole day's suffering, my wife announced that she could handle the new situation and was willing to carry on with the holiday. I was SO relieved! But it seemed then, and still does, that she now held all the strings. She alone had the power to decide whether or not the family holiday would go ahead. It seemed like the declaration of my sexuality could seriously backfire on me and indeed punish me, in that I would be deprived of our time with the boys.

Do you know how or why you gave – and give - your wife all the power in the relationship?

In retrospect I think I learnt at this stage that declaring my sexuality wasn't going to be a good thing. It was loaded with risk, so perhaps it was wiser to keep it a secret if the consequences of declaring it were going to be dire. And so my life carried on.

Being a father was enormously difficult for me in the early days. With the arrival of a maternity nurse soon after the birth of our first son, I felt my role had been completely hijacked. Right up until then I'd been totally involved, attending NCT classes[142], reading and educating myself, attending every antenatal appointment, helping prepare the baby's room. Out of the blue I learned that a maternity nurse, paid for by my wife's father with no consultation with me, had been employed to live with us and look after the baby for the first weeks. I was outraged!

I felt emasculated. My mother had emasculated me growing up, being so strong and dominant a woman. She wouldn't close the door while on the loo, or would sunbathe with her top off, ignoring me as if I wasn't male. At church she'd run her hands up and down my thighs in her soft leather gloves. What the hell did my dad – or my brothers think – sitting right next to us? I loved it but... All her confessions to me, such as about the details of her 'change of life', were so wrong. She'd say how her friends thought I was so marvellous to listen to all her private things.

Doesn't this say something about her relationship with your father? You became a sort of surrogate partner?

Absolutely. I don't think she had affairs but she flirted with other men, was much sought after. It just wasn't appropriate to tell me: I was a teenager.

---

[142] NCT classes: Natural Childbirth Trust classes for parents to be.

So your mother trained you to prioritise her needs and wants over your own and here is your wife doing that, with everything about the wedding and your children's births decided by her.

Her father was castrating me with his money by paying for everything with no discussion with me. In retrospect I should have stood up for myself, been firmer that I didn't want this nurse around, but then I felt I wasn't the one having the baby and maybe my wife didn't have the confidence to be a mother. I recall clearly collecting my wife and first son from hospital and all three of us sleeping in one bed and how wonderful and scary that was.

The next day the maternity nurse arrived and kept the baby in her room all night, bringing him to my wife only for feeding. In the daytime she'd be off on long walks with him. The whole situation was unreal. I remember going to my studio, feeling how strange it all was. And, as if we hadn't learned our lesson this first time, she returned for our second son. God, I feel so embarrassed writing this. Why didn't I stand up for myself?

I guess you'd been well trained to have no contact with your needs, but to put the wishes of others first?

That's it. I'd been so used to being taken over by my mother that I was out of touch with what I wanted. I think W couldn't stand up to her own sisters and her father, so she complied with whatever they decided. I felt so low in self-esteem; I'd accept their rules, however unwillingly.

Not an auspicious start to parenting together as partners?

No, I found the boys' early years very challenging. W was, and remains, always wedded to her work. I was only working two days a week so had the boys alone a lot when I wasn't teaching. At times I really couldn't manage: I remember ringing helplines sometimes. I knew no other men in my position. In retrospect I was alone too much and totally unsupported.

The younger one used to have the most terrible tantrums that I didn't know at all how to deal with. There were times I felt completely impotent. I used to lose my temper a lot, shouting and sometimes hitting the boys I am now ashamed to say. What returns to mind are horrendous Sunday suppers at the kitchen table – they were farcical yet I insisted on continuing them. I remember train journeys when the boys just kicked each other under the table, with me always having this feeling of impotence to stop something, to arrest it, to take control, undermining my confidence – 'I am a useless father.'

At school we had two 'out Sundays' a term and couldn't get home so the parents would come and we'd go to a hotel for lunch. My mum used to fill the mini with sweets. This reminds me of the times when I'd pick the boys up at school and try so hard to get it all right and it never seemed to be and was so painful. I had no experience of being parented daily or of proper family life.

Did you have a nanny yourself?

Yes, I completely adored her. She lived on our farm and being the youngest, I spent a lot of time with her while my parents were away with their racehorses. First thing I'd do when arriving home from boarding school was to go on my bike to talk with her. The wonderful thing was she sat and listened to me.

Coming Out 2

My next experience of coming out concerned my collection of gay mags[143] that I had stashed away in a hiding place in my bedroom. One

---

[143] Gay mags: gay oriented porn magazines found in shops at the time called 'Books and Mags', a vital part of gay & bi men's lives before the Internet.

day, fancying a wank, I went to my secret place but, alas, no magazines! I thought perhaps I had forgotten that I'd moved them so continued looking everywhere. No luck! I began to grow quite panicky: where had they gone? Or, indeed, who had moved them? All sorts of fantasises arose. Had my sons found them, had my wife? Had the workmen, who had recently worked on our house, and were they going to use them as blackmail?

Eventually I decided to take the plunge and explained my predicament to my wife. She hadn't seen them or moved them, why not try looking again. When I did I found them straight away. Had I created this situation to remind W of my sexuality? Now she knew I kept a stash of gay magazines for masturbation purposes. Perhaps she knew anyway and it was no surprise to her. Indeed, she didn't appear shocked, disturbed or surprised. It was as if we were discussing what we were going to eat for supper.

What does this mean: there was nothing left to declare?

Not long after this my dad's cousin died – he was an artist and gay – and his partner invited me to their home to see if I wanted anything from his studio. This visit resulted in my declaring my sexuality to J after he enquired about the state of my marriage. I think he also had his suspicions.

Consequently I returned to London armed with new gay mags and artists materials. Following this, I placed an ad in a mature gay gentlemen's publication because my friend told me I would have much more chance realistically, of meeting an older man. This advert got at least half a dozen replies, which I duly followed up. This was all new territory for me. The first guy I met for coffee and didn't see again. Another guy invited me to lunch at his place and, looking back, I am shocked by the risk I took in going to the house of someone I'd never met before.

Has gay sex been closely associated with risk for you?

He picked me up at the tube and took me back to the house where he'd cooked a meal. The place gave me the creeps a bit. Downstairs was all shuttered up apart from the kitchen. We had drinks on the patio, then the meal, then sex. I was relieved when the time came to be driven back. Anything could have happened in that house!

A similar experience took place another time when I was asked to lunch again only this time there was no sex, only a pat on the bum! I cannot imagine doing any of this nowadays and don't know where I got the energy and inspiration from fifteen years ago. Maybe my desire was the driving force?

I didn't fancy any of these guys. Because of the nature of the magazine they were all quite elderly. Finally I visited a guy in Ealing where I had tea. He turned out to be an ex trolly-dolly![144] He was retired and had started art classes so he was delighted that I was an artist. He showed me all his work, which seemed to take forever, and we decided to meet again when I returned from a trip to Cornwall.

I went to supper and we ended up in his bed. I continued to see him for two or three years, usually for supper on a Saturday night. I had to become very inventive about making excuses for going out but, strangely, found this quite easy. The nights with A became predictable. He always cooked the same meal – very airline – prawn cocktails and steak – and a bought pudding! The table was always beautifully laid. As I had to catch the last train the evening was quite fraught because we were against the clock. Drinks, dinner, sex and out of the door by 10.30! He offered me Amyl Nitrate[145], which gave me

---

[144] 'Trolly-dolly': Polari (secret gay language) term for male flight attendant.

[145] Amyl Nitrite, or 'poppers': chemical nitrites inhaled for recreational purposes - relaxes involuntary muscles, opens blood vessels, causing a 'rush', especially as an aphrodisiac. Isopropyl nitrite became popular due to a ban on isobutyl nitrite in the EU in 2007. More rarely sold is the compound, butyl nitrite. Part of club

the most amazing orgasms.

What a gamble I was taking! Would my mission be over in time to collect two dependent little boys from school? The clash of my contrasting worlds! I guess this ties up with the theme of danger and sex. Would I be found out, would I be trapped in a stranger's house, which almost happened? I took enormous risks because I was so naïve.

A became fed up with me always having to rush for the last train. One time I did stay the night when W had gone away with the boys. I had such a disturbed night and felt so uncomfortable waking next to him in his bed that I couldn't wait to get home. After this we met less and less.

One thing A used to do which really irritated me was to select clothes for me from an Oxfam shop where he volunteered. I would have to go through nightmare rigmarole of trying them all on as soon as I arrived. Once I put the whole lot in a dustbin. I felt that by clothing me, he was trying to get closer or even to own me. I found it quite creepy that he would be thinking about me while he was working, selecting things for me. Having said all this there were one or two garments I enjoyed wearing, despite the associations.

I am struck again at this point, Robert, by the association of sex and gayness set alongside a real disconnectedness from affection, warmth, loving even. It seems that, as with D, 'closeness' feels threatening – like you are being taken over by the other.

This is the big dilemma in my life – wanting an intimate relationship yet running a mile when it's offered. I yearn for closeness but think that, if someone gets too close, they'll find out stuff about me they don't like.

---

culture: the 1970s to 1980s disco scene and the 1990s rave scene made their use popular.

What of the future - for you, for your marriage, for your self-expression and satisfaction with your life?

Reading back over my story, it appears that there were several opportunities to 'come out' that I either missed or failed to take advantage of. If I had capitalised on those opportunities, I wonder what my life would be like now. I think back to when I returned from New York and told friends of my encounter with D: was I not telling them I was gay? I recall that it seemed more important telling them this than how many designs I'd sold! I remember keeping it up my sleeve as a card to play as if it would make me a more interesting person. I don't recall anyone being particularly surprised or shocked.

Returning to London, everything that had been so exciting and liberating just seemed to vanish. I had no gay friends and therefore no one on whom to model myself, or to talk to. Up until that point my sexual life had been so barren: I'd never gone out with anyone or had sex with anyone and all my friendships were platonic. Basically, not knowing what to do with my newfound sexuality, I brought the lid back down and went into retreat. It felt like my encounters with D were isolated incidents, never to be repeated. Why didn't I carry on where I'd left off in New York?

The future

Since turning sixty recently, I have felt differently about life, seeing myself as perhaps only having one more decade left to 'play'. By 'play' I suppose I mean to see where I can go with my gay side. At the same time I worry and grow increasingly anxious about the idea of growing old with W, especially with our sons gone from home.

Basically I don't want to grow old and look back on my life with regrets of a life unfulfilled sexually, emotionally and creatively. So, recently I have taken steps to try to meet someone by joining a gay social site and I have met two guys so far. One I've met up with twice to go to exhibitions: I enjoy being in his company very much.

My dilemma is that I don't want to leave W for a big empty hole. I feel I'm too old to start again on my own. But I have to remind myself that it wouldn't be the same loneliness as before, simply because I do now have a family.

Meanwhile, I am trying to put my energy into the next phase of my life. I recently took voluntary redundancy from the job I've had for twenty-three years. I feel excited and scared. Excited because I have brought about change: scared because I am uncertain of the future. My aim is to make myself do activities I find uncomfortable and that I will have to muster a bit of courage to tackle. I am determined not to stagnate. I have learned how important it is to have creative pursuits outside home and joining a local drama group has paid dividends. When I participate in a drama class, I feel I can let go and be anybody - how good that is. It's amazing to have an arena in which I can do anything (almost) and not be judged.

I do realise that, for so much of my life I have been, am still too much, my own prisoner. For example, within the confines of my home I hardly express myself at all, so my family only experience a one-dimensional person, which is not only harmful to me, but to them as well, because I am denying them the full, rounded Robert, too. I made a decision somewhere along the road that I was only allowed to be a certain person at home - it is very hard to change that after so many years.

CHARLES'S STORY

Introduction to Charles

Having worked for more than five years on this book with the nine other men whose stories precede this one, I was struck by the importance – and the courage – of their 'coming out' again in this way. I felt I wanted to examine and tell my own story along similar lines, to 'turn the tables' – or the therapist's chair at least – upon myself. I have therefore included my story in the same format as the others, as if interviewing myself, in order to emphasise and to honour the equality of each of our unique journeys. I hope this contributes to the richness of the book.

* * *

My story is about an unusual, if dysfunctional, upbringing in which I was always different from those around me and needed to develop my own values, my own moral compass. It's especially interesting that, once mostly freed from the original oppressions of school, home, media and environment and reborn, as it were, into a 1960s London melting pot as a young adult, I was able to experience my polyamorous, fluid sexuality as natural, as Freud intimated that most of us would if released from our societal chains. Then I re-formed myself almost twenty years later in a similar melting pot and came out somewhat differently but with my original self intact.

This sense of difference is hugely significant and comes to the fore repeatedly throughout this book, as it does through the life stories of many people whose experience of their own sex and gender made it difficult for them to fulfil cultural expectations of being properly a boy, or male in acceptable ways. The work of Judy Grahn[146] – for the longer historical body – and Mark Thompson's books, 'Gay Soul', 'Gay Spirit' and 'Gay Body'[147] as well as those by Mitch Walker[148] give us deeper understandings and often forgotten background for this important distinction.

Mine is a story of engagement with the inner and outer processes of life: an organic and developmental story of growing and of contrasting seasons. Eschewing rules, norms, other people's judgements, categories or predetermination seems to have been my life's work. In some ways this is an accidental benefit of lax parental guidance and poor education. There are so many ways of being ourselves, living our selves, why do we often allow them to be so limited – or determined by others?

One interesting dimension in my story is that it's not sexuality or gender which is the main source of my anxiety, insecurity or low self-value, but my earliest experiences of family and the lack of safety, lack of nurture or feedback which left me so painfully fearful and alone as a child. Under such circumstances, one might have expected a different sexuality to be further undermining but I have experienced it mainly just as another aspect of my difference. This is not to say, however, that I didn't experience shame and doubt about my desires all through my early years.

Loss of a brotherly love is significant here as in some other stories, as well as lack of a father's love and an unstable, chaotic home life.

---

[146] Grahn: 'Another Mother Tongue.' Op.cit.

[147] Mark Thompson: http://www.markthompsongayspirit.com

[148] Mitch Walker: radical gay activist, author, Jungian psychologist based in Los Angeles. See: www.uranianpsych.org

Some recent research shows this latter factor to be disproportionally present in the early lives of gay and bi men: it will be fascinating to discover what the connection, if any, could possibly be.

It appears that I have moved between male and female attractions and loves without difficulties, choosing when necessary on the basis of my heart and the quality of my relationship with a particular person. Sexual and intimate connections were mutually made and enjoyed, mostly without comparisons or off-the-peg prescriptions for their worth. I have come to appreciate that this flexible sexuality relies upon having a strong sense of individual morality, feeling solid with one's own beliefs and values. This is not, however, the whole story and there were times, especially several years in my early adulthood before I married, when I became overwhelmed by confusing desires and relationships.

Nevertheless, working in the field of human sexualities and gender identities, as I have for more than twenty-five years, I am optimistic that the transcending of categories will increase further with time and that the truly magical diversity of human sexual and relational experience and expression will be allowed to flourish.

The work we are doing at Pink Therapy[149] presently is all in these directions, changing our 'remit' recently, for example, from the somewhat limited 'LGBT' designation of the 1970s to the much more inclusive term, 'Gender and Sexual Diversity' (GSD) to incorporate asexualities, kink identities,[150] intersexualities[151], gender-bending[152]

---

[149] Pink Therapy: the largest independent training and therapy organisation in the UK working with sexualities and genders in non-pathologising ways. More details in 'Resources: Finding good therapy' section. See: www.pinktherapy.com

[150] Kink: the term derives from the idea of a "bend" ("kink") in one's sexual behaviour, in contrast with 'straight' or 'narrow' sexual mores. Kink practices (cf.BDSM) go beyond those usually considered conventional as a means of heightening the intimacy between sexual partners. See: https://ncsfreedom.org

and many others. Language is vital in shaping and reflecting developments in thinking. Behaving also needs to fit.

This is a story of two great loves in my life, one with a woman and one with a man – along with a wide range of other relationships over time – all experiences which generated great gains, whatever heartaches were also involved. Personal connection overrode gender in these instances. I have considered myself bisexual, straight or gay mostly according to lived experience at any one time. If language were more accurate, I might have described myself as 'gaying', 'bi-ing' or 'hetting'! I do, on the other hand, acknowledge a profound, deeply existential sense of myself as 'different' – a candidate for 'outrider', 'scout' or 'medicine man' maybe in other cultures, other tribes. Wanting, like everyone, to belong and be connected with my tribe – actually, various tribes – and feeling very deep commitment to them, I have at the same time kept a part of myself on the edge, fearing to be subsumed.

Like Bruce, Alex, Nigel and others, I have 'turned my life around' with the help of good, affirmative therapy and group work and I highly recommend others to seek such support. It is so important that, when we are in pain or struggle and summon up the courage to reach out, we find the right kind of help. We are more vulnerable than ever at these times and there are dangers in wrong choices. I imagine that many people reading this book will be in such a struggle

---

[151] Intersexualities: People whose five sex characteristics - chromosomes, gonads, hormones, internal reproductive anatomy and/or external genitalia - are not all typically male or female. See: http://www.ukia.co.uk

[152] Gender-bending: Term referring to transgressing, or 'bending', expected gender roles; sometimes a form of social activism in response to assumptions or generalisations about genders. Some gender-benders do identify with the gender they were assigned at birth yet challenge the norms of that gender through atypical behaviour and appearance. Also known as 'gender-fucking.'

themselves and feel confused as to where to get the help they need. It is vital to go to safe places for appropriate support and advice, as discussed in the Resources section on 'Finding good therapy' at the end of this book.

Informal social support is also crucial and no one can come out fully and successfully without connecting with 'allies' – others who know about your struggle, who are further along the path or who simply accept your fears, conflicts and ambivalence without judgement or agendas whatever their own sexuality may be.

CHARLES'S STORY

I think it's pivotal that my first real experience of 'gayness' was in a delightful, loving, domestic setting when the famous choreographer, John Cranko[153] and his partner moved into a house a few doors from ours when I was about four and I became their 'house child', as it were: an adored and encouraged, sensitive, blonde boy desperate for adult affection and stimulus missing at home. I put all sorts of treasured things in my life since then down to their gift in taking me into their sparkling and brilliant household filled with music, colour, fruit, flowers and fascinating people. I'd started already somehow, inexplicably, to 'talk posh' in contrast with my own family's London accents, but my identification with this male couple must have influenced my early determination to live a life much more like theirs than like that of my family of origin, and contributed to an internal drive to survive the threats which surrounded me and somehow become free of the cultural scripts and expectations to which I was subject.

How did you relate to other males growing up? What did you learn about maleness?

Men and boys were always frightening and desirable in equal measure as well as somewhat alien. My father was an uneducated, alcoholic and violent man who tyrannised our isolated, impoverished London

---

[153] John Cranko: (1927 – 1973) South African choreographer with Sadler's Wells Ballet, later the Royal Ballet, and Founder of Stuttgart Ballet.

family. I was mostly terrified of his presence and rage, especially physically. I tried from an early age to use my intellect to transcend this fear – even studying Gandhi's methods of non-violence and passive resistance as a young boy – but it has, in fact, remained in my body for life and expressed itself through a range of psychological and physical symptoms. My father and I made no real connection at all otherwise – he was often unable to recall my name – and one effect of this has been, at best, a fierce independence in me and, at worst, great difficulty in entrusting myself to be cared for, or guided by, others or to accept leaders or mentors.

My half-brother, six years older than me, was mostly absent in my memory until I was thirteen or so, then he became very powerfully present while sharing my bedroom. A physical, muscular, manly, swimmer's body in the next bed! I don't remember us holding or touching one another except when he sneaked in and caught me while I was 'holding court' to imaginary friends beneath the blankets at night and he'd pretend to be Dracula suffocating me and scare the life out of me.

I do remember his beauty and its effect on me, his attractiveness to women as well as an enviable ability to be one of 'the lads', which I never managed. Because of the frightening circumstances of our lives growing up, and the different impact from, and responses to, these in each of us, he and I did not manage to bond in ways I found satisfying, so I have always lived with a great loss – an internal sense of a brother's absence – and longed for a brotherly presence. I have a sensitive and warm-hearted brother but it's always been very hard for us to find ways to truly connect. Now that he is struggling with multiple cancers, we are enjoying easier connection than previously and that's a curative pleasure.

Another, much younger, brother died in infancy from pneumonia and encephalitis when I was about eight or nine only to compound the wider feeling of loss.

Men were generally tough and 'hard', without sensitivity or imagination, without kindness or any soft aspect, difficult to love or to get any love from. They were physically competent doers who had impact, being organised to get what they wanted. There were no other significant adult males in my environment growing up, except now and then for some gangster uncles, a few teachers and some foster parents. They were not interested in arts or aesthetics on the whole or in philosophy, books or nature, ideas or emotions: all my own major preoccupations then and since. At school and in the neighbourhood I was therefore never one of their number and, by the time of secondary school, felt like an honorary girl of some sort, afraid of most of my peers. I hung out with the senior girls at school and on the whole avoided the company, often hostile, of other boys.

Queer boys then were 'queens'! Perhaps that's why I flirted for a time with very 'feminine' looks: make up, long hair, jewellery and gorgeous fabrics, almost dresses. It's scary now to think how young I was when I was going to secret Soho[154] bars dressed like this alone – having changed in the phone box near my home – to try to work myself out from others' responses; how vulnerable I was to exploitation.

I always felt physically – and sexually – inferior to other boys and, later, to other men. I was tall and very skinny, pale, prone to accidents and illness, inhibited, uncoordinated and nervous. I couldn't catch a ball and was scared of getting hurt. I developed an acute self-hatred about my body early on and acted this out at times in masochistic rituals of flagellation or inflicting pain. Male bodies mesmerised me. I am still cowed and at the same time fascinated by other men's physical skill, ease, grace, potency and playfulness.

It saddens me today that I never appreciated the ways in which I was physically or otherwise attractive and couldn't allow compliments

---

[154] Soho: Central London district famous for nightlife, sex and bars.

to sink in. Ironic then – or maybe not – that I became a successful photographic model when I was sixteen with my version of the 'new look': androgynous, intense and 'wasted' long before punks. This actually made me attractive to males and females who had an 'alternative' bent.

I can still find all-male environments scary and avoid them. However, doing 'men's work'[155], participating in male therapy groups, going to gay clubs and working with a lot of men myself has changed this anxiety and discomfort. Actively fathering three boys, two of whom are now adults, and having the daily, permanent example of my own loving male partner, I have latterly come to immensely value ways in which I now see that it is possible to be masculine individually and with each other. I am happy to have wide-ranging, excellent, reciprocal friendships nowadays with men who are gay, straight and bi.

And what of your relationships with females and your learning about them?

---

[155] Men's work: deriving largely from the legacy of the men's movement, which consisted of networks of men involved in activities relating to men and gender in the late 1960s and 1970s alongside, and often in response to, the women's movement and feminism. Though they share many hallmarks of therapeutic, self-help groups, men's movement groups increasingly view personal growth and better relations with other men as useless without accompanying shifts in social relations and ideologies that support or marginalise different ways of being men. More feminist male activists are concerned with deconstructing male identity and masculinities. Taking a cue from early feminist critiques of traditional female gender roles, the men's liberation movement uses the language of sex role theory to argue that male roles are similarly restrictive and damaging to men. Some 'men's liberationists' have disingenuously decontextualised gender relations to argue that, as gender roles are equally harmful to women and men, both are equally oppressed!

My elder sister died just before my birth. I spent decades not properly knowing about that or understanding the impact on our family dynamics or on me. My younger sister was born a year and a half after me and I found it easy to love, and want to protect, her except during her own teenage rebellion when she became as tough and unavailable as the men around her in order not to be put down by them. She and I accompanied each other through most of the horrible tribulations of our childhood: at foster homes, children's homes, boarding schools and on the rough streets of central London in the fifties and sixties. Our relationship remains strong and very loving as a result. She was as much criticised for being a 'tomboy' (or boyish) as I was for being too 'girlie'[156]: maybe we both over-identified with the parent we most needed to make contact with? We remain companions still as well as close witnesses and comforts to one another in our present lives.

My mother is, without doubt, the most formative model in my life. A sweet and loving soul, naturally warm and bright, fun and good at bonding, she led a sadly deprived and difficult life of consistent suffering right up to the end. She mixed martyr qualities with an indomitable spirit, an incredible capacity to endure and survive. I was always formed around wanting life to be better for her and, mostly, felt powerless to make it so. This has profoundly affected my relationships with others, especially women, my political activism and even my professions as a teacher of disenfranchised people and a psychotherapist specialising in work with clients from persecuted minorities.

Since childhood I have thus found relating to girls and women easier than to males. I hung out with girls at secondary school, feeling ostracised by boys and, I now see, separating myself from them in

---

[156] These are some of the means by which the enactment of 'gender' in prescribed ways is policed eventually even by our children. This often has nothing to do with sexuality, in fact, but harms the free expression and relationships of us all.

order to avoid further hurt and failure. The huge majority of my friends and colleagues have been female. I think this is due to social factors affecting gender, too, such as the way girls are encouraged to focus on relational and emotional aspects of life and boys on activities and competition. My work and interests have been, for the most part, those ascribed to females in this society.

The women around me were mostly poor, hard working, working-class, struggling hard in post-war Britain to build decent lives and homes for their children and to find some pleasure. I saw women as copers, organisers, the ones who held everything together and cared for men and children. They weren't soft, glamorous or soppy as in movies, but tough and resilient. They were badly treated despite this, with low status. They were practical and realistic, not sensual: bodies were functional, not sources of pleasure. Bathing, for example, held no sensual aspects, especially in a shared metal bath once a week or an unheated bathroom shared by four families. Although there was some 'rude' or flirty badinage sometimes between women and with, or about, men, I never got the impression that sex was much to write home about.

I was 'taken up' by several women teachers as a talented, bright boy in need of extra encouragement, introduced to art, politics, music, culture and education, even to the extent of staying with them at their homes (no 'child protection' then!) I also made some important connections with strong women through politics: amazing former suffragettes, vegetarians, naturists, communist leaders and campaigners who became 'midwives' in my development in ways I have, sadly, rarely allowed men to be. I have, I realise appreciatively, never been abused by a woman.

My girlfriends were of a great variety: working class at first, they and their families a bit bemused by me; later middle-class and more interested. I had good intellectual connections with several of them and lighter, fun connections with others; dancing, clothes, clubs, politics, emotional chatter, men. I always lacked the confidence to ask, so they always made the running, took the romantic – even the sexual –initiative. I took pleasure in their loving warmth, their bodies, in sexual connection, in domesticity, sharing inner worlds of thoughts and feelings, in being romantic, sensual, soft, kind, providing, care-taking. I suppose, to be honest and with retrospect, women have been mainly my sisters, sometimes aspects of a mother and, less frequently, truly my lovers.

It's been harder to find connections with which to bond male to male. Interestingly, one of the outcomes of this for me, as for many bi and gay men, is to make sex into that bond, that currency. Indeed, in gay male subcultures, the irony is that it is sometimes hard to find relational, affectionate connections between men that are not sexual. Between male lovers this can be a problem over the longer term when it's difficult for either man to take adequate account of internal or relational matters.

How and when did you become aware of being 'different' sexually?

In so many ways I always felt 'different': to the rest of my family, to the kids I was growing up with and found so hard to relate to, or be liked by, to how boys were meant to be, to the expectations, life scripts and opportunities presented by my class, my subculture, my inadequate schools. Different in every possible way! I became a communist and a pacifist in my early teens and spent all my time campaigning for CND[157], against apartheid and fascism, learning about art and literature, designing things. None of my available peers were doing this. My 'queerness', first labelled by hostile others before I

---

[157] CND: The Campaign for Nuclear Disarmament, started in 1957 to campaign for unilateral nuclear disarmament in the UK and tighter international controls on nuclear and other weapons..

was sexually aware, became merely another strand – possibly even an explanation – for such differences. It went some way to explain the constant physical and verbal bullying I experienced everywhere growing up.

My first romantic love was when I was five and a new boy's father asked if I'd take care of him as I'd been at the school a term already: he had slightly olive skin, jet black hair, incredibly long black eyelashes and was Italian: the beginning of a lifelong love of that country and its people for me. I adored him and was so happy to have him to look after and to be my loyal companion for many years until we went to different secondary schools.

Can you recall your early sexual experiences?

I actually cannot remember what my first sexual experience was and maybe that's just as well, given how unprotected I was. At primary school I remember seeking children out for naughty games, often of my invention, involving showing our 'willies' or getting naked under one pretext or another (cf. Alan). At children's homes and boarding schools a bit later there were numerous experiments with bodies shared with boys and girls together. My fertile imagination seemed to be the source of much of this as well as other kinds of play. I do remember persuading a group of kids in one children's home to capture others in the woods where we played freely and drag them as prisoners to our camp where I was arraigned as a formidable leader, who demanded naked supplication whilst wielding birch branches. Were these early experiments with BDSM[158] or an attempt to garner

---

[158] BDSM: term from 1969 for a variety of erotic practices involving dominance & submission, role-play, restraint and other interpersonal dynamics. People who don't consider themselves as practicing BDSM may engage in a range of these, so that inclusion in a 'BDSM community' or subculture depends on self-identification and shared experience. Interest in BDSM ranges from one time

stature and power somehow?

I also remember being 'touched up'[159] regularly at around eight or nine by a male shopkeeper locally, being sexually assaulted by older children and a couple of adults as a young child and then by a male teacher in the first few years of secondary school. Two of us were chosen to stay behind for treats, to go into the technical drawing stock-room and pull our shorts down or his trousers – originally to be amazed at his scars from a shell in the war! I was oppressed enough by then to have internalised the idea that I caused the abuse in some way simply by being me and somehow giving out the wrong signals. Of course, through shame, the other boy and I never told anyone at all, or even spoke together about what we were doing.

I discovered cruising at 'The Biograph'[160] cinema by accident when I was ten or so and men started playing sexually in the dark. Only years later did I discover that this place was a gay landmark. I was always passive and quite mesmerised rather than taking any initiative: scared and fascinated at once. The same is true of encounters at the

---

experiment to a lifestyle, and there is discussion over whether BDSM or kink (op.cit.) sexual identity constitutes a form of sexual orientation or not. See Resources section for links.

[159] 'Touched up': vernacular phrase for inappropriate sexual touching.

[160] 'The Biograph': Britain's first cinema, opened as the Electric Theatre in May 1909 in Wilton Road, London. By the 1960s it was still doing great business, mainly because it had become a gay meeting place. The tabloid 'News of the World' had banner headlines, 'Close Down this Cinema of Vice' with a description of scandalous events, with constant moving by the audience and frequent visits to the gent's toilet. Despite this exposé nothing much changed apart from the appointment of a 'bouncer' and films being played with lights on. Great double bills continued, men continued to cruise and the occasional 'tourist', lured in by the programme, would complain to have their money refunded or else settle in. The Biograph eventually became the only operating cinema in the Victoria area. Closed now.

many 'cottages'[161] around Victoria Station when I was a young teenager. Despite being chosen frequently for sex by strangers, I managed to remain very insecure about my body, desirability or sexual prowess for most of my life and think now that my bodily fearfulness had a huge impact on this. It always seemed that more powerful others, adults at first but later even my peers, determined what happened, when and how, knew what they wanted and how to get it, and that I merely had to conform and be grateful in some sense for having been selected. At the same time I was acutely ashamed that I was.

I had regular, almost daily, sex in a compartment on the short train journey to school with a male commuter by the time I was sixteen. This was terribly exciting, partly because of the danger of discovery by my school-mates when they boarded the train a little later, partly having a 'real' man evidently so attracted to me, all to myself in a private space and more than once – an embryonic gay relationship.

Gay sex was, of course, illegal at the time and I was acutely aware of that. Before 1967[162] the atmosphere I remember is one of tangible fear and mystery. There were frequent cause célèbres like Gielgud[163],

---

[161] 'Cottages': not cute thatched homes but public toilets, magazine shops and dark byways in which men and boys would meet for sex with strangers at a time when being gay was illegal and making contact with other men difficult.

[162] 1967. Change in UK law regarding homosexuality following the Wolfenden Report of 1957 partly influenced by the Montagu scandal (footnote 19 below)

[163] Sir John Gielgud: 1904 – 2000, British Shakespearean actor, director and producer. Shortly after he was knighted in 1953, Gielgud was convicted of "importuning for immoral purposes" (cottaging) having been arrested trying to pick up a man in a public lavatory. Deeply humiliated, Gielgud avoided Hollywood for over a decade for fear of being denied entry. There was discussion about whether his career could endure the ignominy but, instead of being rejected by the public, he received a standing ovation at the opening of his

Montagu[164], film stars and so on when the whole country seemed to bray and hiss and call for sacrifice. I saw it all over my father's 'News of the World'[165] every Sunday and, again, was scared and gripped equally! Maybe this is why I developed my lifelong fascination for Oscar Wilde and his 'passion'[166]. This lust for scandal came very close to home when Cranko's house, my sanctuary, became part of the

---

next play in Liverpool, partly because of the support of his popular co-star, Dame Sybil Thorndike.

[164] Lord Montagu: (b.1926) Tory politician tried for offences against boy scouts after which a witch-hunt was unleashed. Acquitted, Montagu was convicted of homosexual offences in 1954 with journalist Peter Wildeblood and landowner Michael Pitt-Rivers in a case that made headlines around the world and scandalised 'high society'. During the trial, Wildeblood dramatically admitted being gay, one of the first British men to make a public declaration while homosexuality was an offence carrying a maximum life sentence. Although he denied allegations of sex with a male nurse, Wildeblood's admission convinced the all-male jury to find the trio guilty. Wildeblood and Pitt-Rivers were jailed for 18 months. When the three were led out to start their sentences, the crowd burst into applause, mirroring sympathy for them across the country and outcry over the length of their sentences. Montagu always denied the charges. He did come out later as bisexual and to mark the 40th anniversary of homosexuality being decriminalised, he took part in a documentary about the case and its aftermath, 'A Very British Sex Scandal', broadcast on Channel 4 TV in July 2007.

[165] 'News of the World': vile bestselling tabloid newspaper in Britain from 1843 to 2011, when it was closed due to a telephone hacking and bribery scandal.

[166] "Oscar Wilde's passion" or "the love that dare not speak its name": From the poem, 'Two Loves' (1894) by Lord Alfred Douglas, with whom the brilliant author & playwright became besotted. Mentioned at Wilde's indecency trial, it is usually interpreted as a euphemism for homosexuality. Wilde regarded his rise and fall as a Christ-like 'passion'– described in his long prose poem to Douglas from prison, 'De Profundis' (1897).

Profumo affair[167] once it was identified as one of the venues at which Stephen Ward[168], Christine Keeler and others mixed with members of the aristocracy and royal family, crooks and prostitutes. I remember feeling personally implicated although I was just fifteen by then - and I remember how much I wanted to be.

We had a neighbour who was friendly with my mum, who was camp and sweet, a musician I think. His being 'that way', 'like that' or 'one of them' came up often in comments between locals or rows between my mum and dad. I feared even then that I was the same. Of course television, which was new to us, gave terrible examples, too: Liberace[169] and Danny La Rue[170] were spectacular in denial, whereas

---

[167] Profumo affair: 1963 British political scandal named after John Profumo, Secretary of State for War. His affair with Christine Keeler, reputed mistress of an alleged Soviet spy, followed by lying in the House of Commons when questioned about it, forced the resignation of Profumo and damaged the reputation of Harold Macmillan's government, leading soon afterwards to its collapse.

[168] Stephen Ward: (1912 – 1963): osteopath and artist, notorious as a central figure in the 1963 Profumo affair (op.cit.) Ward introduced the married cabinet minister and MP, Profumo, to 'showgirl' Christine Keeler at a house party at Lord Astor's stately home, Cliveden in the summer of 1961 with fatal consequences. (Ward killed himself just before a trial) See: 'Scandal' 1989 film of the affair based on 1987 Anthony Summers' book, 'Honeytrap.' Also Lloyd Webber's 2014 musical 'Stephen Ward.'

[169] Valentino Liberace: (1919 – 1987) world-renowned American pianist and vocalist, whose career spanned four decades of concerts, recordings, cinema and television. During the 1950s–1970s he was the highest-paid entertainer in the world and embraced a lifestyle of flamboyant excess both on and off the stage, whilst denying his homosexuality publically. A multi-award-winning Steven Sodenburgh 2013 film about his extravagant life and love affair with Scott Thorson, 'Behind the Candelabra' starred Matt Damon and Michael Douglas.

Frankie Howerd[171] and Kenneth Williams[172] were a lot more fun. All were pretty scary consequences, however, to a growing boy, of being 'one of the Wilde sort'.

I wore make up sometimes, pan stick and eyeliner, long hair and chunky rings and had girlfriends at school make me clothes from Liberty oddments – floral or paisley ties and shirts and the lowest hipsters you can imagine staying up. My headmaster at my last school waited for me at the gate and banished me from the premises saying, "This school is not a brothel!" I was only interested in Art for Art's sake and Literature and refused to take part in any other curricula, especially 'games' which I eventually gained permission not to attend through a campaign lasting several years and costing me dear. I had so many serious accidents when forced to 'play'– team games, gymnastics, sports days and so on – that I was finally begged not to return and spent every Wednesday morning while the rest of the school 'did games' doing just what I pleased around all the London art galleries.

What about sexual and romantic relationships as you grew older?

My first 'partner' combining a romantic with a partially erotic connection was R at a children's home ostensibly run by her alcoholic

---

[170] Danny La Rue:(1927 – 2009) an Irish entertainer known for his extravagant singing and drag impersonations on British stages and television who always denied his homosexuality publicly.

[171] Frankie Howerd: (1917 - 1992): camp English comedian and comic actor whose career was described by a friend as "a series of comebacks."

[172] Kenneth Williams: (1926 – 1988) British comic actor and comedian. One of the main ensemble in 26 of the camp 'Carry On' films, he appeared in numerous television and radio shows, especially the outrageous 'Round The Horne' radio series which delighted those in the know (gay listeners) with its clever use of innuendo and 'Polari' - a secretive gay slang of the times.

mother. We would drag her bed into the tree house and sleep together overnight entwined, kissing and cuddling, stroking and soothing one another – we were both extremely wounded – but never more than that. I was around twelve and she eleven by then.

Next came TC through our joint political campaigning in the West End of London in the evenings and at weekends. I was fourteen and he around seventeen and exotically Chinese. I loved his flatter face and straight thick black hair, his squarer, muscular, more developed body. He'd ride me home on his motorbike and I'd climb through his bedroom window to avoid detection by his brutal parents. He was the first and only one to fuck me until I was in my thirties.

I had a permanent girlfriend, H., in the last years at secondary school. She was working-class, boyish, highly sexual and really 'into' my body and me, opening up a whole new experience of myself. I'd never felt so much desired. We were expected by her family to marry but, once I fully realised this, I knew it wouldn't be right for us. I had a part-time job as a domestic cleaner and had formed a sexual relationship with a Wildean client forty-five years my senior, who had great wealth and style and lived a gay bachelor life in Marylebone. It fascinated me and resonated deep inside with something I'd known since my earliest days in the house of John Cranko. I didn't feel abused by him, merely encouraged along my path.

By this time I was spreading my wings, finding myself wanted in ways I could never have imagined, forming highly charged romantic relationships with at least two males and three females at once from all classes and backgrounds. I would usually have a male and a female lover at the same time and, as honesty was a prized value at that time, be sure each knew about the other and openly negotiate time together with them. Sex and sexuality suddenly wasn't such a problem for me any more although the complexities of multiple relationships eventually were. It felt wholly right for me to be sexual with anyone with whom the attraction and desire were was mutual, regardless of gender. At last I had moved into what was most natural for me.

A major attachment, begun as pen-pals, was with A, who was two or three years older and starting at university in Sussex. He was my first proper gay relationship: we were very much in love and I moved in with him as soon as I moved out of the flat of his female friend whose lover I was by then. It was the sixties after all! We were boyfriends, lovers and monogamous, which seemed quite a relief, for about eighteen months, which included my residential stay in a so-called 'therapeutic community' following several suicide attempts and my girlfriend's termination of pregnancy. I was struggling to find a stable identity and rewarding work. I owe him a great deal for this gentle, kind, equitable relationship, a good beginning to life as a gay man.

How then did you come to be married at twenty-one?

S, another childhood friend of A's, became figural in our lives and it was she who soon became my wife. We all shared much in those generous years – unsurprisingly, Truffaut's 'Jules et Jim'[173] was our favoured film! We shared hectic weekends in London and Sussex and holidays in Italy with other romantic friends, all with almost no money, forming a kind of Pre-Raphaelite group of our own. They were great favourites, along with the Decadents and Aesthetes[174] of the 1890s on whom I became something of an expert. I had thick, shoulder-length waves as in their paintings, kiss-swollen lips, mascara, 'snake' hips, big jewellery, velvet capes, silver topped canes and lace

---

[173] 'Jules et Jim': Truffaut's 1962 highly acclaimed film about a 'love triangle' based on H-P Roché's 1953 semi-autobiographical novel about his relationship with male writer Franz Hessel and his wife, Helen Grund, starring Jeanne Moreau, Oskar Werner and Henri Serre.

[174] Pre-Raphaelites, Decadents and Aesthetes: overlapping artistic movements between about 1845 and 1900 in Europe.

cuffs. Jagger, Bolan and Bowie[175] were yet to ascend to stardom but all the signs were there by then of a growing fascination with androgyny and blurred gender boundaries. I was chosen by 'The Sunday Times magazine'[176] as 'the face of the year'.

In the beginning S would happily stay with A and me and there was little conflict. She and I fell madly in love. After a little while she needed me to make a choice between her and A and, consulting my heart alone, I knew I loved her most. I had no doubt at all. A was as generous as ever.

S and I set up home together in our teens in a whirlwind of happy optimism, marred only by the separation of her own glamorous and socially idealised parents at exactly the same time. We married after two incredibly happy years living together on very little and filled our lives with work, friends and the extraordinary cultural life of early seventies London. We honeymooned for a baking month in an exquisite Italian villa loaned by an aristocratic friend. I became twenty-one on our honeymoon, S was nineteen. Life was rich, full and marvellous: we had good jobs, good friends, a new rented flat in Islington, our health and one another. Then suddenly, after six months, she left.

S's parents' separation had a deep effect on her and she felt insecure and trapped by marriage at an early age, unsure whether it was possible to trust the happiness and love we also seemed to have as true and lasting. I could not accept losing her and went into overdrive to try everything to reconnect. I was obsessively attached to

---

[175] Jagger, Bowie, Bolan: Mick Jagger of The Rolling Stones, David Bowie and Marc Bolan became hugely popular British 'gender-bending' performers and role models over the coming decade.

[176] 'Sunday Times magazine': Culture and style supplement to major British Sunday newspaper, was extremely influential in the 60s and 70s and pioneering in photo-journalism.

reclaiming her as the single great love of my life even though she was 'seeing' a new man. Defeated eventually, I tried to establish some kind of life without her and, after many months, a female former school-friend moved in with me and we comforted each other, though neither of us ever doubted that S was the only one who counted.

Then S had a change of heart and it really was that. She returned and we somewhat naively ignored what had happened in our excitement at being together again. We made another home, worked hard and had two beautiful sons. This was everything I ever wanted: the stable, loving, aesthetic, warm family home I'd yearned for since birth. We had a lot of stress with our parents, with health issues – mostly mine – with poverty and through over-committing ourselves to too many causes.

Looking back, I am amazed at how we managed all we did at such a young age. Eventually the stressors won out, however, and my wife left again, this time with the boys, unable to be clear about her unhappiness and her goals but sure she had to go. This was the most devastating thing ever to happen to me and threw my world, my health and my spirit into turmoil. It took me a decade to begin to truly recover.

Was your sexuality a factor in your wife's dissatisfaction?

Not directly – to my knowledge. We enjoyed a rich, fulfilling sex life together for almost fourteen years, during which I had no strong desire to connect sexually with men or other women: husbanding and fathering really was satisfying and deeply curative for me, hugely rewarding. I had no other sexual or romantic partnerships except during our separation. I know S felt threatened all through our relationship by my potential 'gayness' and attractiveness to men and women; we had gay friends and I'd still wear make up and dress up for parties. Our lives were not really hetero-normative,[177] except for our sexual relationship. No, it was more the 'legacies' from our lives before we met which had so great an impact.

What are you referring to as 'legacies'?

I can only speak of my own. I had a nervous breakdown at six and from then on was in psychoanalytic treatment, several sessions a week, all through primary school. At secondary school, I started years of psychological medication as well – another 'queer' thing about me compared with my peers! I was diagnosed as manic-depressive and then lived up to the diagnosis: on antidepressants, tranquillisers, Valium for anxiety; suicide attempts; another breakdown; being hospitalised. Alongside, and obviously bound up with this, my whole life had been marked by 'physical' illness and accidents with something like twenty stays in hospital. I credit S with 'saving' me from life in a residential mental hospital due to her dedication in not allowing me to 'sink' into despair in the early days of our romance. I never quite shook off this legacy, however, and it affected how I was able to be and to cope within our marriage with two little boys, constant illness and extremely stressful teaching jobs in inner city schools. I know I was quite a strain to live with and that S did her very best to make our marriage work.

How have you managed to free yourself from these patterns since then?

Soon after our separation, following a dreadful period of illness and depression and a life-changing accident, I discovered Humanistic

---

[177] Another ghastly modern term meaning to take the norms of heterosexuality as a given, as the only real or healthy way, as superior values, attitudes and behaviours.

psychotherapy.[178] Thus began a healing journey of thirty years' individual and group therapy and then training, during which I have learned to connect with others for support, feel safer in groups, appreciate my deep sanity, build resilience in place of endurance and to reject identification with illness, manic depression and psychotropic medication. I learned to reach out – and inside myself– and to live a much more fulfilling life.

Two years after our separation I began another journey. Once I'd finally accepted, with huge difficulty, that my wife and I could not retrieve what we had so fortunately had together before, I returned to a world mirroring what Freud called the 'polymorphous perverse'[179]: a world of multiple relationships, genders, sexualities and possibilities, like the one I'd temporarily inhabited as a teenager. While I experimented I also dug deep inside myself.

Then I fell profoundly in love: something I was sure I couldn't ever have again. I met the man I have loved and lived with ever since, J. We have delighted in co-parenting my two sons and, for the past ten years, his son – he was donor for some lesbian friends and is an active father. This year we became besotted grandparents. We have built a rich, full, committed, passionate and multi-layered life around a deep relationship, which we live within a wide range of social, familial and cultural environments.

––––––––––––––––––

[178] Humanistic psychotherapy: see footnote in Philip's story.

[179] Freud's 'polymorphous perverse' refers to the infant's first five years of life. In 'Infantile Sexuality' (1910) Freud theorized that humans are born with unfocused libidinal drives; that our modes of pleasure, including sexual satisfaction, are multifarious. This polymorphous perverse sexuality then progresses through distinct oral, anal and phallic stages. Only subsequently do children learn to constrain sexual drives within social norms such as heterosexual genitality. For Freud, 'perversion' is a non-judgmental term used to designate behaviour outside socially acceptable norms. We know better nowadays.

Do you, then, today regard yourself as polymorphous, bisexual or gay?

I still regard myself on a deep level as not wanting or needing to be categorised, as not a thing, preferring to see myself as a living organism in a constant process of flux, growing itself. For ease of communication, and to feel some comfort in community, I call myself and our love together 'gay.' I am proud now to be fully what I have been since birth and that is 'queer.' I do not prescribe anything about other people or other possibilities. I revel in the diverse relationships I enjoy every day. I am only interested in love and commitment and in making a strong contribution through my work.

I long for a time when we can transcend categorising one another and ourselves and fully realise the wonder of our diversity in all its manifestations. Meanwhile we must work with the tools we have and where we are up to in our evolving. I try to stay at the exploring edge (a queer position throughout history)[180] at the same time as being deeply and passionately involved.

What of your relationships with your children?

They have been the greatest gift I can imagine. Having felt very unsuccessful at being a child and young person myself, and having been so unhappy and frightened growing up, fathering my boys has just allowed my heart to go on expanding and expanding. I sometimes feel I'll burst with love and gratitude. It has been an incredibly healing experience for me to attempt being the father I wish I had found for myself. It has been the most beautiful, educative, illuminating thing to have them grow alongside me and become the spectacular adults they

---

[180] See for example 'Gay Soul' and 'Gay Spirit' edited by Mark Simpson as well as Judy Grahn's ground-breaking book, "Another Mother Tongue' unearthing the special roles occupied by queer people in all times and places.

are today, just exactly the kind of men with whom I would wish the world to be populated. I feel extremely close to them, indeed at times the pain of even a slight separation from them is almost physically and spiritually intolerable, although I know that their integrity and distinctness is healthy.[181]

Coming out to them wasn't really an issue as nothing had changed in them or me, just in the gender of my partner and they took to him very quickly. He is brilliant with children and young people. They were extraordinarily able to understand this at a natural level although, of course, they then had to deal with the homophobia and sexism around them, especially in schools and amongst boys, between whom heterosexuality is so fiercely policed. We had to deal with this too and the most disappointing aspect of that was the intransigent sexism buried within gay male subcultures at the time regarding men and children. Our sons were always an intrinsic part of our lives and love and my partner became another father to them in every possible respect. I do believe that consistency of love is the key determinant of children's happiness – of everyone's happiness.

In what other ways has your life changed since you reconnected with your original queerness?

Interestingly, the parallel journey to the relational, sexual one, and clearly connected with it, has been a complete change in career. Leaving school without useful qualifications, I was desperate to return to study and become a teacher, which I had always felt was my purpose or mission. When I was newly married I did so with considerable support from my wife: another thing for which I will ever be grateful to her. She and I really struggled financially, having

---

[181] Khalil Gibran's lovely poem on parenting from 'The Prophet' (1923) 'Your children are not your children: They are the children of Life's longing for itself' - has always reassured me.

our first son with me being a student. I taught at all levels of education from infant school to postgraduate level at university, spending fifteen years leading initiatives in tertiary education in inner London at the heyday of the ILEA[182]: wonderful, radical, innovative times of complete commitment and amazing social progress. A real privilege.

Once separated from my wife, having moved city to be near my sons and lost my house and job, I plunged deeply into working with a superb psychotherapist, Rex Bradley at Spectrum,[183] who later encouraged me to consider training as a therapist. I took a lot of convincing: still attached, I suppose, to earlier life-scripts describing me as neurotic, sick, weak, even at times mad. To say nothing of the relationship between psychology and queerness: 'arrested development' and 'perverted' were their phrases. I hadn't wholly grasped the humanism in 'Humanistic'! But I did see how some of the psychotherapy training could help my work in education with disenfranchised groups, so I undertook it.

My training was immensely challenging and hugely freeing for me over the next thirty years and I continue enjoying it today. Since then I have been immersed in therapy, human development, research and sexual politics, following my initial outrage[184] at the retrogressive

---

[182] ILEA: Inner London Education Authority established as having primary responsibility for education in inner boroughs once the Greater London Council replaced the London County Council in 1965. Abolished by a Conservative government hostile to its progressive policies in 1990.

[183] Rex Bradley: (1946-2010) Humanistic Psychotherapist and trainer; Formerly Director of Spectrum and Vice Chair of UKCP. See: www.rexbradley.wordpress.com. Spectrum: largest humanistic therapy and training centre in the UK based in Finsbury Park, London See Resource section: Organisations as well as: http://www.spectrumtherapy.co.uk

[184] As a result of this outrage I founded and chaired for many years the UK Association for Lesbian, Gay & Bsexual Psychologies to campaign to overcome homophobia in psychology and therapy.

position of psychology and therapy in relation to sexualities and gender, especially having worked so hard for so long in progressive education at the cutting edge regarding diversity and equality with many pioneering colleagues. I cannot imagine a richer working life.

I spent ten important years in a men's group led by Terry Cooper[185] at Spectrum too, learning not to fear men – straight or gay – and to reclaim positive aspects of my disowned maleness. I also led the longest lasting gay men's therapy group in the world there for twenty-three years.

Would you do anything differently? What would you advise another married gay or bi man to consider, or to do, to best help himself?

I'd prioritise getting specialist support as early as possible: initially in the form of trustworthy individual therapy and, after a time, with groups as well as with other gay and bi men online and face-to-face. I would recommend his carefully coming out to one trusted other person at a time, increasing honesty with his wife and regarding the intersecting processes as ones to be shared as well as ones which he alone must work through. I highly recommend supporting these changes through bibliotherapy and cinetherapy.[186] Most of all, I'd put energy into the gradual bringing out of one's own homophobia, biphobia, shame and guilt (all common aspects of internalised

---

[185] Terry Cooper: Humanistic and Formative Psychotherapist and trainer. Co-Founder & Director of Spectrum (see footnote 183 above); pioneer in Formative Psychology and men's groups in the UK, as well as in working formatively with dreams. See: www.spectrumtherapy.com

[186] Bibliotherapy and cinetherapy: using books and films to support one's own therapeutic journey totally invaluable as resources!! See Resources section for details of films and books.

oppression[187]) and the building of resilience and courage with the help of allies.

I have seen over and over again the possibilities of loving, satisfying, creative relationships made manifest in this process and the greater happiness and fulfilment that results. I wish him, and indeed everyone involved, all the very best of luck.

---

[187] Internalised Oppression: see footnote in Alex's story.

RESOURCES SECTIONS

Resources Section 1
Organisations

Adult Children of Straight-Gay Marriages (ACSGM)

Confidential support group for over 18 year olds who grew up in families where one parent is straight and the other gay.
www.adultchildrenofgayfathers.com

Alternate Path (Yahoo support board)

This group is for wives only.
groups.yahoo.com/group/alternatepath/

Bi Guys' Wives

For women married to bisexual men. Also offers support to bi men who want to come out to their wives.
groups.msn.com/BiGuysWives

Children of Lesbians and Gays Everywhere. (COLAGE)

Support & info for children of GLB&T parents, parental tips for coming out to them, a webpage, newsletter, etc.
www.colage.org San Francisco based.

Children of Mixed Orientation Marriages

The child's identity can be in crisis when a parent changes theirs. Children can have happy lives, too, if the parents join forces on behalf of the children they created.
groups.yahoo.com/group/ChildrenOfMixed-Orientation

Coming Out as Married Lesbian or Bi

Listserv for women realising they are gay or bi while married.
groups.yahoo.com/group/COAMLB/

Gay Husbands

Coming out workshops which will only help if the participant is willing to leave his spouse afterwards.
www.gayhusbands.com

Gay Husbands, Straight Wives. US/Canada based

Bonnie Kaye's website, newsletter, radio show, articles, chat lines, books - all supporting straight wives.
www.gayhusbands.com/index.html

How

Support group for husbands out to their wives.
e-mail frazer.jones@ gmail.com to gain membership.

MAILL

Listserv for married and previously married lesbians and married women questioning their sexuality.
groups.yahoo.com/group/maill/

Married Bisexual Women's Support Group

Support group for lesbians & bi women (only) in committed heterosexual relationships
groups.yahoo.com/group/marriedbifemsupport/

I am Married but Gay

Experience group features support, personal stories and experiences, advice, chat, talk, forums, videos, pictures and resources.
www.experienceproject.com

Married Gay

For gay, bi and lesbian people married to – or in a relationship with - the 'opposite' sex and their spouses or partners.
www.marriedgay.com UK based.

Men married to Lesbians

Small group, but good place for men to share.
groups.yahoo.com/group/mmtl

Monogamous Mixed Orientation Marriages

Help for living with SSA within a framework of monogamy.
groups.yahoo.com/group/MMOMW/

New Hugs-Couples2 Group

List is for couples in mixed orientation marriages who want to make their relationship work. Both spouses must join.
groups.yahoo.com/group/HUGS_Couples2/

Parents, Friends and Families of Lesbians & Gays (PFLAG)

Info. & advocacy for LGBT persons and family members
www.pflag.org Washington based.

Sexuality Information & Education Council of the U.S.

Info. on sexuality & reproductive health.
www.siecus.org New York based.

Relate

Relationship counselling, sex therapy, LGBT issues etc. Trusted trained relationship counselling services throughout UK.
relate.org.uk

Straights Lounge

For straight spouses married, separated or recently divorced from GLBT spouses, in Mixed Orientation Marriage, who want to connect

with individual straight spouses of the opposite gender, for purposes of friendship, mutual support and/or romance.
groups.yahoo.com/group/StraightsLounge/

Straight Partners Anonymous (SPA). UK based

Online, face-to-face & Facebook members support group
www.straightpartnersanonymous.co.uk

Straight Spouse Connection

www.straightspouseconnection.com

Articles & online dialogue for straight spouses.

Straight Spouse Network (SSN). New Jersey based

In 35 years Straight Spouse Network has become an international organization devoted to supporting heterosexual spouses of glbtq partners and mixed-orientation couples through support groups. Provides information about family issues & mixed-orientation marriages to professionals, community organizations & media.
www.ssnetwk.org
ssnaustralia@gmail.com
straightspousenetwork.co.nz

Wives of Bi/Gay Husbands

Support group for wives only.
groups.yahoo.com/group/wivesofbigayhusbands/

Women in Life Loving Other Women

Listserv for women who are lesbian, bi, poly, or searching, married to men, divorced or in between.
groups.yahoo.com/group/willowgals/

ASEXUALITY:

www.asexuality.org
www.facebook.com/pages/AVENues/113213305413321
asexualeducation.tumblr.com/
https://www.facebook.com/aceawareness
Carrigan, M., Morrison, T & Gupta, K (2013): I do not miss what I do not want: Asexual identities, asexual lives. Special issue of Psychology & Sexuality journal, 4 (2).

Cormier-Otano, Olivier. Accredited integrative and psychosexual therapist in the Pink Therapy directory, working in London.
See his presentation, 'Doing Without: A Therapist's Findings' at: www.youtube.com/watch?v=H-cI61oeOOE
Contact him at: www.oliviercounselling.co.uk
asexualitystudies.org

BISEXUALITY:

Bisexuality & biphobia info at Stonewall:
www.stonewall.org.uk/at_home/sexual_orientation_faqs/2696.asp

Barker, M.; Richards, C.; Jones, R., et al: The Bisexuality Report. Open University.
Free download:
www.open.ac.uk/ccig/files/ccig/The%20BisexualityReport%20Feb.2012.pdf
www.biuk.org
www.Bi.org
www.bisexualindex.org.uk
www.biresource.net
bisexuality.wikia.com

BDSM:

bdsmfordummies.wordpress.com
en.wikipedia.org/wiki/BDSM
www.londonfetishscene.com
dir.yahoo.com/society_and_culture/sexuality/activities_and_practices/
bdsm/organizations/
www.fetlife.com Like a kinky Facebook where people create profiles,
have discussions and offer good advice

BOARDING SCHOOLS:

BOARDING SCHOOL SURVIVORS

Founded in 1990, **BSS** raises public consciousness about the psychological effects of sending children away to school and the social system that has encouraged this. Their book, 'The Making of Them: the British Attitude to Children and the Boarding School System'[188] received wide acclaim from doctors, therapists, educators and general readers. It describes the history and social context of boarding, as well as the process of de-constructing a 'strategic survival personality.'

Since 1990 BSS has run therapeutic workshops for adults who have recognised that they may have paid a price for their education and look to understand and heal their wounds. These have allowed many people to leave aspects of their past behind and develop their true potential.

They also offer relationship counselling and therapy for individuals and those in relationships, as well as specialist supervision and training for professionals.
www.boardingschoolsurvivors.co.uk

---

[188] Nick Duffel: 'The Making of Them': 2000: Lone Arrow Press.

BOARDING CONCERN

Boarding School Survivors has a sister organisation called BOARDING CONCERN which aims to keep in touch with ex-boarders and arrange annual conferences on themes important to ex-boarders. Boarding Concern works to raise awareness and monitors developments in the boarding industry through its advocacy arm. They welcome ex-boarders who would like follow-up support for their experiences and/or like to take part in advocacy. *www.boardingconcern.org.uk.*

Marcus Gottlieb

A psychotherapist in the Pink Therapy Directory, in private practice specialising in groups for boarding school survivors. *marcusgottlieb.com*

BOARDING RECOVERY

A group of accredited psychotherapists and trained counsellors who specialise in working with 'boarding school survivors'. *www.boardingrecovery.com/*

Books and articles on impacts of boarding:

Duffell, Nick & Bland, Robert: The Making Of Them: The British Attitude to Children and the Boarding School System. Lone Arrow Press. 2000.

Fry, Stephen: Moab Is My Washpot. Arrow. 2004.

marcusgottlieb.com/articles/working-with-gay-boarding-school-survivors/

Lambert, Royston: The Hothouse Society. Weidenfeld & Nicolson. 1968.

Monette, Paul: Becoming a Man: Half a Life Story. Abacus. 1994.

Raphael, Frederic: A Spoilt Boy: A Memoir of a Childhood. Orion. 2003.

Schaverien, Joy: Boarding School: The Trauma of the 'Privileged' Child. Journal of Analytical Psychology, 2004, vol. 49, pp. 683-705.

FAITH AND RELIGIOUS COMMUNITIES:

ISLAM

Imaam

Imaam supports LGBT Muslim people, their families and friends, to address issues of sexual orientation within Islam. It provides a safe space and support network to address issues of common concern through sharing individual experiences and institutional resources. Imaan promotes Islamic values of peace, social justice and tolerance and aspires to bring about a world free from prejudice and discrimination against all Muslims and LGBT people.
www.imaan.org.uk

The Muslim Alliance for Sexual and Gender Diversity

Works to support, empower and connect LGBTQ Muslims and seeks to challenge root causes of oppression, including misogyny and xenophobia. MASGD aims to increase acceptance of gender and sexual diversity within Muslim communities, and to promote a progressive understanding of Islam that is centered on in*clusion, justice, and equality.*
www.muslimalliance.org

Safra Project

A resource project working on issues relating to lesbian, bisexual and/or transgender women who identify as Muslim religiously and/or culturally. Set up in 2001 by and for Muslim LBT women. The issues faced by Muslim LBT women. The combination of prejudices based on sexual orientation, gender identity, gender, religion, race, culture and immigration status that they experience are unique and insufficiently addressed.
www.safraproject.org

HINDU

GALVA

International organization dedicated to the teachings of Lord Caitanya, the importance of all-inclusiveness and the Vedic concept of a natural third gender described in Vedic literatures. GALVA also wishes to provide a friendly place where third-gender devotees and guests learn more about Krsna consciousness and advance in spiritual life.
galva108.org/index.html

JEWISH

The Jewish Gay and Lesbian Group

The Jewish Gay and Lesbian Group, founded in 1972 is the longest established Jewish LGBT group in the world. Open to Jewish men and women who are lesbian, gay, bisexual or transgender they welcome non-Jewish partners to all events and non-LGBT & non-Jewish guests to certain events and, although the group is based in London, they have many members across the country.

Primarily a social, rather than religious, group most religious events tend to follow Progressive/Reform traditions. Recently they have attracted many orthodox members and we are ensuring that events are suitable for all. There are occasional kosher Friday night meals in members' homes to which all members are invited. These add a new dimension to the group alongside a long running tradition of monthly Friday night services along Progressive/ Reform lines.
www.jglg.org.uk

CHRISTIAN

The Lesbian and Gay Christian Movement

The Lesbian and Gay Christian Movement is a UK based international charity, which challenges homophobia and transphobia, especially within the Church and faith based organisations, as well as working to create, and praying for an inclusive church. Started in 1976, LGCM continues to grow despite opposition and has members world-wide from all major denominations as well as none. Membership is open to all regardless of sexual orientation or faith as long as they uphold LGCM's Statement of Conviction. *www.lgcm.org.uk*

RECOVERY FROM SEXUAL ABUSE:

www.survivors.org.uk
www.malesurvivor.org/
www.oprah.com/oprahshow/The-Road-to-Recovery-7-Steps-to-Help-a-Male-Sexual-Abuse-Survivor-Heal
www.menweb.org/sexabuse.html
www.workingtorecovery.co.uk/shop/reclaiming-our-lives-a-workbook-for-males-who-have-experienced-sexual-abuse
Mike Lew: (2004) Victims No Longer: The Classic Guide for Men Recovering from Sexual Child Abuse. Harper Collins, New York.

RESOURCES SECTION 2
Therapy

FINDING GOOD THERAPY

An excellent resource for people looking for good sexualities and diversity-aware therapy is the guide:
www.pinktherapy.com/en-gb/findatherapist/choosingatherapist.aspx

For people embarking on counselling or therapy training programmes to check the ethics of the courses beforehand, try *www.pinktherapy.com* for advice.

COUNSELLING AND PSYCHOTHERAPY:

Only a couple of decades ago homosexuality was considered by the World Health Organization to be a mental illness. This pathologising of sexual variation has affected the way many therapists view sexual difference. We are all judged through a heterosexual lens of what is 'normal'. Indeed, today people who wish to change their gender, or others who enjoy consensual BDSM sexual relationships can still find themselves diagnosed as mentally disordered.

It is only recently that some therapists have begun to be aware of, and gain specialist training in, the special issues and requirements of working with bi, gay, trans and other sex and gender diverse clients. Most practicing counsellors and therapists and psychologists have no special knowledge or training in working with these issues and, indeed, many were trained on courses that pathologised and discriminated against gender and sexual minorities. It is therefore imperative that those seeking support research carefully the therapist's own training, background, attitudes and knowledge before embarking on a course of therapy with them. Pink Therapy has also compiled a list of useful questions to ask a therapist or counsellor with whom you are considering working.[189] If possible see more than one therapist and then decide who you feel is best to help you.

Most relationship therapists still talk of working with 'marriages' and 'couples' and this may be a clue as to how open they are to the special concerns and circumstances with which GSD clients might be dealing within their relationships. Mixed-orientation relationships have attracted almost no attention in the therapy world until now so most therapists are unfamiliar with the dynamics of such partnerships. There has also been very little knowledgeable help for 'straight' spouses in dealing with their feelings - shock, hurt, anger, powerlessness, grief, and self-blame – on learning that their partner was gay or lesbian and it can be assumed that this necessarily means the break up of their relationship. Beware!

PINK THERAPY

I have no hesitation in insisting here that the best place to start to find ethical, professional therapists or counsellors to work with issues highlighted by this book would be Pink Therapy, the largest specialist UK provider of such services for gender and sexuality diverse clients, for training other professionals in the issues and raising public awareness.

Pink Therapy welcomes the whole spectrum of different gender and sexual expressions and all those engaged in consensual, albeit transgressive, sexualities seeking a place to understand and be understood. These include, but are not restricted to people who identify as asexual, celibate, polyamorous, non-monogamous, or

---

[189] http://www.pinktherapy.com/en-gb/findatherapist/choosingatherapist.aspx

swingers and those involved in BDSM or Kink lifestyles or practices, anyone on the gender spectrum from cross dressers/transvestites, gender queer, intersex and those living with variations in sex development, androgynes, third sex/two spirit, to those living full time as transgenderists or trans men and women.

Fourteen Associate Therapists positively identify as having gender or sexual minority lived-experience. As well as a large, regularly updated resources guide (under 'Knowledge') the website also hosts the UK Directory of Pink Therapists – see below.
www.pinktherapy.com

PACE

PACE is London's leading charity promoting the mental health and emotional well being of the lesbian, gay, bisexual and transgender community.
www.pacehealth.org.uk/

LONDON FRIEND

LONDON FRIEND is a charity that promotes the social, emotional, physical and sexual health and well being of lesbian, gay and bisexual people, including transgender people who identify as lesbian, gay or bisexual and all those unsure of their sexuality.
www.londonfriend.org.uk/

DIRECTORIES:

DIRECTORY OF PINK THERAPISTS

The most reliable directory in the UK related to issues discussed in this book is Pink Therapy's online directory of therapists of all sexualities and gender identities who work with gender and sexual diversity clients from a non-judgmental standpoint.
www.pinktherapy.com/en-gb/findatherapist.aspx

Such practitioners believe that sexual or gender difference is just that: a difference. They believe that what is 'sick' are some of society's prejudicial attitudes and they pay acute attention to the social contexts in which clients live. Living with stigma and oppression creates additional pressures and people of diverse gender and sexual identity often benefit from emotional and psychological support to help deal with these.

OTHER DIRECTORIES

If you can't find someone near to where you live or work in Pink Therapy's directory, you could check the following online directories of the major accrediting psychotherapy and counselling organizations in the UK. We would encourage you to look specifically for people who say they work with gender and sexual diversity clients in an affirmative manner and to check this out when you call.

British Association for Counselling and Psychotherapy at:
www.bacpregister.org.uk

United Kingdom Council for Psychotherapy website:
www.psychotherapy.org.uk/index.html

Association of Independent Psychotherapists at:
referrals@aip.org.uk

Counselling Directory is another national directory and information portal listing qualified therapists
www.counselling-directory.org.uk

Find Counselling Services is another reliable UK wide database of counsellors and counselling services
www.findcounsellingservices.co.uk

Search the register of the British Psychological Society for a clinical or counselling psychologist at:
www.bps.org.uk

AVOIDING BAD THERAPY:

Beware the 'Conversion', 'Reparative' or 'Ex-Gay' practitioners.

See: Wayne Besen's website for 'Truth Wins Out' campaigning group reveals the truth behind Reparative Therapy
www.truthwinsout.com/

Read: Drescher, Jack & Zucker, Kenneth: Ex-Gay Research: Analyzing the Spitzer Study in Relation to Science, Religion, Politics and Culture. Routledge, 2006.

Watch: discussion between Pamela Gawler-Wright and Shelley Bridgman on effects of Reparative therapy.
www.youtube.com/watch?v=MVEc1kqBMIc

The Human Rights Campaign has excellent reporting on 'Conversion therapy' here:
www.hrc.org/resources/entry/the-lies-and-dangers-of-reparative-therapy

So does the professional body for psychotherapy in the UK on this page:
www.psychotherapy.org.uk/reparative_therapy.html

An early port of call for those needing help with recovering from what's happened to them in the 'ex-gay' movement could be:
www.beyondexgay.com

Formal apologies from ex gay movement leaders can be seen here:
www.youtube.com/watch?v=aDiYeJ_bsQo

The latest news on progress banning ex gay, conversion or reparative 'therapies' as this book went to press were to be seen here:
www.pinknews.co.uk/topic/reparative-therapy/

RESOURCES SECTION 3:
BIBLIOTHERAPY & CINETHERAPY

I highly recommend the frequently updated KNOWLEDGE section of www.pinktherapy.com for useful books for clients and web resources.

Also the online encyclopaedia at: www.glbtq.com

And the unrivalled expertise of 'Gay's The Word' community bookshop in London at: www.gaystheword.com

BOOKS & ARTICLES ON BEING GAY OR BI & MARRIED:

Ball, Aimee Lee. "When Gay Men Happen to Straight Women in 'O: The Oprah magazine' (December 2004): 236-39, 259-63.

Barbetta, Dr. Francine: A Pebble in his Shoe: a Straight Man with a Gay Spouse. 2008: USA.

Butler, Katy. "Many Couples Must Negotiate Terms of 'Brokeback' Marriages." New York Times (March 7, 2006): Section F, 5.

Buxton, Amity Pierce
Contact: www.straightspouse.org

Paths and Pitfalls: How Heterosexual Spouses Cope When Their Husbands or Wives Come Out.

The Best Interest of Children of Gay and Lesbian Parents in 'The Scientific Basis of Child Custody Decisions'

The Other Side of the Closet: The Coming Out Crisis for Straight Spouses and Families, revised 1994, NY, Wiley.

Family trauma immediately after disclosure by educator who founded the Straight Spouses Network.

Thoughts on a Father's Coming Out to his Children.

Works in Progress. How Mixed Orientation Couples Maintain their Marriages after Wives Come Out.

Browder, Brenda Stone: On the Up and Up: A Survival Guide for Women with Men On the Down Low. 2005: Kensington Press, USA

Cram, Heather: You're What ?: Survival Strategies for Straight Spouses. 2008: Langdon Street Press, USA.

Grever, Carol: My Husband is Gay: A Woman's Guide to Surviving The Crisis. 2001:Crossing Press. Freedom, Ca. Personal stories of 26 women offer guidance in facing immediate issues.

Grever, C. & Bowman, D.: When Your Spouse Comes Out: A Straight Mate's Recovery Manual: 2008: NY, Haworth Press. The only one to discuss underlying psychological issues with a therapeutic approach.

Gross, Jane. "When the Beard Is Too Painful to Remove." New York Times (August 3, 2006).

Gochros, Jean Scharr: When Husbands Come Out of the Closet: 1989: NY, Harrington Park Press. Academic approach for women with gay or bi partners.

Komuves, Louella Christy: Silent Sagas, Unsung Sorrows: Heterosexual Wife, Homosexual Husband. 2006: iUniverse.

Krome, Mary A.: Left in His Closet. 2010: Tate Publishing, Arizona, USA.

Lee, Jennifer: My Ex is Having Sex With Rex. 2007:Illinois, USA.

Marie, Joy: The Straight-Up Truth About the Down-Low: Women Share Their Stories of Betrayal, Pain and Survival. 2008: Creative Wisdom Books, USA.

Matos McGreevey, Dina: Silent Partner: A Memoir of My Marriage. 2007: Hyperion Books, USA.

Pearson, Carol Lynn: Goodbye I Love You. The true story of a wife, her homosexual husband, and a love that transcended tragedy. 2008, Cedar Falls Inc., Springville, Utah, USA.

Rogak, Lisa: Pretzel Logic: a Novel. 1999: Williams Hills Press, USA.

Vaughan, Diane: Uncoupling: Turning Points in Intimate Relationships. 1986: Oxford University Press.

Whitehead, Sally Lowe: The Truth Shall Set You Free: A Memoir. 1999: John Knox Press, Westminster.

FROM A LESBIAN, BI OR GAY PERSPECTIVE:

Abbott, Deborah and Ellen Farmer: From Wedded Wife to Lesbian Life: Stories of Transformation. 1995: The Crossing Press. Freedom, California.

Bozett, Frederick, and Dean, Patricia Forni, and Sussman, Marvin B (Eds): Homosexuality and Family Relations. 1990: Routledge, New York, NY,

Cassingham, Barbe and O'Niel, Sally: And then I Met This Woman: Previously Married Women's Journeys into Lesbian Relationships. 1993: Mother Courage Press, Atlanta, USA.

Fleisher, Joanne: Living Two Lives: Married to a Man and in Love with a Woman. 2005: Alyson Books, Los Angeles.

Hutchins, Loraine and Lani Kaahumanu (eds): Bi Any Other Name: Bisexual People Speak Out. 1994: Alyson Books, Reno, NV, USA.

King, J.L.: On The Down Low: A Journey Into the Lives of Straight Black Men Who Sleep With Men. 2005: Harmony, NV., USA.

Klein, Fritz: The Bisexual Option. 1993: Routledge.

Mattson, Martha: Amazons: The Forgotten Tribe. 1998: Amazon Press, USA.

Strah, David: Gay Dads: a celebration of fatherhood.

Strock, Carren: Married Women Who Love Women. 1997: Routledge.

White, Mel: Stranger at the Gate: To Be Gay and Christian in America. 1994: Plume Books, USA.

Whitney, Catherine: Uncommon Lives: Gay Men and Straight Women. 1990: Dutton Adult Books, USA.

MIXED ORIENTATION FAMILY & CHILDREN:

I strongly recommend the new magazine for alternative families in the UK:

www.wearefamilymagazine.com

Bernstein, Robert: Straight Parents, Gay Children: keeping Families Together. 1995: Avalon Books.

Buxton, Amity Pierce: From Hostile to Helpful in 'Home Fronts'.

Corley, Rip: The Final Closet: The Gay Parents Guide for Coming Out to their Children. 1990: Miami, Florida: Editech Press.

Fairchild , Betty & Hayward, Nancy: Now That You Know: What Every Parent Should Know About Homosexuality. 1981: Harcourt Paperbacks.

Garner, Abigail: Families Like Mine: Children of Gay Parents Tell It Like It Is. 2005, Harper Paperbacks.

Glick, Daniel: Monkey Dancing: A Father, Two Kids and a Journey to the Ends of the Earth. 2003: Public Affairs Press, USA.

Gottlieb, Andrew R. (Ed): Life Curves: Sons Talk About Their Gay Fathers.

Howey, Noelle & Samuels, Ellen (Eds): Out of the Ordinary: essays on growing up with gay, lesbian and transgender parents

MacPike, Laralee: There's Something I've been Meaning to Tell You. 1989: Naiad Press.

Norman, Terry L.: Just Tell the Truth: Questions Families Ask When Gay Married Men Come Out. 1998: Prehension Publications

Stewart, Terry: Invisible Families for parents of lesbian or gay children. 2008:Heartflags Books. Aims to help conservative families talk openly, heal rifts and achieve a loving understanding: valued for its' insights and guidance. It also contains an interesting introduction to issues relating to Maori and Polynesian people.

Turan, Ali: We Are Family: Testimonies of Lesbian and Gay Parents. 1996: Continuum International Publishing.

Looks at the reality of being lesbian or gay and a parent, ways & means of achieving parenthood, benefits and challenges of pink parenting in Britain. Based on interviews. Issues examined include: taboos and myths surrounding same-sex parenthood; artificial insemination; surrogacy; adoption & fostering; custody; what to tell children; what to tell neighbours; what kids think of their queer parents.

Web resources for LGBT Parents

www.wearefamilymagazine.co.uk

www.pink-parenting.com

Pink Parents: *www.onespace.org.uk*

www.gayfamiliesinthemaking.wordpress.com

www.gaydads.co.uk

www.gaymums.co.uk

www.gayparentmag.com

www.invisibleparents.eu

Lesbian & gay parenting booklist: *www.parentbooks.ca*

Proud 2 b Parents Greater Manchester:
m.taylor-roberts@manchester.gov.uk

Stonewall resources for parents and families: *www.stonewall.org.uk*

USEFUL BOOKS FOR PROFESSIONALS:

PINK THERAPY TRILOGY:

Davies, D and Neal, C. (eds.) (1996). Pink Therapy: a guide for counsellors and therapists working with lesbian, gay and bisexual clients. Buckingham: Open University Press.

Davies, D and Neal, C. (eds.) (2000) Therapeutic Perspectives on Working with Lesbian, Gay and Bisexual Clients. (Pink Therapy Vol. 2) Buckingham: Open University Press.

Neal, C. and Davies, D. (eds.) (2000) Issues in Therapy with Lesbian, Gay and Bisexual Clients. (Pink Therapy Vol. 3) Buckingham: Open University Press.

* * * *

Alexander, C. J. (1997) Growth and Intimacy for Gay Men: A Workbook. Binghampton NY: Harrington Park Press.

Ali, T. (1996) We Are Family: Testimonies of Lesbian and Gay Parents. London: Cassell.

Barker, M and Langdridge, D. (2010) Understanding Non-Monogamies. Abingdon: Routledge.

Barrett, J. (2007) Transsexual and Other Disorders of Gender Identity: a practical guide to management. Oxford: Radcliffe Publishing.

Baldwin, G. (1993) Ties that Bind: the SM/Leather/Fetish Erotic Style: Issues, Commentaries and Advice. San Francisco: Daedalus Publishing

Beckerman, N.L. (2005) Couples of Mixed HIV Status: Clinical Issues and Interventions. Binghampton, NY: Haworth Press.

Bereznai, S. (2006). Gay and Single… Forever? New York: Marlowe & Co.

Besen, W. (2003) Anything But Straight: unmasking the scandals and lies behind the ex-gay myth. New York: Harrington Park Press.

Bettinger, M. (2001) It's Your Hour: A Guide to Queer Affirmative Psychotherapy. Los Angeles: Alyson Books

Bigner, J. J. & Wetchler, J. L. (Eds.) (2004) Relationship Therapy with Same Sex Couples. Binghampton: Haworth Press Inc.

Bohan, J. S. and Russell, G. M. (eds) Conversations about Psychology and Sexual Orientation. New York: New York University Press.

Bornstein, K. (1998) My Gender Workbook. London: Routledge.

Boswell, J (1981) Christianity, Social Tolerance and Homosexuality: Gay People in Western Europe from the Beginning of the Christian Era to the 14th Century. University of Chicago Press.

Brent, B. (2002) The Ultimate Guide to Anal Sex for Men. San Francisco: Cleis Press.

Butler, C., O'Donovan, A and Shaw, E. (2010) Sex, Sexuality and Therapeutic Practice: A manual for therapists and trainers. Hove: Routledge.

Carl, D. Counselling Same Sex Couples New York: WW Norton

Carrol, L. (2010) Counselling Sexual and Gender Minorities. Upper Saddle River NJ: Merrill

Clarke, V., Ellis S.J, Peel, E. and Riggs, D.W. Lesbian, Gay, Bisexual, Trans and Queer Psychology: An introduction. Cambridge: Cambridge University Press.

Coyle, A. and Kitzinger, C. (eds.) (2002) Lesbian and Gay Psychology: New perspectives. BPS/Blackwell

das Nair, R., and Butler, C. (eds.) (2012) Intersectionality, Sexuality and Psychological Therapies: Working with lesbian, gay and bisexual diversity. Oxford: BPS/Blackwell

D'Augelli, A. R. & Patterson, J. (Eds.) (1995). Lesbian, gay and bisexual identities over the lifespan: psychological perspectives. New York: Oxford University Press.

Davies, D. (1996): Fundamental Issues in gay affirmative therapy, homophobia and coming out Part 1 (4 chapters) of Pink Therapy: a guide for counselors and therapists working with lesbian, gay & bisexual clients. Open University Press, Buckingham.

Davies, D. (2007) Not in front of the Students in 'Therapy Today' Journal. UK, February 2007.

Davies, D (2012) Sexual Orientation in C. Feltham & I. Horton (eds) The Sage Handbook of Counselling and Psychotherapy. 3rd edition. London: Sage Publications.

Denman, C. (2004) Sexuality: A Biopsychosocial Approach. Basingstoke: Palgrave.

Drescher, J. (1999) Psychoanalytic Therapy and The Gay Man. New York: Haworth Press Inc.

Drescher, J, D'Ercole, A, Schoenberg, E. (eds.) (2003) Psychotherapy with Gay Men and Lesbians: Contemporary Dynamic Approaches. New York: Haworth Press Inc.

Drescher, J. and Zucker, K (eds) (2006) Ex-Gay Research: Analyzing the Spitzer Study and Its Relation to Science, Religion, Politics and Culture. New York: Harrington Park Press.

Evosevich, J. M. & Avriette, M. (2000) The Gay and Lesbian Psychotherapy Treatment Planner. New York: John Wiley & Sons

Feinberg, L. (1996) Transgender Warriors: Making history from Joan of Arc to Dennis Rodman. Boston: Beacon Press.

Glassgold, J.M and Iasenza, S. (eds) (1995) Lesbians and Psychoanalysis: Revolutions in Theory and Practice. New York: The Free Press.

Grahn, J. (1991) Another Mother Tongue: Gay words, gay worlds. Beacon Press.

Greenan, D, and Tunnell, G. Couple Therapy with Gay Men New York: Guilford Press

Greene, B. (ed) (1997) Ethnic and Cultural Diversity among Lesbians and Gay Men. Sage Publications.

Guter, R and Killacky, J. R. (Eds.) (2004) Queer Crips: Disabled Gay Men and Their Stories. Binghampton: Harrington Park Press.

Haule, J. R. (1996) The Love Cure: Therapy Erotic and Sexual. Spring Publications

Heyward, C. (1995) When Boundaries Betray Us: Beyond illusions of what is ethical in therapy and life. San Francisco: HarperSanFrancisco.

Houlbrook, M. (2005) Queer London: Perils and Pleasures in the Sexual Metropolis, 1918-1957. University of Chicago Press.

Hutchins, L. & Kaahumanu, L. (Eds.) (1991). Bi any other name. Boston, MA: Alyson Publications.

Isay, R. A. (1989) Being homosexual: Gay men and their development. New York: Avon Books.

Israel, G.E. and Tarver, D.E. (1997) Transgender Care: Recommended Guidelines, Practical Information and Personal Accounts. Philadelphia: Temple University Press.

Jacques, T. (1993) On the Safe Edge: A manual for SM play. Toronto: Whole SM Publishing

Jivani, A. (1997). It's Not Unusual: A History of Lesbian and Gay Britain in the Twentieth Century. London: Michael O'Mara Books Ltd.

Johnson, S. M. and O'Connor, E. (2001) For Lesbian Parents: Your Guide to Helping Your Child Grow Up Healthy, Happy and Proud. New York: Guilford Press.

Johnson, S. M. and O'Connor, E. (2002) The Gay Baby Boom: The Psychology of Gay Parenthood. New York: New York University Press.

Kort, J. (2008) Gay Affirmative Therapy for the Straight Clinician. New York: Norton.

Kane-DeMaios, J. A. and Bullough, V.L. (2006) Crossing Sexual Boundaries: Transgender Journeys, Uncharted Paths. New York: Prometheus Books.

Keane, H. (2002) What's Wrong with Addiction? Melbourne: Melbourne University Press.

Karasic, D. & Drescher, J. (Eds.) (2005) Sexual and Gender Diagnoses of the Diagnostic and Statistical Manual (DSM): A Re-evaluation. Binghampton, NY: Haworth Press Inc.

Kaufman, M., Silverberg, C., Odette, F. (2003) The Ultimate Guide to Sex and Disability: For All of Us who Live with Disabilities, Chronic Pain and Illness. San Francisco: Cleis Press.

Langdridge, D and Barker, M (eds) (2008) Safe, Sane and Consensual: Contemporary Perspectives on Sadomasochism. Basingstoke: Palgrave.

Lee, J. A. (Ed.) (1991) Gay Midlife and Maturity. Binghampton, NY: Harrington Park Press

Lev, A. I (2004) Transgender Emergence: Therapeutic guidelines for working with gender-variant people and their families. New York: Haworth Press Inc.

Lev, A. I (2004) The Complete Lesbian and Gay Parenting Guide. Berkley Publishing.

Ley, D. (2012) The Myth of Sex Addiction. Plymouth UK: Rowman & Littlefield

Lingiardi, V & Drescher, J. (Eds.) (2003) The Mental Health Professions and Homosexuality: International Perspectives. Binghampton: Haworth Medical Press.

Mallon, G. P. (2004) Gay Men Choosing Parenthood. New York: Columbia State University Press.

Malebranche, J. (2006) Androphilia: A manifesto rejecting the gay identity and reclaiming masculinity. Baltimore: Scapegoat Publishing.

Martell, C. R, Safren, S. A, Prince, S. E. Cognitive-Behavioural Therapies with Lesbian, Gay and Bisexual Clients. New York: Guilford Press.

Mathy, R.M, and Kerr, S.K. (Eds.) (2003) Lesbian and Bisexual Women's Mental Health. Binghampton: Haworth Press.

Mason-John, V. & Khambatta, A. (1993). Lesbian talk: Making black waves. London: Scarlett Press.

Merilee Clunis, D and Dorsey Green, G (1988) Lesbian Couples. Seattle: Seal Press.

Merla, P. (Ed.) (1996). Boys like us: gay writers tell their coming out stories. New York: Avon Books

Moon, L. (Ed.) (2008) Feeling Queer or Queer Feelings? Radical Approaches to Counselling Sex, Sexualities and Genders. London: Routledge.

Moon, L. (Ed.) (2010) Counselling Ideologies: Queer challenges to heteronormativity. Farnham: Ashgate

Moore, L. (Ed.) (1997). Does your mama know? An anthology of black lesbian coming out stories. Texas: Redbone Press

Neal, C. (1993): Queer in the Head in Self & Society. Journal of Association for Humanistic Psychotherapy. (AHPP) Autumn, UK.

Neal, C. (2000): We Are Family: Working with Gay Men in Groups in Neal, C. & Davies, D. Issues in Therapy with Gay, Bisexual and Transgender Clients' Open University Press, Buckingham. (Chap. 7)

Neal, C. (2013): A Body of Experience in Transformations. Journal of Psychotherapists and Counsellors for Social Responsibility (PCSR), Summer 2013.

Newman, F. (2004) The Whole Lesbian Sex Book San Francisco: Cleis Press.

Orbach, S. (2000) The Impossibility of Sex: Stories of the intimate relationship between therapist and patient. Scribner Book Company.

Ortmann, D.M and Sprott, R.A. (2013) Sexual Outsiders: Understanding BDSM Sexualities and Communities. Plymouth UK: Rowman & Littlefield.

Outland, O. (2000). Coming Out: a handbook for men. New York: Alyson Books

Pepper, R. (2005). The Ultimate Guide to Pregnancy for Lesbians: How to Stay Sane and Care for Yourself from Preconception Through Birth. 2nd Edn. San Francisco: Cleis Press

Pimental-Habib, R.L. Empowering the Tribe: A positive guide to gay and lesbian self-esteem. New York: Kensington Books.

Pierce Buxton, A. (1994) The Other Side of the Closet: The Coming-Out Crisis for Straight Spouses and Families. New York: John Wiley & Sons.

Pope, K.S., Sonne, J.L., Holroyd, J. (2005) Sexual Feelings in Psychotherapy: explorations for therapists and therapists-in-training. Washington DC: American Psychological Association.

Purnell, A. (2004) Transsexed and Transgendered People: A Guide. London: Gendys.

Ravenscroft, A. (2004) Polyamory: Roadmaps for the Clueless and Hopeful. Santa Fe: Fenris Bros

Rashid, N. & Hoy, J. (Eds.) (2000). Girl 2 Girl: the lives and loves of young lesbian and bisexual women. London: Diva Books

Rose, S., Stevens, C., Parr, Z. et al. (Eds.) (1994). Bisexual Horizons London: Lawrence & Wishart.

Schmitt, A. & Sofer, J. (Eds.) (1992) Sexuality and Eroticism Among Males in Moslem Societies. Binghampton, NY: Harrington Park Press.

Shaw, L., Tacconelli, E., Watson, R. and Herbert, C. (2009) Living Confidently with HIV. Gloucester: Oxford Development Centre.

Shelley, C. (Ed.) (1998) Contemporary Perspectives on Psychotherapy and Homosexualities. London: Free Association Books

Shernoff. M. (2006) Without Condoms: Unprotected sex, gay men and barebacking. Routledge.

Shidlo, A, Schroeder, M, and Drescher, J. (eds.) (2002) Sexual Conversion Therapy: Ethical, clinical and research perspectives. New York: Haworth Medical Press.

Smith, A. & Calvert, J. (2001). Opening Doors: Working with older lesbian and gay men. London: Age Concern.

Stowe, J. R. (1999) Gay Spirit Warrior: An empowerment workbook for men who love men. Forres: Findhorn Press.

Sweasey, P. (1997) From Queer to Eternity: Spirituality in the lives of lesbian, gay and bisexual people. London: Cassell.

Sue, D.W. (2010) Microaggressions in Everyday Life: Race, gender and sexual orientation. Hoboken, NJ: Wiley.

Taormino, T. (2008) Opening Up: A guide to creating and sustaining open relationships. San Francisco: Cleis Press.

Trenchard, L. & Warren, H. (1984). Something to tell you... The experiences and needs of young lesbians and gay men in London. London: London Gay Teenage Group

Thompson, M. (1994) Gay Soul: Finding the heart of gay spirit and nature. San Francisco: HarperSanFrancisco.

Thompson, M. (1997) Gay Body: a journey through shadow to self. New York: St Martin's Press.

Waugh, R. (Ed.) (2000). Dykes with baggage: the lighter side of lesbians in therapy. Los Angeles: Alyson Publications.

Wilson, G and Rahman, Q (2005) Born Gay: The Psychobiology of Sex Orientation. London: Peter Owen Pubs.

Whitman, L. (Ed.) (2010) Telling Tales about Dementia: Experiences of caring. London: Jessica Kingsley.

With many thanks to **Dominic Davies**, Founder and Director of Pink Therapy for permission to use his invaluable booklist.

BIBLIOTHERAPY & CINETHERAPY

BOOKS & FILMS FOR YOUR OWN JOURNEY:

A highly selective list companions contributors have found valuable.

Downs, Alan: The Velvet Rage: Overcoming the Pain of Growing Up Gay in a Straight Man's World. Da Capo Press, 2006. So many clients have been inspired and encouraged by this book.

Driggs, J. et al: Intimacy Between Men: How to Find and Keep Gay Love Relationships. Plume, 1991.

Easton, Dossie & Liszt, Catherine: The Ethical Slut: A Guide to Infinite Sexual Possibilities. Greenery Press, Ca.1998. Groundbreaking and wise handbook.

Gideonse, Ted: From Boys to Men. 2006: Da Capo Press, Cambridge, Mass., USA. A stunning collection of essays, not coming out stories exactly, but about what it is like to be different, aware of that difference from the earliest of ages and the magical variety of such differences.

Helminiak, Daniel: What the Bible Really Says About Homosexuality. Alamo Square Dist. Inc., 1994

Howey, Noelle & Samuels, Ellen: Out of the Ordinary: essays on growing up with gay, lesbian and transgender parents.

Isay, R. A. (1989) Being homosexual: Gay men and their development. New York: Avon Books

Isensee, Rik:
Are You Ready? The Gay Man's Guide to Thriving at Midlife.

The God Squad, a spoof on the "ex-gay" movement.

Growing Up Gay in a Dysfunctional Family: A Guide for Gay Men Reclaiming Their Lives. Prentice Hall Trade, 1992.

Love Between Men: helping gay couples resolve conflicts by meeting the underlying needs of both partners.

Reclaiming Your Life: a guide for gay men in recovery from early abuse, homophobia, and self-defeating behaviour.

We're Not Alone: a young adult novel.

All available from Rik's website: *gaytherapist.com*

Johnson, Brett K.: Coming Out Every Day: A Gay, Bisexual or Questioning Man's Guide. Oakland, Ca., 1997.

Kort, Joe:

Gay Affirmative Therapy for the Straight Clinician.

10 Smart Things Gay Men Can Do To Find Real Love

10 Smart Things Gay Men Can Do To Improve Their Lives

All available from Joe's website at: *www.joekort.com*

Maupin, Armistead: Tales of the City. Series of novels about gay San Francisco. HarperCollins, NY, 1994

Marcus, Eric: Is It A Choice? Answers to the Most Frequently Asked Questions About Lesbian and Gay People. Harper One, 2005.

McNaught, Brian: Now That I'm Out, What Do I Do?: Thoughts on Living Deliberately. St. Martin's Press, 1997.

MIND: How to cope with doubts about your sexual identity. National Association for Mental Health free leaflet.

Nicolson, Nigel: Portrait of a Marriage: Vita Sackville-West and Harold Nicolson. Futura Publications, 1975.

Nimmons, David: The Soul Beneath the Skin: The Unseen Hearts and Habits of Gay Men. St Martin's Press, United States, 2004

Ramer, Andrew: Two Flutes Playing: Spiritual Journey for Gay Men. Alamo Square Press, 1997.

Rowbotham, Sheila: Edward Carpenter: A Life of Liberty and Love. Verso, 2008. Biography of the 'father' of the modern gay movement.

Stowe, John R.: Gay Spirit Warrior: An Empowerment Workbook for Men Who Love Men. Findhorn Press, 1999.

Tóibín, Colm: Love in a Dark Time. Picador, 2002. An important collection of essays on a wide range of gay creative lives.

CINETHERAPY:

A few great films to help you on your way.

After Stonewall: 1999 documentary directed by John Scagliotti about 30 years of gay rights activism since the 1969 riots.

Amphetamine: 2010 Hong Kong film starring Byron Pang and Thomas Price. The story of a Chinese fitness trainer, Kafka, who meets Daniel, a business executive. Directed by acclaimed Chinese film-maker, Scud, the stage name of Danny Cheng Wan-Cheung, this award winning film explores themes traditionally regarded as 'taboo' in Hong Kong society in an unusually convention-defying way. One of four such films by Scud, the other three are City Without Baseball, 2008, Permanent Residence, 2009 and Love Actually... Sucks! 2011.

Before Stonewall: The Making of a Gay and Lesbian Community: 1984 American documentary about the LGBT community prior to the 1969 Stonewall riots. Directors: Robert Rosenberg, Greta Schiller, John Scagliotti.

Breakfast with Scot: 2007 Canadian comedy about parenting and gay life, adapted from the novel by Michael Downing.

Brokeback Mountain is a 2005 American epic romantic drama by Ang Lee, adapted from a 1997 short story by Annie Proulx, with the screenplay written by Diana Ossana and Larry McMurtry. The film stars Heath Ledger, Jake Gyllenhaal, Anne Hathaway and Michelle Williams and depicts the complex romantic and sexual relationship between two men in the American West from 1963 to 1981.

But I'm a Cheerleader: 1999 satirical romantic comedy directed by Jamie Babbit and written by Brian Wayne Peterson. Natasha Lyonne stars as an apparently happy heterosexual high school cheerleader. However, her friends and family are convinced she is gay and send her to a residential in-patient conversion therapy camp to cure her lesbianism. Megan soon realizes that she is indeed a lesbian and, despite the therapy, gradually comes to embrace her sexual orientation.

Cachorro: ('Bear Cub' in English): 2004 Spanish gay-themed (in particular, the gay bear community) written and directed by Miguel Albaladejo, about a bearish gay man who ends up looking after his nephew while his sister goes to India. He develops a fatherly bond with the boy as well as forcing him to alter his lifestyle. 'Cachorro' describes any young, furry animal such as a cub or puppy.

Chef's Special ('Fuera de carta'): 2008 Spanish film directed by Nacho García Velilla that centers on the decision to come out. It focuses on men who have had relationships with women to hide their own sexuality, to the point of having children. The film also deals with the theme of single parents.

Jihad for Love: 2007 documentary on the coexistence of Islam and homosexuality. Directed by Parvez Sharma and produced by Sharma and Sandi DuBowski.

Latter Days: 2003 American romantic comedy-drama about a gay relationship between a closeted Mormon missionary and his openly gay neighbor. Written and directed by C. Jay Cox. The first film to openly portray the clash between The Church of Jesus Christ of Latter-day Saints and homosexuality.

Portrait of a Marriage: (BBC, TV drama): 1990. www.youtube.com/watch?v=khL_Y5ZO3Mc. Directed by Stephen Whittaker. Real-life relationships between feminist writer Vita Sackville-West, novelist Violet Keppel and Vita's politician husband Harold Nicolson in 1920s England. Broadcast in four episodes.

Stonewall: 1995 historical comedy-drama. Inspired by the memoir of that title by gay historian Martin Duberman: a fictionalised account of the weeks leading up to the Stonewall riots. Director: Nigel Finch.

Save Me: 2007. Robert Cary film about a drug-addicted gay man admitted into an ex-gay programme run by Gayle and her husband Ted. Premiered at the 2007 Sundance Film Festival.

Stonewall Uprising: 2010 American documentary examining events surrounding the Stonewall riots of June 28, 1969.

Trembling Before G-d: 2001 American documentary about gay and lesbian Orthodox Jews trying to reconcile their sexuality with their faith. Director: Sandi DuBowski.

XXY: 2007 Argentine-Spanish-French drama written and directed by Lucía Puenzo, which tells the story of a 15-year-old intersex person, the way her family copes with her condition and the ultimate decision that she must eventually make as she finds her gender identity. It was nominated for eight awards.

Word Is Out: Stories of Some of Our Lives: 1977 documentary featuring interviews with 26 gay men and women. Directed by six people collectively known as the Mariposa Film Group.

www.channel4.com/programmes/father-ray-comes-out/4od

www.channel4.com/programmes/coming-out-to-class/4od

www.channel4.com/programmes/the-joy-of-teen-sex/4od

See also the KNOWLEDGE section of *www.pinktherapy.com* for regularly updated book and film lists, video clips and articles.